Common Knowledge about Chinese History

The Overseas Chinese Affairs Office of the State Council

China Overseas Exchanges Association

中国历史常识

国务院侨务办公室
中国海外交流协会

前言

《中国历史常识》、《中国地理常识》和《中国文化常识》是中华人民共和国国务院侨务办公室、中国海外交流协会委托南京师范大学、安徽师范大学和北京华文学院分别编写的一套华文教学辅助读物，供海外华裔青少年通过课堂学习或自学的方式了解中国历史、地理、文化常识，也可供家长辅导孩子学习使用。我们希望学习者通过学习，初步了解、掌握中国历史、地理和文化的知识，进而达到普及、弘扬中华文化和促进中外文化交流的目的。

根据海外华文教学的实际情况和需求，我们分别选编了中国历史的重大事件和重要人物，进行客观记述；选取了中国地理最主要的自然特点和人文特征，进行概略描述；筛选了中华文化和民俗风情的精华，加以介绍。突出体现科学性、思想性和实用性的编写原则，在编排设计等方面力求有所创新。

在上述三本书的编写过程中，苏寿桐、王宏志、臧嵘、侯明、刘淑英、李芳芹等参加了《中国历史常识》的审稿工作；王永昌、乐平兰、刘淑梅、毕超、徐玉奎、董乃灿、张桂珠、李文君等参加了《中国地理常识》的审稿工作；张英、张猛、董明、武惠华、陶卫、杨二林等参加了《中国文化常识》的审稿工作。在此，谨表示诚挚的谢意。

书中考虑不周或疏漏之处，祈盼使用者不吝赐正，以期再版时修订。

编　者

2001年12月

Preface

The Overseas Chinese Affairs Office of the State Council of the People's Republic of China and China Overseas Exchanges Association commissioned Nanjing Normal University, Anhui Normal University and Beijing Chinese Language College to respectively write this set of auxiliary Chinese language teaching materials, namely, *Common Knowledge about Chinese History*, *Common Knowledge about Chinese Geography* and *Common Knowledge about Chinese Culture* which acquaint overseas Chinese teenagers with basic knowledge on these subjects through class education or self-teaching. Parents can also use them to help their children with study. Moreover, we hope this set of books can offer a wider group of readers some rudimentary knowledge about Chinese history, geography and culture, thus promoting cultural exchanges between China and other countries.

According to the actual condition and needs of overseas Chinese language teaching, in this set of books, we objectively narrate important events and figures in Chinese history; briefly describe the major natural and cultural features of Chinese geography; carefully select and introduce the essence of the Chinese culture, habits and customs. We have tried to introduce new ideas in typesetting, design and so on and to embody scientific, ideological and practical principles in the writing.

We are deeply grateful to Su Shoutong, Wang Hongzhi, Zang Rong, Hou Ming, Liu Shuying and Li Fangqin for revising *Common Knowledge about Chinese History*, Wang Yongchang, Yue Pinglan, Liu Shumei, Bi Chao, Xu Yukui, Dong Naican, Zhang Guizhu and Li Wenjun for revising *Common Knowledge about Chinese Geography*, and Zhang Ying, Zhang Meng, Dong Ming, Wu Huihua, Tao Wei and Yang Erlin for revising *Common Knowledge about Chinese Culture*.

Advice is welcomed if there were any mistake in the books. We will revise them when republishing the books.

Compilers

December, 2001

目录 Contents

中国古代史
Period before the Opium War of 1840

中国历史的开篇——先秦
The Dawn of Chinese History—The Pre-Qin Period

封建大一统时期——秦、汉
The Period of Great Feudal Unity—The Qin and Han Dynasties

目录 Contents

封建社会的继续发展和民族政权并立时期——
五代、辽、宋、夏、金、元
The Continued Development of Feudal Society and the Co-existence of Ethnic
Regimes—The Five Dynasties, and the Liao, Song, Xia, Jin and Yuan Dynasties

目录 Contents

统一的多民族国家进一步发展和封建社会由盛而衰时期——明、清（鸦片战争以前）
Further Development of the Unitary Multi-ethnic Country and Decline of Feudal Society—The Ming and Qing Dynasties (Before the Opium War of 1840)

中国近代史
Modern Period

目录 Contents

现代中国
Contemporary Period

概述
Introduction

先秦，指中国历史上秦始皇统一中国以前的漫长历史时期。

大约在170万年以前，中国人的祖先就生活在云南的元谋县境内，我们把这作为原始社会的开端。在陕西的蓝田、北京的周口店等地，都有原始人类的遗址。古书中记载了不少关于中国人祖先的传说，其中最有名的是炎帝、黄帝和尧、舜、禹的传说。

约公元前2070年，中国第一个王朝夏朝建立，其统治时间长达400多年。第二个王朝是商朝，也叫殷朝（因为商朝初年，多次迁都，最后迁到殷——今河南安阳，并在那里统治了300多年）。商朝是当时世界上的一个大国，统治时间长达500多年，留下了甲骨文、青铜器等许多极其珍贵的史料、文物。第三个统一的王朝是西周，都城在今天的西安。后来西周的都城被少数民族攻占，周王室被迫迁都到今天的洛阳，历史上叫做东周，西周与东周的时间共约800年。东周分为春秋和战国两个时期，春秋时期，国家分裂成许多小国；到了战国时期，形成了七个力量强大的国家，这些国家通过改革进入了封建社会，并为后来秦的统一奠定了基础。

与世界历史对照，当古埃及、古巴比伦、古印度文明发展进步之时，中国正经历文明勃兴的夏、商、西周王朝。当欧洲希腊、罗马城邦国家繁荣之时，正是中国春秋战国思想文化昌盛的时代。东西方文明交相辉映，地中海地区和中国，逐渐形成世界两大文明的中心。

中国历史的开篇—**先秦**

The Dawn of Chinese History —
The Pre-Qin Period

The pre-Qin period refers to remote antiquity, before Emperor Qinshihuang united China for the first time.

Ancestors of the Chinese people lived in present-day Yuanmou County, Yunnan Province, about 1,700,000 years ago. We regard this time as the beginning of primitive society. There are sites of primitive people in Lantian, Shaanxi Province, and Zhoukoudian, near Beijing, and other places. There are many legends about the ancestors of the Chinese people recorded in ancient books, the most famous of which are the legends concerning Yandi, Huangdi, Yao, Shun and Yu.

About 2070 BC, the Xia Dynasty, the first dynasty to emerge in China, was founded. It lasted for over 400 years. The second dynasty was the Shang Dynasty (also called the Yin Dynasty, as it changed its capital several times, and finally settled in Yin, today's Anyang in Henan Province). The Shang Dynasty was a great power in the world at that time. It existed for over 500 years, and left a lot of extremely precious historical materials and artifacts such as inscriptions on bones and tortoise shells and bronze wares. The third dynasty was the Western Zhou Dynasty, the capital of which was Hao, today's Xi'an in Shaanxi Province. Driven from Hao by invading tribes, the Zhou ruling house moved its capital to today's Luoyang, in Henan Province, from which time it was known to history as the Eastern Zhou Dynasty. Western and Eastern Zhou lasted about 800 years altogether. Eastern Zhou is divided by historians into the Spring and Autumn Period (770 - 476 BC) and the Warring States Period (475 - 221 BC). During the Spring and Autumn Period, the country split into many small rival vassal states; by the time of the Warring States Period, they had coalesced into seven powerful states. It was in the Warring States Period that the foundations were laid for feudalism and the forthcoming unification of China under the Qin Dynasty.

When the ancient Egyptian, ancient Babylonian and ancient Indian civilizations were developing, the Xia, Shang and Western Zhou dynasties were flourishing in China. When the Greek and Roman city states were in their heyday in Europe, the thought and culture of the Spring and Autumn and Warring States periods prospered. The Mediterranean area and China gradually came to be the centers of the world's two main civilizations.

中国境内最早的人类
The Earliest Human Beings in China

中国是世界文明古国，也是人类的发源地之一。中国到目前为止是世界上发现旧石器时代的人类化石和文化遗址最多的国家，其中重要的有元谋人、蓝田人、北京人、山顶洞人等。

元谋人　1965年，在云南省元谋县，考古人员发现了两颗远古人类的牙齿和一些粗糙的石器。

经科学家鉴定，这是远古人类的遗骨、遗物，距今大约170万年。在元谋发现的远古人类我们称为元谋人。元谋人是中国境内目前发现的最早的人类。

北京人　1929年，在北京西南周口店龙骨山山洞里发现了远古人类的头盖骨，后来在这个遗址中又先后发现了五个头盖骨。在这里发现的远古人类我们称为北京人。北京人生活在距今约70万年至20万年，他们保留了猿的某些特点，但已经能够使用工具劳动。北京人把石块敲打成粗糙的石器，还把树枝砍成木棒，用来采集植物，捕捉动物，加工食物。北京人已经会使用天然火。火的使用是人类进化过程中的一个很大的进步。

山顶洞人　1930年，在北京西南周口店龙骨山顶部的山洞里，发现了距今约18,000年的人类遗骨。我们把他们称作山顶洞人。山顶洞人的模样和现代人基本一样。

山顶洞人用的还是打制石器，但有的制作很精细。他们已经懂得磨制和钻孔技术，会制造骨针等骨器，会用骨针缝制兽皮衣服，还会用有钻孔的兽骨、兽牙、石珠、海蚶 (hān) 壳做装饰品。他们已懂得人工取火，靠采集植物、打猎、捕鱼得到食物。

山顶洞人按母亲的血缘关系组成氏族。同一氏族的成员居住在一起，共同劳动，共同分配食物。

1

1. 江苏南京北阴阳营出土的玉串饰 (新石器时代)
   These jade ornaments were found in the army unit of Beiyinyang, Nanjing City, Jiangsu Province (Neolithic Period)
2. 北京周口店猿人洞遗址
   The Peking Man Site at Zhoukoudian
3. 北京人头部复原图
   A replica of the head of Peking Man
4. 山顶洞人头部复原图
   A replica of the head of Upper Cave Man

China is not only a country with an ancient civilization, it is also one of the birthplaces of the human race. China so far ranks first in the number of human fossils and cultural sites dating from the Paleolithic Period, among which there were traces of Yuanmou Man, Lantian Man, Peking Man and Upper Cave Man.

Yuanmou Man In 1965, archeologists found two ancient human teeth and some rough stone tools in Yuanmou County, Yunnan Province.

After examination, it was confirmed that they dated back some 1,700,000 years, making Yuanmou Man the earliest human found in China so far.

Peking Man In 1929, human skulls were found in caves on Mount Longgu in Zhoukoudian, in southwest Beijing. Later, five more human skulls were found there. They were determined to be relics of Peking Man, who lived around 700,000 to 200,000 years ago. Peking man had some ape-like characteristics, but he mastered the arts of making and using tools. He chipped stones into rough implements and chopped tree branches into sticks to gather vegetation, hunt animals and process food. He also learned to use natural fire, which marks a milestone on human evolution.

3   4

小资料 Data

旧石器时代

原始人用石块敲打出来的石器叫打制石器，使用这种石器的时代就叫做旧石器时代。旧石器时代经历了二三百万年，那时人们过着采集和渔猎的生活。

Paleolithic Period

The period in which chipped stone implements were used is called the Paleolithic Period. The Paleolithic Period lasted for two to three million years. People of that period lived by gathering, hunting and fishing.

新石器时代

大约从八九千年前开始，原始人已经普遍使用磨制石器。使用磨制石器的时代叫新石器时代。新石器时代已出现农业和牧业。

Neolithic Period

Around 8,000 - 9,000 years ago, primitive people already used ground stone implements. The period in which ground stone implements were used is called the Neolithic Period. During the Neolithic Period agriculture and animal husbandry appeared.

Upper Cave Man In 1930, human bones dating from about 18,000 years ago were found in caves near the top of Mount Longgu in Zhoukoudian. Upper Cave Man's appearance would have been almost the same as that of modern man.

Upper Cave Man also used chipped stone tools, some of which were exquisitely made, and the tools show that he had already mastered grinding and drilling techniques. He made bone needles to sew animal skins to make clothing, and used animal bones and teeth, stone beads and shells as ornaments. He knew how to make fire, and got food from gathering, hunting and fishing.

The Upper Cave people formed the matriarchal clans. Clan members lived together, worked together and shared their food.

中国古人类化石分布略图
Sketch Map of Distribution of the Fossils of Ancient Human Beings in China

1. 山顶洞遗址
   The site of one of the Upper Caves
2. 北京人头盖骨
   The skull of Peking Man
3. 元谋人牙齿
   The teeth of Yuanmou Man

华夏之祖
Ancestors of the Chinese Nation

华夏部落
Huaxia tribe

涿鹿
Zhuolu

黄帝
Huangdi

炎帝
Yandi

东夷部落
Dongyi tribe

蚩尤
Chiyou

苗蛮部落
Miaoman tribe

黄帝和禹传说时期地域示意图
Sketch Map of the Legendary Period of Huangdi and Yu the Great

—— 传说中八大部落集团的分布地区
Distribution area of the eight legendary tribal groups

—— 黄帝氏族东移路线
Eastward migration route of Huangdi's tribe

黄帝氏族部分东移路线
Eastward migration route of part of Yandi's tribe

传说中洪水泛滥的地区
Legendary flooded area

× 主要战场 Main battle site

1. 陕西宝鸡市炎帝祠
   Yandi Mausoleum, Baoji, Shaanxi Province

中国人常说自己是"炎黄子孙"，这个说法跟传说中的人物黄帝和炎帝有关。

大约4,000多年以前，中国黄河流域一带住着许多氏族和部落，其中比较著名的是以黄帝、炎帝为首领的两大部落。

黄帝和炎帝两个部落在黄河流域，势力强大。在东方还生活着一个势力也很强大的部落叫九黎部落，九黎部落的首领叫蚩尤（chīyóu）。相传，当时的九黎族人已经使用铜造的兵器，打起仗来非常勇猛，常常进攻别的部落。

传说蚩尤部落为了扩大自己的地盘，同炎帝部落发生了战争。炎帝部落战败，向黄帝求援。黄帝与炎帝联合起来大战蚩尤。这次战争发生在涿鹿（zhuōlù，今河北省境内）。在战斗中，忽然天昏地暗，大雾弥漫，连对面的人也看不见。黄帝使用指南车，帮助士兵识别方向，追击蚩尤，结果蚩尤被捉住杀死。

涿鹿之战后，黄帝和炎帝两个部落为了争夺对其他各部落的领导地位，又发生了冲突，最后黄帝部落取得了胜利。两个部落进一步结合在一起，其他部落也纷纷加入黄帝部落的联盟，共同开发中原地区。各部落在语言、习惯、生产、生活等各方面的交

小资料 Data

三皇五帝

三皇是中国古代传说中远古时期的帝王，通常的说法是指燧(suì)人、伏羲(xī)、神农。

五帝是中国古代传说中远古时期的帝王，时代比三皇略晚。五帝通常指黄帝、颛顼(zhuānxū)、帝喾(kù)、尧和舜。

The Three Kings and the Five Emperors

The three kings were legendary kings in China in remote antiquity. They were Sui Ren, Fu Xi and Shennong.

The five emperors were legendary emperors of China, who reigned a little later than the three kings. They were Huangdi, Zhuan Xu, Di Ku, Yao, and Shun.

1. 指南车
   A south-pointing chariot
2. 蚩尤像
   A drawing of Chiyou
3. 湖南炎陵县炎陵内的炎帝像 (传说炎帝死后葬于此地)
   A statue of Yandi inside the Yandi Mausoleum, Yanling County, Hunan Province (According to legend, Yandi was buried here.)

流逐渐加强，经过长期的融合和发展，形成了华夏族的主体。

华夏族是汉族的前身，是中华民族的主要组成部分。华夏族把黄帝、炎帝看做自己的祖先，称自己为"炎黄子孙"。直到今天，汉族人和许多兄弟民族还习惯这么说。

1

Chinese people often refer to themselves as "descendants of Yandi and Huangdi". This refers to the legendary heroes Yandi and Huangdi.

Over 4,000 years ago, there lived many clans and tribes in the Yellow River valley, among which the two tribes led by Huangdi and Yandi, respectively, were the most prominent.

To the east of the Yellow River valley was the territory of the Jiuli tribe, with Chiyou as its chieftain. It is said that the Jiuli people already had bronze weapons, and were a warlike group.

2

Legend has it that the Jiuli attacked Yandi's tribe. The latter was defeated, and turned to Huangdi for help. Huangdi allied himself with Yandi, and defeated Chiyou at a place called Zhuolu (in today's Hebei Province). During the battle, a dense mist descended, and all was in confusion. However, on his chariot Huangdi had an instrument which constantly pointed south. In this way, he rallied the allied forces. Finally, Chiyou was captured and killed.

After the Battle of Zhuolu, conflicts arose between the tribes of Huangdi and Yandi for hegemony of all the tribes. At last, Huangdi prevailed, and ruled over all the tribes of the Central Plains. Eventually, they merged their languages, customs, and production and living habits, to form the Huaxia people.

The Huaxia people were the predecessor of the Han people, and the principal part of the Chinese nation. The Huaxia people regarded Huangdi and Yandi as their ancestors, and called themselves "descendants of Yandi and Huangdi".

3

大禹治水和中国历史上第一个王朝

Yu the Great Harnesses the Flood, and the First Dynasty Is Founded

大禹 (yǔ) 是传说中夏后氏部落的首领，原称"禹"，也称"夏禹"。传说尧 (yáo) 的时候，黄河发大水，洪水冲毁了村庄和房屋，人们只能住到树上和山顶上。洪水给人民带来了极大的灾害。那时，炎黄部落联盟的首领尧任用鲧 (gǔn) 治理洪水，鲧采用筑堤堵水的办法治水，遭到了失败。尧之后，担任部落联盟首领的舜 (shùn) 杀死了鲧，然后命令鲧的儿子禹继续治水。禹吸取了鲧的教训，改用疏导的方法治水，让洪水顺着河道流向大海。禹辛勤地工作，传说他在外治水13年，三次经过家门都没有抽时间进去看看。最后，禹终于制服了水患。人们感谢禹，尊称他为"大禹"。

由于禹治水成功，得到舜的"禅 (shàn) 让"，舜征得各部落首领的同意，推举禹为自己的继承人。舜死后，禹便成为部落联盟的首领。

1. 大禹像
   A portrait of Yu the Great
2. 大禹治水图
   Yu the Great Harnessing the Floods

1. 夏朝的彩陶鼎 (河南二里头遗址早期遗物之一)
   The colored tripod, *ding*, of the Xia Dynasty (Erlitou culture of Henan)
2. 浙江绍兴大禹陵
   Yu the Great Mausoleum, Shaoxing, Zhejiang Province
3. 河南禹州市大禹雕像
   A statue of Yu the Great, Yuzhou, Henan Province

1

那时洪水刚刚平定，草木茂盛，野兽危害人民，禹派人教百姓开辟耕地；还派人教导人民耕种田地，收获粮食。于是人民的生活渐渐安定下来。禹又对苗族发动战争，阻止他们进入黄河流域，巩固了华夏族在中原地区的地位。禹之后，部落联盟首领的权力大大加强了。

约公元前2070年，禹建立夏朝，是中国历史上第一个王朝。后来禹死了，他的儿子启继承了禹的位置，引起有扈 (hù) 氏部落的反抗。启打败了有扈氏以后，他的地位得到了各部落的承认。从此世袭制代替了禅让制。夏朝历经400多年，最后一个王叫桀 (jié)，他是个暴君，政权非常腐朽。那时黄河下游的商国强大起来，起兵灭夏，大约在公元前1600年建立了商朝。

小资料 Data

禅让制

是中国古代部落联盟推选领袖的制度。相传尧是陶唐氏部落的首领，后被推举为部落联盟领袖。尧老了，征询了四方部落首领的意见，推选了舜为继承人。舜是有虞 (yú) 氏部落的首领，聪明能干。尧对舜进行了三年的考察，最后选定他为部落联盟首领。舜年老时也采取了同样的办法推选了夏后氏部落的首领禹接替自己的位置。

Abdicating and Handing over the Throne

In ancient China, power was passed on to the next generation by means of abdication by the ruler of the alliance of tribes. According to legend, Yao was chieftain of the Taotang tribe, who was chosen to be head of the alliance. In his old age, Yao consulted the other tribal chieftains, and chose Shun, head of the Youyu clan, as his successor. In the same way, Shun chose Yu, leader of the Xiahou clan, to be his successor.

Yu the Great was the chieftain of the legendary Xiahou clan. He was originally called Yu or Xiayu. According to legend, the Yellow River flooded during the reign of Emperor Yao, and the people were forced to abandon their villages, and go to live in trees or on mountaintops. The flood brought great misery to the people. Emperor Yao, the chieftain of the Yan-Huang tribal alliance, appointed Gun to harness the flood. Gun built dikes to keep back the water, but failed. Shun, who succeeded Yao, killed Gun, and appointed Gun's son Yu to continue with the flood-harnessing work. Yu adopted the dredging method to lead the flood waters to flow along river courses into the sea. Yu worked very hard. It was said that during the 13 years he spent taming the floods, he passed his home three times, but did not enter until his task was completed. As a result of his successful efforts, the people bestowed on him the title "Yu the Great", and Shun chose Yu as his successor, with the approval of the tribal chieftains.

Following the taming of the floods, vegetation and wild beasts grew rampant, threatening the survival of the people. Yu taught his subjects the art of agriculture, and thus how to dominate the land and feed themselves in a regular and organized way. He also repelled invasions by the Miao tribe, and consolidated the Huaxia people's supremacy in the Central Plains.

Around 2070 BC, Yu established the Xia Dynasty, the first dynasty in Chinese history. After Yu's death, his son Qi succeeded to the throne. Crushing an attempt to overthrow him by the Youhu clan, Qi established the system of hereditary rulers.

The Xia Dynasty lasted over 400 years. Its last king, Jie, vilified in the ancient records as a tyrant, was overthrown by the leader of the kingdom of Shang on the lower reaches of the Yellow River in 1,600 BC.

小资料 Data

二里头文化

1952年在河南登封二里头村，考古工作者发现了大型的夏朝宫殿遗址和其他丰富的遗物。后来在别的地方也发现了相同类型的文化遗址，人们把这种类型的文化遗址叫二里头文化。二里头文化是一种青铜时代的文化。

Erlitou Culture

In 1952, archeologists discovered the locations of Xia palaces and many other Xia relics in Erlitou Village, Dengfeng County, Henan Province. Sites of the same type of Bronze Age culture, collectively called Erlitou culture, were found in other places later.

武王伐纣
King Wu Attacks King Zhou

1

商朝后期政治混乱，最后一个王是纣 (zhòu) 王。他只知道自己享乐，根本不管人民的死活，是个残暴的君主。

商纣王在首都北边的沙丘养着各地送来的珍禽异兽，在首都的南边修建鹿台，用来存放无数的珍宝财物。他还造了"酒池"，里面装满了美酒；还造了"肉林"，里面挂满了香喷喷的熟肉。纣王每天和妃子、大臣们在"酒池"、"肉林"中嬉戏游乐。他修建的巨大仓库里，装满了从全国各地掠夺来的粮食。他还发明了很多残酷的刑罚，其中一种叫"炮烙 (pàoluò) 之刑"，就是把涂满膏脂的铜柱放在燃烧的炭火上，强迫犯人在上面行走，犯人站不住，就掉在炭火中活活烧死。

商纣王不听任何人的劝说，他的叔叔比干因为向他提意见而被他挖心处死。另一个大臣劝他说，这样将会有亡国丧命的危险。商纣王却回答说，他的性命是有上天保佑的，谁也不能把他怎么样！

那时，渭水流域的周国，迅速发展。周原来是商的属国。周文王一心要治理好自己的国家，重视农业生产，待人宽厚，重用人才。吕尚（俗称姜太公）就是他发现的。吕尚帮助周文王整顿政治和军事，对内发展生产，使人民安居乐业；对外征服各部族，不断扩大疆土，周的势力逐步强大。

公元前11世纪中期，周文王死后，他的儿子即位，这就是周武王。周武王得到吕尚和叔旦（即周公旦）的帮助，国家兴盛。这时候，商朝的统治更加腐朽。周武王联合西方和南方的部落，进攻商纣王。双方在牧野（今河南省境内）大战。商朝的军队中大部分是奴隶，他们平时恨透了纣王，不但不抵抗，还纷纷起义，引导周军攻入商朝首都。商纣王自焚 (fén) 而死。商朝终于灭亡。周武王得到了各个部落和各个小国家的拥护，于公元前

武王伐纣路线图
Sketch Map of King Wu's Route of Campaign against King Zhou

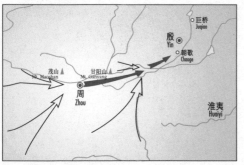

➡ 周武王进攻商纣的方向
　King Wu's route of advance
⇨ 进攻商纣的各部落的会兵方向
　Tribal reinforcements' route of advance

1046年建立了周朝，定都镐（hào）京（今陕西西安西南），历史上称为西周。

The last monarch of the Shang Dynasty, King Zhou, is said to have been a cruel despot who neglected state affairs and abandoned himself to sensuous pleasures.

In the meantime, a vassal kingdom of the Shang Dynasty called Zhou (a different Chinese character from that used as the name of King Zhou) was growing powerful in the Weishui River valley. The king of Zhou, named Wen, was an able and enlightened administrator who valued agriculture and made good use of talented people. Assisted by his able prime minister, Lu Shang (also known as Jiang Taigong), King Wen made his realm rich and powerful.

In the mid-11th century BC, King Wen died, and his son came to the throne as King Wu. The new ruler, assisted by Lu Shang and his own uncle Duke Zhou, led an alliance of tribes against the tottering Shang Dynasty, and toppled King Zhou at the Battle of Muye (in today's Henan Province). The victory was aided by a revolt of the Shang army, which consisted mostly of conscripted slaves. King Zhou burnt himself to death, and his throne was taken by King Wu. King Wu founded the Zhou Dynasty in 1046 BC, and located his capital in Hao (southwest of today's Xi'an, Shaanxi Province). This era, until the capital was moved eastward to Luoyang in 770 BC, is known as that of the Western Zhou Dynasty.

小资料 Data

姜太公钓鱼，愿者上钩

姜太公，姜姓，吕氏，名尚，字子牙，又称太公望。传说他曾经在渭水边钓鱼，希望能看到从这里经过的周文王。他的鱼钩是直的，上面没有鱼饵，而且离水面很高。他一边钓鱼，一边说："快上钩呀，愿意的就快上钩。"有一天周文王发现了他，于是就高兴地邀请他帮助自己治理国家。以后人们就用"姜太公钓鱼，愿者上钩"来比喻做一件事情是心甘情愿的。

Jiang Taigong's Way of Fishing

Jiang Taigong was an ambitious man of the Lu clan. There is a story that he used to sit by the Weishui River, at a spot which King Wen often passed, holding a fishing rod high above the water. His fishhook was straight with no bait on it. He would say, "Rise to the hook. Those who are willing, please rise to the hook." One day King Wen passed by, and invited him to help administer the country. The phrase "Jiang Taigong's going fishing" means that someone is volunteering to do something.

1. 周公像
   A portrait of Duke Zhou
2. 姜太公像
   A statue of Jiang Taigong
3. 姜太公钓鱼石
   The rock with an indentation, which many believe was made when Jiang Taigong sat fishing

春秋五霸
The Five Hegemons of the Spring and Autumn Period

1. 齐国的殉马坑（在今天的山东省境内，殉马数量很多，大约有600匹，是齐国国力强大的一个证明。）
   Horses sacrificed upon the burial of a noble of the State of Qi in modern Shandong Province (A total of 600 immolated steeds have been found in Shandong, indicating the wealth and power of Qi.)
2. 齐桓公像
   A portrait of Duke Huan of Qi
3. 管仲像
   A portrait of Guan Zhong
4. 越王勾践剑
   The sword of Gou Jian, ruler of the State of Yue

👉 **小资料 Data**

"春秋"的来源

春秋是中国历史上的一个时代名，它代表公元前770年—公元前476年这一历史时期。中国古代的一部史书《春秋》记载了这一段时期的历史，因而用"春秋"作时代名。

The Origin of "Spring and Autumn"

The history of the years from 770 BC to 476 BC is recorded in an ancient document known as The Spring and Autumn Annals, hence the name "Spring and Autumn Period".

春秋初年诸侯国有一百多个。各诸侯国为了争夺土地和人口，发生混战。力量强大的诸侯国一面不断吞并弱小的国家，一面争夺霸权。春秋时期先后起来争当霸主的有齐桓公、宋襄公、晋文公、秦穆公、楚庄王，历史上称为"春秋五霸"。还有一种说法，"春秋五霸"指齐桓公、晋文公、楚庄王、吴王阖闾（hélú）、越王勾践。

齐国是春秋时期东方一个富裕的国家。齐桓公在大政治家管仲的辅佐下，在政治上和经济上进行了一系列改革，发展生产，使齐国强大起来。齐桓公率兵击退山戎等少数民族的进攻，又率领齐、鲁、宋等八国的军队讨伐中原的楚国，阻止了楚军的北进，威信大增。公元前651年，齐桓公召集各诸侯国订立盟约，周天子也派人参加，齐国称霸中原的时代开始了。

齐桓公之后，宋襄公一心想接替齐桓公做霸主，但没有成功。晋文公做了国君以后采取了一系列措施，很快使晋国成为北方一大强国。当时南方的楚国也想称霸。公元前632年，晋国和楚国进行了一场大战，楚军大败，晋国从此成为中原的一大霸主。晋楚之间的争霸持续了一百多年，后来楚庄王打败晋军，做了中原的霸主。秦穆公本来也打算向东发展，到中原去做霸主，没能成功，转而向西扩大地盘，独自称霸西方。

吴国和越国都是长江下游的国家。这两个国家都不大，但也加入了争霸战争。晋楚争霸时，吴国在晋国的支持下曾经攻破楚国的都城。后来吴越两国进行了多次战争，各有胜负。公元前494年，吴王夫差大败越国，越国成为吴国的属国。越王勾践经过10年的艰苦准备，终于灭掉了吴国。后来勾践又率军北上，成为春秋时期最后一个霸主。

In the early Spring and Autumn Period (770 - 476 BC) the Zhou Kingdom was divided into over 100 vassal states, all squabbling over land and population. Strong states annexed weak ones and contended for hegemony over all the others. During this period, Duke Huan of Qi, Duke Xiang of Song, Duke Wen of Jin, Duke Mu of Qin and King Zhuang of Chu became the hegemons in succession, and were called the "five powers of the Spring and Autumn Period". Some historians rank the "five powers" as Duke Huan of Qi, Duke Wen of Jin, King Zhuang of Chu, King Helu of Wu and King Goujian of Yue.

Qi was a rich state in what is now Shandong Province. With the aid of the able statesman Guan Zhong, Duke Huan of Qi carried out a series of political and economic reforms, which helped the state to flourish and greatly enhanced its military power. In 651 BC, Duke Huan convened a meeting of the rulers of all the states, at which envoys from the Son of Heaven of Zhou (the Son of Heaven was the titular sovereign, and had little real power) were present. A treaty of alliance was concluded, and the period of Qi hegemony commenced.

In 632 BC the State of Jin defeated the State of Chu to rule the roost in the Central Plains. However, the fight for hegemony went on between two states for 100 years, until King Zhuang of Chu smashed the Jin army and made himself the hegemon. In the meantime, Duke Mu of Qin was expanding his territory to the west, and the State of Yue, located on the lower reaches of the Yangtze River, finally absorbed its long-time rival State of Wu. Gou Jian, King of Yue, led his army north, and made himself the last hegemon of the Spring and Autumn Period.

春秋列国形势图
Sketch Map of the Main Powers during the Spring and Autumn Period

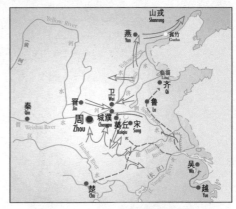

- 周王城 Capital of the Zhou Dynasty
- 各国都城 Capital of the vassal states
- 吴国进军路线 Wu's route of advance
- 越国进军路线 Yue's route of advance
- 齐、楚扩张路线 Qi and Chu's routes of expansion

👉 小资料 Data

退避三舍

晋文公曾经因为晋国内乱，在外流亡了19年，得到过楚成王的隆重接待。为了感谢楚成王，晋国和楚国作战时，遵守以前的诺言，把军队撤退了三舍（1舍约30里）。后来人们用"退避三舍"比喻主动让步，不跟人相争。

Retreating 90 Li

As a mark of gratitude to King Cheng of the State of Chu, who had harbored him for 19 years after he had been expelled from his own state, Duke Wen of Jin withdrew his troops 90 li (one li is equal to 1/2 km) when he found himself in an alliance against Chu. The phrase later came to be used to mean showing forbearance.

战国七雄
The Seven Powers of the Warring States Period

1. 带矛胄(战国兵器)
   The spear heads from the Warring States Period
2. 战国水陆攻战铜壶拓片
   A rubbing of the pattern on the bronze pot
3. 战国水陆攻战铜壶
   The bronze pot incised with scenes of a battle on both water and land (Warring States Period)

春秋时期无数次战争使诸侯国的数量大大减少。到战国时期，七个实力最强的诸侯国是齐、楚、燕(yān)、韩、赵、魏(wèi)、秦，并被称作"战国七雄"。

战国初期，韩、赵、魏三家结成联盟，打败了齐、秦、楚等大国，成为较强盛的国家。后来这个联盟破裂，齐国、秦国却逐渐兴盛起来。

战国中期，魏国军队攻打赵国，赵国请齐国帮助退兵。魏国内部空虚，大军事家孙膑(bìn)带领齐国的军队直接去打魏国的首都。魏国军队本已攻破赵国首都，听见自己的国家情况危急，便急忙从赵国撤军去救魏国，刚走到半路，就遇上了埋伏的齐国军队，齐国军队堵住魏国军队，打了个大胜仗。这就是中国历史上著名的战例——"围魏救赵"。

两年后魏国进攻韩国，齐国的军队在孙膑的指挥下围魏救韩。齐军假装后退。第一天撤出后营地留下的炉灶足够做10万人的饭；第二天留下的炉灶只够做5万人的饭；第三天留下的炉灶减少到只够做3万人的饭。魏军从炉灶的数量推测，以为齐军大量逃亡，于是挑选了精锐的士兵，追赶齐军，一直追到马陵(今河南省境内)，结果被埋伏在这里的齐军彻底打败。这就是著名的"马陵之战"。两次战役后齐国取代了魏国称霸中原。

战国后期，秦国越来越强盛，其他6个国家都不能单独抵抗秦国，于是就想联合起来，共同抵抗秦国。秦国为了打败其余的六国，挑拨六国之间的关系，促使他们都和秦国亲近。各国为了自身的利益，一到关键时刻常常不能齐心合力，结果给了秦国机会。秦

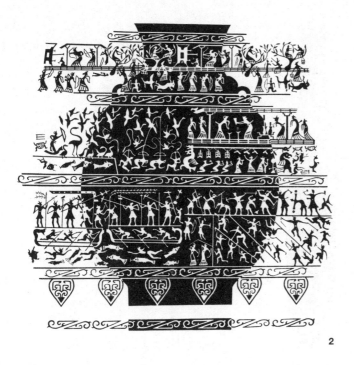

2

国前后征服了其他国家，并灭了周王室，统一了中国。

3

By the time of the Warring States Period (475 - 221 BC), only seven vassal states remained, the rest having been absorbed by Qi, Chu, Yan, Han, Zhao, Wei and Qin. These seven states were called the "seven powers of the Warring States Period".

In the early Warring States Period, Han, Zhao and Wei formed an alliance, and defeated Qi, Qin and Chu, separately. Later the alliance broke up, while Qi and Qin gradually gained in strength.

In the mid-Warring States Period, the State of Wei attacked Zhao. Zhao asked the State of Qi for help.

战国形势图
Sketch Map of the Warring States

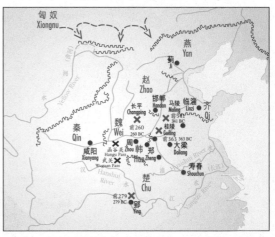

1. 虎纹铜矛鐏 (战国兵器)
   A bronze spear head with tiger-carving (made
   during the Warring States Period)
2. 镂空虎纹戈 (大约是春秋—战国时代的
   兵器)
   A spear head with tiger-carving (made during
   the Spring & Autumn Period and Warring States
   Period)

The great military strategist Sun Bin led the Qi army against the Wei capital. Alarmed at the threat to their own lightly-defended state, the Wei troops, who had already occupied the Zhao capital, withdrew, and Zhao was saved. On their way back to Wei, the Wei forces were ambushed by the Qi army, and were crushingly defeated. This was a famous battle in Chinese history, and gave rise to the saying "Besieging Wei and saving Zhao".

Two years later, Wei launched an attack against the State of Han. The Qi army, again under the command of Sun Bin, besieged Wei and saved Han. Then the Qi army pretended to retreat. On the first day they left behind enough camp fire sites to cook food for 100,000 soldiers, the second day enough for 50,000 soldiers, and the third day only enough for 30,000 soldiers. The Wei commander speculated that the Qi soldiers were deserting in great numbers. When the Wei forces caught up with a small force of the Qi army at Maling (in today's Henan Province), they were ambushed and put to flight by the full strength of the Qi troops. Qi later replaced Wei as the hegemon of the Central Plains.

In the late Warring States Period, Qin became stronger and stronger. The other six states allied against the growing power in the west, but Qin cleverly sowed discord among them, and they could never form a united front against it. Qin vanquished the other states one by one, abolished the Zhou ruling house, and united China under the Qin Dynasty.

商鞅变法
Shang Yang's Reform

公元前361年，秦国的新国君秦孝公即位。他下决心要使秦国强大起来，于是下了一道命令，说谁能使秦国强大，就封谁做官。

1. 商鞅奖励耕织
Shang Yang's reform was to reward farming and weaving.

商鞅 (yāng) 原来是卫国人，听到了这个消息，就来到秦国。商鞅和秦孝公谈论国家大事，一连谈了几天几夜。秦孝公非常赞同商鞅的主张。公元前356年，秦孝公任用商鞅，开始改革旧的制度。

商鞅起草了一个改革的法令，但又怕老百姓不相信他，就叫人在都城的南门竖了一根很高的木头，并说，谁能把木头搬到北门，就赏谁十金。很多人都以为这是开玩笑。商鞅知道老百姓不相信他，就把赏金提高到五十金。人们在木头旁议论纷纷，终于有一个人把木头扛起来，一直扛到了北门。结果商鞅真的赏给那人五十金。这件事在秦国引起了轰动，商鞅说到做到，在老百姓中有了威信，于是商鞅就把新法令公布了出去。

商鞅变法共进行了两次，变法的主要内容有：①废除了井田制，打破过去土地上的界限，国家承认土地私有，允许自由买卖。②生产粮食布帛 (bó) 多的人可以免除徭役 (yáoyì)。在战争中军功越大，授予的爵 (jué) 位越高，赐给的土地和房子也越多。旧贵族没有军功，就不能享受特权。③在全国设置31个县，由国君直接派官吏管理。

新法令刚刚开始推行，就遭到了旧贵族的强烈反对。太子的两个老师鼓动太子反对变法，商鞅就处罚了那两位老师，一个割掉了鼻子，一个在脸上刺了字。这样，大家就不敢反对了。

经过商鞅变法，秦国的经济得到了发展，军队战斗力得到了加强，成为战国后期最强大的国家。

小资料 Data

商鞅之死

商鞅变法遭到旧贵族的强烈反对。秦孝公死后，商鞅被诬告谋反，结果被车裂而死。车裂是古代一种非常残忍的死刑，就是把人的四肢和头分别拴在五辆马车上，让马向不同的方向奔跑，撕裂人的肢体。

The Death of Shang Yang

After his patron Duke Xiao died, Shang Yang was accused of treason by the old Qin aristocracy, and put to death by being torn apart between five chariots.

In 361 BC, Duke Xiao came to the throne of the State of Qin. Determined to make Qin a powerful state he set about looking for men of talent to help him do so. Shang Yang, of the State of Wei, offered his services to Duke Xiao, and in 356 BC was given the task of reforming Qin's institutions.

Shang Yang thought up a novel way to win the confidence of the population, so that the people of Qin would back his reform. He had a log placed near the south gate of the capital of Qin, and announced that he would give 10 pieces of gold to anyone who carried the log to the north gate. When nobody took up the offer, Shang Yang raised the reward to 50 pieces of gold. Finally a man shouldered the log, and carried it to the north gate. Shang Yang was as good as his word, and handed over 50 gold pieces to the man.

Sure of the confidence of the people of Qin, Shang Yang set about a suite of reforms, which included private ownership of, and transactions in, land, exemption from corvee labor for producers of large amounts of crops or cloth, lavish rewards for people of military distinction, and the division of the state into 31 counties which were supervised by officials directly appointed by the duke.

Members of the aristocracy of Qin felt that their position was threatened by the reform, and tried to stir up opposition to it. This anti-reform party was led by two tutors of the heir-apparent. Shang Yang moved swiftly. He had the pair punished by having the nose of one of them cut off and the face of the other tattooed.

Shang Yang's reform had a great deal to do with Qin's emergence as the most powerful state in the late Warring States Period.

灿烂的青铜文明
Brilliant Bronze Civilization

小资料 Data

司母戊大方鼎

商朝后期制造，河南安阳出土，腹部呈长方形，腹内铸"司母戊"三字。鼎高1.33米，长1.1米，宽0.78米，重832.84千克，是至今为止发现的最大的出土青铜器。

The Simuwu Square *Ding* cauldron

The Simuwu square ding cauldron was manufactured in the late Shang Dynasty. It was unearthed in Anyang, Henan Province. The belly of the cauldron is rectangular in shape. The vessel is 1.33 m tall, 1.1 m long and 0.78 m wide. It weighs 832.84 kg, making it the biggest item of ancient bronze ware existent in the world.

1. 编钟（战国早期文物，分上下三层，共悬编钟64件，至今仍能演奏乐曲。）
   The set of chimes unearthed from the tomb of Marquis Yi of Zeng

商朝的青铜器制造很发达，后期制造的司母戊鼎（dǐng），是现今世界上发现的最大的青铜器。另一件四羊方尊，造型雄奇，工艺高超，是商朝青铜器中的精品。

先秦时期，青铜还被用来制造乐器。春秋战国时期，盛行"钟鼓之乐"（一种以编钟与鼓为主要乐器所演奏的音乐）。1978年在湖北随州曾侯乙墓中出土的大量文物中，以整套编钟最为珍贵。编钟共有64件，以大小和音高为序组成8组，悬挂在铜木结构的三层钟架上。整套编钟音律准确，音色优美，音域宽广，它在地下埋藏了2,000多年，今天依然能用它来演奏音乐。

The manufacture of bronze wares reached its zenith during the Shang Dynasty. The Simuwu square *ding* cauldron, made in the late Shang Dynasty, is the biggest item of bronze ware existent in the world. A *zun* wine vessel with the heads of four goats carved on it, also dating from the Shang Dynasty, is one of the finest examples of bronze ware known.

During pre-Qin times, bronze was also used to make musical instruments. In the Spring and Autumn and Warring States periods, chimes were popular musical instruments played at court and religious ceremonies. In 1978, a complete set of chimes was excavated from the tomb of Marquis Yi of Zeng in Suizhou, Hubei Province. A total of 64 chimes divided into eight groups according to their different sizes and pitches hung on a three-layer stand of bronze and wood. The chimes have a beautiful timber and wide range, and can still be played after being buried for over 2,000 years.

1

哈雷彗星和《甘石星经》
Halley's Comet and the *Ganshi Classic of the Constellations*

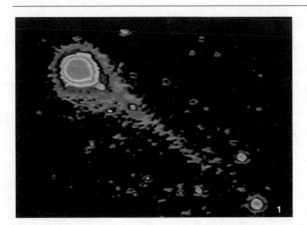

中国人很早就注意观察天象。古书上关于夏朝时流星雨和日食的记载，是世界天文史上最早的记录。春秋战国时期，天文学已取得了相当高的成就。鲁国的天文学家在对天象的观测中，观测到37次日食，其中33次已被证明是可靠的。现在世人通称的哈雷彗星，早在公元前613年就被载入鲁国史书《春秋》中，这是世界上关于哈雷彗星的最早的记录。

这一时期还出现了天文学专著，齐国人甘德著《天文星占》八卷，魏国人石申写了《天文》八卷，后人将它们合为一部，称《甘石星经》，这是世界上现存最早的天文学著作。书中记录了水、木、金、火、土五大行星的运行情况，以及它们的出没规律。书中还记录了800个恒星的名字，有121个的位置现在已经被测定。甘德还用肉眼发现了木星的卫星，比意大利天文学家伽利略在1609年用天文望远镜发现该星早2,000多年。石申则发现日月食是天体相互掩盖的现象，这在当时也是难能可贵的。为了纪念石申，月球上有一座环形山就是用他的名字命名的。

The Chinese people have paid great attention to astronomical phenomena since very early times. Meteor showers and solar eclipses which occurred as far back as in the Xia Dynasty are recorded in ancient books, and are thought to be the earliest astronomical accounts. By the Spring and Autumn and Warring States periods, astronomy had reached quite a high level of sophistication. Astronomers of the State of Lu observed 37 solar eclipses, among which 33 have been proved accurate. The earliest record of an

appearance by Halley's Comet (613 BC) is contained in the chronicle of Lu known as the *Spring and Autumn Annals.*

During this period there appeared specialized works on astronomy. Gan De of the State of Qi wrote a work titled *Astronomy and Astrology* in eight volumes, and Shi Shen of the State of Wei wrote his *Astronomy,* also in eight volumes. Later, the two works were combined as the *Ganshi Classic of the Constellations.* The earliest astronomical work extant in the world, it records the motions of Mercury, Jupiter, Venus, Mars and Saturn. There also recorded the names of 800 stars, the positions of 121 of which have been ascertained. Gan De discovered Jupiter's moon with the naked eye, 2,000 years earlier than the Italian astronomer Galileo, who discovered it with an astronomical telescope in 1609. Shi Shen discovered the reason for solar and lunar eclipses. A crater on the moon has been named after Shi Shen.

🖝 小资料 Data

哈雷彗星

1682年英国人哈雷发现了一颗彗星，并推算出它的运行轨道，人们将这颗彗星称为"哈雷彗星"。西方人对这一彗星的发现比中国人晚了2,000多年。

Halley's Comet

Halley's Comet gets its name from Sir Edmond Halley, an English astronomer who, in 1682, discovered the comet and calculated its orbit. Chinese astronomers, however, had recorded Halley's Comet 2,000 years earlier.

1. 哈雷彗星（在中国古代历史书中有数百条彗星记录，关于哈雷彗星的记载尤其详尽。图为中国云南天文台1985年12月13日拍摄的哈雷彗星。）
   Halley's Comet as photographed on December 13th, 1985, by the Yunnan Observatory
2. 《春秋》记载哈雷彗星（孛星）的书页
   The earliest record of an appearance by Halley's Comet is contained in the chronicle of the *Spring and Autumn Annals.*
3. 唐代紫微恒星图
   The depiction of Purple Forbidden Enclosure (a Chinese Star region) was drawn during the Tang Dynasty.

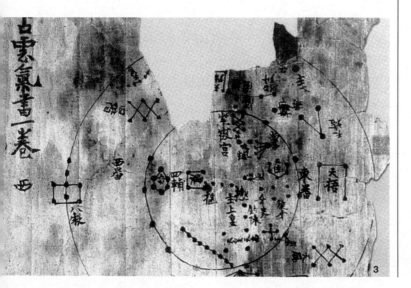

大教育家孔子
Confucius, the Great Educator

小资料 Data

六经

即儒家的六部经典:《易》、《诗》、《礼》、《乐》、《尚书》、《春秋》,它们是由孔子亲自整理编订的,是孔子对中国古代文化发展作出的不朽贡献。

The Six Classics

The Six Classics are six ancient works considered central to the Confucian canon, namely, *The Book of Changes, The Book of Songs, The Book of Rites, The Book of Music, The Book of History* and *The Spring and Autumn Annals*. These works are said to have been compiled and edited by Confucius himself. They are immortal contributions Confucius made to the development of ancient Chinese culture.

孔子(公元前551年—公元前479年),名丘,字仲尼,春秋末期鲁国陬邑(zōuyì,今山东曲阜东南)人,是儒家学派的创始人。

孔子是个大思想家,首先,他提出"仁"的学说,即要求统治者能够体贴民情,爱惜民力,不要过度压迫剥削人民。其次,他主张以德治民,反对暴政。

孔子又是个大教育家,在那个时代,只有贵族子弟才能够受教育。孔子提倡"有教无类",他收学生,不论他们地位贵贱,都一律平等地进行教育。孔子兴办私学,打破了官府对文化教育的垄断。据说孔子教过的学生有3,000多人,其中著名的有72人。孔子主张"因材施教",对不同的学生,进行不同的教育。他教育学生:学习知识要经常复习,"温故而知新";学习态度要老实,"知之为知之,不知为不知";还要求把学习和思考结合起来。

后来,孔子的学生们将孔子的思想言行记录下来,汇编成《论语》一书,《论语》成为儒家经典之一。孔子的学说成为中国2,000多年封建文化的正统。

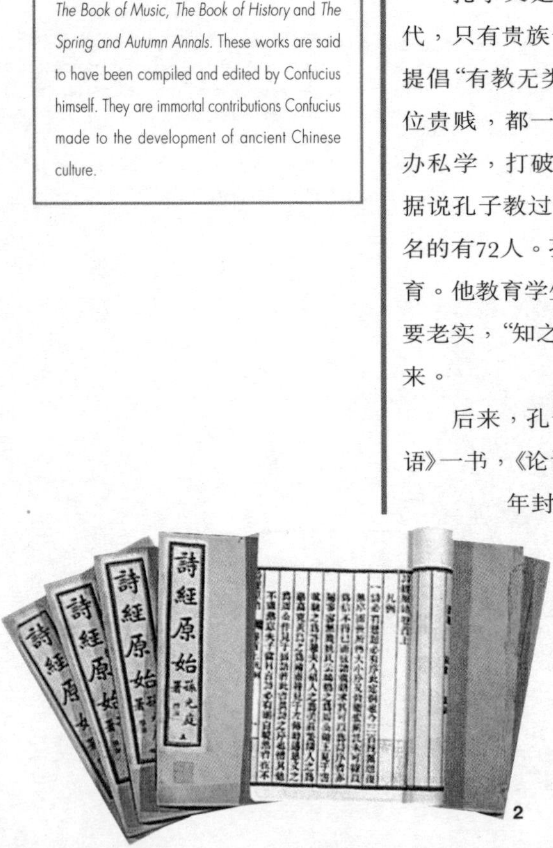

1

2

Confucius (551 - 479 BC) was surnamed Kong and his given name was Qiu, and he styled himself Zhongni. He was born in Zouyi in the State of Lu (in the southeast of today's Qufu, Shandong Province) in the late Spring and Autumn Period. He was the founder of Confucianism.

Confucius was one of the great thinkers that emerged

1. 孔子像
   A portrait of Confucius
2. 《诗经》是中国最早的一部诗歌总集，
   传为孔子所编，收集了从西周初到春
   秋中叶约500年间的诗歌305篇
   The Book of Songs was edited by Confucius. It
   contains 305 songs — some of the oldest pieces
   of Chinese literature — which were collected
   during the 500 years dated from the early
   Western Zhou Dynasty through the Spring and
   Autumn Period.
3. 孔子讲学图
   Confucius Giving a Lecture
4. 山东曲阜孔庙
   Confucius Temple, Qufu, Shandong Province
5. 孔子墓
   Confucius' Tomb

at this time. He advanced the theory of benevolence (*ren*) on the part of rulers toward their people, stressing that the wealth they produced should not be squandered and political rule should be based on virtue, not force.

Confucius was also a great educator. In his time, only children from aristocratic families could receive education. Confucius advocated "treating everyone the same in educating people". He taught his pupils without discrimination, no matter what their social status was. Confucius established private schools and broke the government's monopoly over education. It is said that Confucius taught as many as 3,000 pupils, among whom 72 became very famous. Confucius proposed "teaching students according to their aptitude". He said one should be honest in learning and not pretend to know what one did not know. He told his pupils to review what they had learned regularly during their study, because "new knowledge can be gained by reviewing old knowledge"; he also told his pupils to combine study with thinking.

Confucius' disciples recorded his words and deeds in *The Analects of Confucius*, which is one of the classics of the Confucian school. Confucius' theories formed the orthodox ruling ideology in China for over 2,000 years.

5

诸子百家
The "Hundred Schools of Thought" and Their Exponents

　　春秋战国时期，是中国历史上大变革的时代。社会大变革促进了文化的繁荣。这一时期，出现了老子、庄子、孔子、孟子、荀子、墨子、韩非子等大思想家，他们从不同的立场和角度出发，对当时的社会发表主张，并逐步形成以道家、儒家、墨家和法家等为主的众多派别，在中国历史上被称为"诸子百家"。他们纷纷著书立说，宣传自己的主张，批评别人的观点，出现了"百家争鸣"的局面。

　　老子是道家学派的创始人，著有《道德经》一书，他认为，各种事物都有对立面，如祸和福、有和无、生和灭、贵和贱、上和下、强和弱等都是对立的双方，它们之间会相互转化。

　　墨子开创了墨家学派，主张节约，反对浪费，主张选举品德高尚，有才能的人来做官，并要求人们相互友爱，反对战争。

　　法家最重要的代表人物是韩非，著有《韩非子》一书，他主张"法治"，认为法律应当向全国公布，臣民应该严格遵守；强调用严厉的刑罚来镇压人民的反抗。他提倡改革，提出建立君主专制的中央集权的国家。他的思想后来被秦始皇采用。

Great social changes took place during the Spring and Autumn and Warring States periods, which spurred cultural development. In these periods, there appeared many great thinkers, such as Lao Zi, Zhuang Zi, Confucius, Mencius, Xun Zi, Mo Zi and Han Fei Zi. They stated their views on society from different stands and angles, and gradually formed schools of philosophy represented mainly by the Taoist, Confucianist, Mohist and Legalist schools. These numerous schools and their representatives came to be known as the "Hundred Schools of Thought and their exponents". They wrote books to expound their theories, publicized their propositions and criticized others'

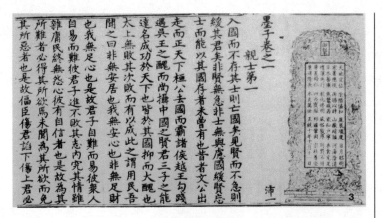

1. 老子像
   A portrait of Lao Zi
2. 荀子像
   A portrait of Xun Zi
3. 墨子主张选贤能之士做官
   Mo Zi advocated appointing those who are noble and talented to be the government officials.
4. 老子著作《道德经》
   Lao Zi's *Dao De Jing (The Classic of the Way and Virtue)*
5. 孟子像
   A portrait of Mencius

viewpoints in a period when "one hundred schools of thought contended".

Lao Zi was the founder of the Taoist School, and wrote *Dao De Jing (The Classic of the Way and Virtue)*. He deemed that all things have their opposites; for example, fortune and misfortune, existence and non-existence, life and death, nobility and baseness, high and low, strong and weak are all pairs of opposite aspects of a unity and can be transformed into each other.

Mo Zi initiated the Mohist School. He encouraged economy and opposed waste. He advocated choosing noble-minded and talented people to be officials to govern the people. And he called on people to love each other and eschew war.

The most important representative of the Legalist School was Han Fei Zi, who wrote *The Book of Han Fei Zi*. He advocated ruling the country by means of strictly enforced laws. He was in favor of a centralized autocratic monarchy. His theories were later adopted by Emperor Qinshihuang, China's first unifier.

世界第一部兵书——
《孙子兵法》

Sun Zi's Art of War — The World's First Treatise on Military Science

1

《孙子兵法》又称《孙子》，是中国古代著名的兵书，也是世界上现存最早的兵书，作者是春秋末期杰出的军事家孙武。孙武是齐国人，后来迁到吴国。那时候，各诸侯国为了争夺霸主的地位，不断地发动战争，社会动荡不安。孙武居住在吴国时，各国的战争吸引他去思考并总结战争的规律。经过艰苦的努力，终于完成了兵书的写作。

孙武将兵书献给了吴王阖闾。吴王任命孙武为大将，让他训练吴国军队。他军纪严明，练兵认真，在他的帮助下，吴国成为春秋时期的一个军事强国。

《孙子兵法》现存13篇，共6,000多字。在这不长的篇幅中，孙武全面论述了对战争的看法。他强调战争中要对敌我双方的情况调查清楚，提出了"知彼知己，百战不殆(dài)"(了解敌人，了解自己，无论打多少仗都不会受损)，"攻其无备，出其不意"(在敌人没有防备时进攻，在敌人意想不到的地方下手)，以及集中优势兵力打败敌人等思想。孙武特别强调"非危不战"(不到危急的时候，不要发动战争)，因为打仗会大大加重人民负担。战国时的军事家孙膑，比孙武晚100多年，他继承了孙武的军事思想，写有《孙膑兵法》。

《孙子兵法》已被译为英、法、日、德、俄、捷等多种文字，这本书虽然讲的是战争规律，但对其他行业也有启示意义，因此在世界上享有很高的声誉。

Sun Zi's Art of War is the earliest work of military science extant in the world. Its author, Sun Wu, was an outstanding strategist in the late Spring and Autumn Period. Sun Wu was born in the State of Qi, later moving to the State of Wu. The endemic wars between the various states at that time caused Sun Wu to think deeply about military strategy. He wrote *The Art of War*, and presented it to the ruler of Wu, who put him in command of his army. In consequence, Wu soon became a major military power in the Spring and Autumn Period.

The Art of War consists of 13 chapters, amounting to some 6,000 characters. In this limited space, Sun Wu expounds his wide-ranging views on war. He emphasizes the importance of "knowing yourself and knowing your enemy", "attacking the enemy unexpectedly" and concentrating a superior force to thoroughly defeat the enemy. He was also probably the first to recommend the use of spies. Sun Wu especially stressed the importance of using war only as a last resort, because war was a grievous burden on the people. Some 100 years later, during the Warring States Period, Sun Bin inherited Sun Wu's military theory, and wrote *Sun Bin's Art of War*.

Sun Zi's Art of War has been translated into English, French, Japanese, German, Russian, Czech and other languages. Because it is deemed applicable to many of life's problems, not just war, it enjoys high international prestige.

👉 **小资料 Data**

三十六计

在《孙子兵法》一书中，孙子共列出了36条计谋，教人们如何去应付战争。他当时提出的"用间"，就是采用间谍战，至今还广为沿用。

在这"三十六计"中，有一条最有名的计谋，那就是"走"。"三十六计，走为上计"早已成了成语，意思是：如果你没有获胜的希望，那最好的办法就是赶紧逃吧。

The 36 Stratagems

In his *Art of War*, Sun Wu lists 36 stratagems, of which the most famous is "When you are hopeless of victory, the best course is to run away". A common saying even nowadays in China is "Of the 36 stratagems, running away is the best".

1. 孙武像
   A portrait of Sun Wu
2. 清代版本《孙子兵法》
   The Qing Dynasty edition of *Sun Zi's Art of War*

2

爱国诗人屈原
Qu Yuan, a Patriotic Poet

屈原 (约公元前340年—前278年) 是中国古代伟大诗人,他出身于楚国贵族,非常有学问。他在楚国做官期间,主张改革,主张联合齐国抵抗秦国,遭到奸臣的排挤反对,被楚王流放,长期在外漂泊。公元前278年,楚的都城郢 (yǐng) 被秦军攻破后,他悲愤绝望,跳进汨 (mì) 罗江自杀。传说屈原投江的日子是中国农历的五月初五,人们为了纪念他,每年的这一天都要赛龙舟、吃粽子。

赛龙舟,是为了把鱼吓走;人们还包粽子喂鱼,这些都是为了让鱼不要去吃沉没在江中的屈原的尸体。后来农历的五月初五演变为中华民族的传统节日——端午节。

屈原生前采用楚国方言,利用民间歌谣的形式,创造出一种新的诗歌体裁,后人称为"楚辞"体。他写了许多优秀的诗篇,以抒情长诗《离骚》最为著名。他的作品表现了他对楚国的深切怀念和为理想而献身的精神,语言优美,想像奇特,融合大量古代神话传说,富有浪漫主义色彩。屈原的诗不仅在中国被广为传诵,还被译为多种外国文字,成为中华民族贡献给人类文化的一份珍贵遗产。

1

1. 屈原像
   A portrait of Qu Yuan
2. 湖北秭 (zǐ)归屈原祠
   The Qu Yuan Memorial Temple in Zigui, Hubei
   Province
3. 每年农历五月初五,各地都会赛龙舟,以纪念屈原
   Drogon-boat races are held on the fifth day of
   the fifth lunar month in commemoration of Qu
   Yuan.

Qu Yuan (340 - 278 BC) was born into an aristocratic family of the State of Chu, and showed a talent for writing poetry at an early age. As a senior official, he tried to warn the ruler of Chu of danger from the State of Qin, but lost his official post due to intrigue, and was exiled. In 278 BC, the capital city of Chu, Ying, fell to an invading army from the State of Qin. Overcome with grief, Qu Yuan threw himself into the Miluo River in northeast Hunan Province. Tradition has it that this occurred on the fifth day of the fifth month by the lunar calendar. In commemoration of this patriotic man of letters, dragon-boat races are held on this day every year. Also, people eat *zongzi* (a pyramid-shaped dumpling made of glutinous rice wrapped in bamboo or

reed leaves). The dragon-boat races are meant to frighten fish away from Qu Yuan's body, and *zongzi* are supposed to be used to feed the fish, so that they would not eat the poet's dead body. The Dragon Boat Festival is one of the highlights of the Chinese calendar.

Adopting the framework of Chu folk ballads and using the Chu dialect, Qu Yuan created a new type of poems, called the "songs of Chu" genre by later generations. His most famous poem is the long lyric work *Li Sao*. Qu Yuan's poetic works are filled with devotion to his native State of Chu, and are enlivened with references to ancient myths. They have been translated into many foreign languages.

小资料 Data

《楚辞》

《楚辞》是继中国最早的诗歌总集《诗经》之后的又一部诗集。由西汉刘向收辑。收入战国屈原、宋玉、景差及汉代贾谊、东方朔、刘向等人的作品，共16篇，其中主要为屈原的作品。

The Songs of Chu

The Songs of Chu (Chu Ci) is a poetry anthology, the second to appear in Chinese history after *The Book of Songs*. *The Songs of Chu* was collected and compiled by Liu Xiang of the Western Han Dynasty. It includes works by Qu Yuan, Song Yu and Jing Chai of the Warring States Period and Jia Yi, Dongfang Shuo and Liu Xiang of the Han Dynasty (206 BC - 220 AD). Of the 16 poems, most are by Qu Yuan.

概述
Introduction

　　秦汉时期，开始于公元前221年，结束于公元220年。秦朝是中国历史上第一个封建大一统的时代，也是统一的多民族国家的奠基时期。秦汉王朝开创的许多制度，为以后历代封建统治者所沿用。

　　秦朝建立于公元前221年，秦始皇采取了一系列巩固统一的措施，建立了一整套的统治制度，中国成为第一个统一的封建中央集权的多民族国家。但是，秦始皇和他的继承者对农民空前残暴的压迫和剥削，导致秦的统治在公元前207年被农民起义推翻。

　　汉朝包括西汉与东汉两个朝代，公元前202年，汉高祖刘邦建立汉朝，定都长安(今西安)，历史上称之为西汉。西汉末年，王莽夺取西汉政权。公元25年，西汉贵族刘秀借农民起义之机，恢复汉朝，定都于今天的洛阳，历史上称之为东汉。东汉末年，政权被农民大起义瓦解，最后结束于220年。两汉时期长达400多年，这个时期社会发展有很多成就，有些成就具有深远的历史影响。今天的汉族、汉字、汉语、汉文化等名称都与汉朝有关。秦汉时期，生产发展迅速，经济繁荣，国防巩固，科技文化事业发达，在医学、天文学、地质学等方面都取得了突出的成就，还涌现出许多著名的政治家、思想家、军事家、科学家、史学家、文学家。特别是造纸术的发明和改进，对世界文化事业的发展作出了巨大贡献。

　　秦汉时期，从地中海、西亚到太平洋东岸，雄踞着4个帝国，其中汉朝与罗马的历史地位尤其重要。随着丝绸之路的开辟，中国辉煌灿烂的文化开始影响世界，当时世界上优秀的文明成就也逐渐融入中国的传统文化之中。

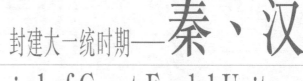

封建大一统时期—秦、汉

The Period of Great Feudal Unity –
The Qin and Han Dynasties

The period of the Qin and Han dynasties began in 221 BC and ended in 220 AD. The Qin Dynasty was the first feudal dynasty to rule the whole of China, and it laid the foundation of a united multi-ethnic country. Many institutions initiated in the Qin and Han dynasties were inherited continuously by later dynasties.

The Qin Dynasty was established in 221 BC by Emperor Qinshihuang, who adopted a series of reforms such as unifying the currencies and writing systems of the previous states. However, the heavy-handed methods of Qinshihuang and his successor led to the overthrow of the Qin Dynasty in 207 BC by a peasant uprising.

In 202 BC, Liu Bang established the Han Dynasty, choosing Chang'an (today's Xi'an) as his capital. In 9 AD, Wang Mang staged a coup, and set up the short-lived Xin Dynasty. The Han Dynasty was restored in 25 AD by Liu Xiu, who moved the capital to the city known today as Luoyang. Subsequently, this period became known to historians as the Eastern Han Dynasty, and the previous one as the Western Han Dynasty. In 220, the Eastern Han Dynasty was overthrown by a peasant uprising. In its over 400 years of existence, the Han Dynasty made achievements in agriculture, defense, science and technology, and culture. Notable among these achievements was the invention of the technique of papermaking, which was a great contribution to world civilization.

During the period of the Qin and Han dynasties, the Silk Road started to connect China with the Roman Empire and the Western world as a whole. With the opening of the Silk Road, China's brilliant culture began to influence the whole world, and the splendid cultural accomplishments of other countries gradually merged into traditional Chinese culture.

中国第一位皇帝
——秦始皇

Qinshihuang — The First Emperor in Chinese History

秦在公元前770年才被封为中国西部一个诸侯国,疆域较小,国力不盛,始终被中原诸侯看不起。但自从实行了商鞅变法后,国力日盛,很快成为战国七雄中的强国。秦王嬴政 (yíngzhèng,公元前259年—公元前210年) 当政以后,发动了大规模的战争。从公元前230年开始,历时10年,先后灭了韩、赵、魏、楚、燕、齐,于公元前221年统一了六国。

嬴政幻想秦的统治能永远继续下去,自称"始皇帝",他的后代称二世、三世,以至千万世。因此,历史上称嬴政为秦始皇。

秦始皇统一后,采取了许多巩固统一的措施。

政治上 在中央,设置了丞相、御史大夫、太尉等职。丞相帮助皇帝处理全国的政务,御史大夫负责监察百官,太尉管理军事,都由皇帝任免。在地方,实行郡县制度,全国划分为36郡(后来增到40多个郡),郡下设县。长官称郡守和县令,也都由皇帝直接任免,负责管理人民。这样,皇帝把统治全国各地的权力牢牢控制在自己手里。

经济上 首先统一度量衡。战国时期,各国的度量衡都不一样,秦始皇统一度量衡,使长度、容量、重量,都有了统一的标准,促进了经济的发展。秦朝还统一了货币。秦政府规定把秦国的圆形方孔钱,作为统一的货币,通行全国。这对促进各民族各地区的经济交流,十分有用。后来各个朝代的铜钱都仿照秦朝的样式。

文化上 第一,统一文字。战国时期,各国的文

秦疆域图
Sketch Map of Qin Territory

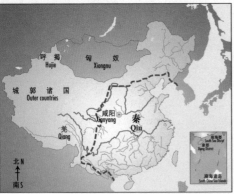

秦统一六国货币简图
The Common Currency of the Qin Dynasty

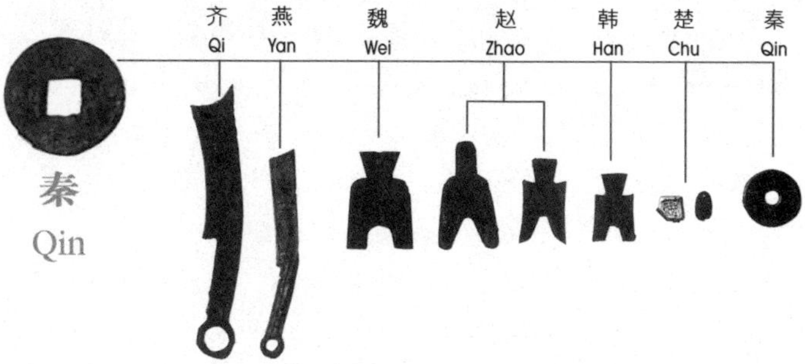

齐	燕	魏	赵	韩	楚	秦
Qi	Yan	Wei	Zhao	Han	Chu	Qin

秦
Qin

1. 秦始皇像(秦始皇,公元前259年—公元前210年,公元前221年统一六国,建立了中国第一个中央集权的封建国家。)
Qinshihuang (259 - 210 BC) united the whole China in 221 BC, and established the first feudal dynasty.

字也都不一样。秦始皇下令统一文字,把简化了的字体小篆(zhuàn)作为标准字体,通令全国使用。接着,又出现了一种比小篆书写更简便的字体——隶书。现在的楷(kǎi)书,就是从隶书演化来的。文字的统一,促进了文化的交流。第二,焚书坑儒,加强思想控制。公元前213年,丞相李斯认为,人们读了古书上的各种观点后,会用那些观点批评时事,这样会不利于朝廷的统治。所以他建议,民间除了医药、种植等书以外,其余的书,尤其是各国史书及诸子书籍应全部烧掉。秦始皇采纳了他的建议。第二年,一些读书人背后议论秦始皇专横武断,滥施刑罚。秦始皇加以追查,最后活埋了460多人。这两件事,史称"焚书坑儒"。

军事上 击败匈奴,修筑长城,安定了北方;在南方,使越族归顺,扩大了民族交往。

秦始皇完成统一大业,结束了长期以来诸侯割据称雄的局面,建立了中国历史上第一个统一的多民族的封建国家。秦朝的疆域,东到大海,西到陇西,北到长城一带,南到南海,人口达到2,000多万。但秦始皇又是暴君,他的残暴统治也对中国历史产生了不良影响。

It was not until 770 BC that the State of Qin came into existence as one of the vassal states in western China. Later, it emerged as one of the seven most powerful states in China, assisted by Shang Yang's reform. King Ying Zheng (259 - 210 BC) embarked on a campaign of expansion. In the space of only ten years, from 230 BC, Qin vanquished Han, Zhao, Wei, Chu, Yan and Qi one after another, and united the whole of China in 221 BC.

1

1. 在秦始皇陵出土的铜车马
   The bronze chariot was unearthed from Qinshihuang Mausoleum.

1

Ying Zheng called himself "The First Emperor of the Qin Dynasty" (Qinshihuang).

Qinshihuang enacted a sweeping series of reforms to consolidate his rule. The government was presided over by a prime minister. The Yushidafu supervised the bureaucracy, and the Taiwei was commander-in-chief of the army. They were all appointed and removed by the emperor himself. The whole country was divided into 36 prefectures (later increased to more than 40), which were in turn divided into counties. The magistrates of the prefectures and counties were also directly appointed and removed by the emperor.

In the Warring States Period, linear measures differed from state to state. Qinshihuang set fixed standards for length, volume and weight, which propelled the development of the economy. The Qin Dynasty also issued a uniform currency. Round coins with a square hole in the middle were used all over China, and set the pattern for the coins of later dynasties.

Of great significance for the development of communication and culture was the standardization of Chinese characters. The first reform of the characters resulted in the seal script (*zhuan*). Then, the official script (*lishu*), a simplified version of the seal script, was devised. Today's regular script (*kaishu*) developed from the official script. In 213 BC, Qinshihuang's prime minister, Li Si, had all books, except for those on medicine and agriculture, burned, in order to strengthen the regime's ideological control of the people. To further guard against dissent, the emperor had 460 Confucian scholars buried alive.

To curb the incessant invasions of the Hun (Xiongnu) nomads in the north, the Qin Dynasty set about building the Great Wall by linking up already existing defensive walls that had been built by various states. In the south, Qinshihuang subdued the Yue people.

Qinshihuang established the first united multi-ethnic feudal country on Chinese soil. Qin's territory, embracing over 20 million people, reached the Pacific in the east, Longxi (west of the Longshan Mountains) in the west, the Great Wall in the north and the South China Sea in the south. However, to achieve this, Qinshihuang had to resort to tyrannical methods.

陈胜、吴广起义
The Uprising of Chen Sheng and Wu Guang

公元前210年，秦始皇在一次巡游中去世。他的二儿子胡亥（hài）即位，称为二世皇帝。秦二世十分残暴，百姓非常怨恨他，社会局势动荡不安。

公元前209年，900多名贫苦农民，在被征去防守边境的途中，遇雨被困于大泽乡（今安徽宿州西南），无法按期赶到边境。按照秦朝法律，误期都得处死。农民被迫死里求生。陈胜、吴广合谋杀死押送的军官，举行起义。陈胜慷慨激昂地说："王侯将相，宁有种乎！"（那些王侯将相，难道都是天生的贵种吗？）中国历史上第一次大规模的农民起义在大泽乡爆发了。

起义军很快攻克了附近的几个县城，不到一个月，队伍就壮大到几万人。陈胜在陈地（今河南淮阳）称王，国号"张楚"。然后，起义军的主力西进，这年9月攻入函谷关，打到秦都城咸阳附近，队伍发展到几十万人。

1. 陈胜、吴广起义图
   A portrait of the Uprising of Chen Sheng and Wu Guang

1. 河南商丘陈胜墓
   Chen Sheng Mausoleum, Shangqiu, Henan Province
2. 陈胜揭竿起义曾攻入函谷关，直逼秦都咸阳
   Chen Sheng once led the peasants to capture Hanguguan Pass and threatened to attack the capital Xianyang.

秦二世得知起义军入关，非常害怕。来不及调集军队，只好派章邯(hán)率领正在建造骊(lí)山陵墓的几十万人迎战，击溃了起义军的主力。不久，吴广被部将所杀，陈胜也被叛徒刺死，起义军虽进行了将近半年的艰苦奋斗，终被秦军镇压。

In 210 BC, Qinshihuang died during an inspection tour. His second son, Hu Hai, succeeded to the throne.

In 209 BC, over 900 poor peasants drafted to guard the boundaries were delayed by rain in Dazexiang (southwest of today's Suzhou in Anhui Province) on their way to their posts. According to the harsh Qin laws, they faced the death penalty, and in desperation, led by Chen Sheng and Wu Guang, they killed the officers escorting them, and rose in revolt. This was the beginning of China's first great peasant uprising.

The revolt spread, and Chen Sheng proclaimed himself emperor. The deaths of Chen Sheng and Wu Guang by treachery and the defeat of the rebels when they were almost at the gates of the capital, Xianyang, gave the second Qin emperor a breathing space.

刘邦和项羽
Liu Bang and Xiang Yu

1. 刘邦像
   A portrait of Liu Bang
2. 项羽像
   A portrait of Xiang Yu

陈胜、吴广起义失败以后，刘邦和项羽继续领导农民反抗秦朝统治。公元前207年，项羽以少胜多，在巨鹿 (今河北平乡西南) 大败秦军主力。同时，刘邦带兵直逼咸阳。秦朝统治者向刘邦投降，秦朝灭亡。

秦朝灭亡以后，项羽自称为西楚霸王，封刘邦为汉王。自公元前206年开始，项羽和刘邦为争做皇帝，进行了将近4年的战争，历史上称为"楚汉战争"。战争初期，项羽实力雄厚，有40万大军；刘邦只有10万人。但是刘邦关注民心，进驻咸阳时，宣布废除秦朝的严酷法令，向老百姓"约法三章"——杀人的要被处死，打伤人以及偷盗都有罪；刘邦还很重视人才，得到萧何、张良、韩信等人帮助。另外，刘邦有富饶的关中作为根据地，因此，刘邦率领的汉军逐渐由弱变强。相反，项羽骄傲自大，不听取意见，放任士兵烧杀抢掠，大失民心。

公元前202年，刘邦率大军攻打项羽，在垓 (gāi) 下 (今安徽省境内) 把项羽的楚军重重包围。夜里，项羽听到汉军军营中的楚歌从四面八方传来，十分吃惊，以为楚的地方全被汉军占领了，项羽悲痛地与虞姬 (yújī，项羽的妾) 诀别，率领800多骑兵突围逃走。汉军紧追不舍，形势十分危急，项羽被迫在乌江 (今安徽和县东北) 自杀。

刘邦战胜项羽后，建立汉朝，定都长安（今西安西北），国号"汉"，历史上称为西汉。刘邦就是汉高祖。

After the uprising led by Chen Sheng and Wu Guang failed, Liu Bang and Xiang Yu continued to lead peasants against the Qin Dynasty. In 207 BC, Xiang Yu with a small force routed the main body of the Qin army at Julu (southwest of today's Pingxiang in Hebei Province). At the same time, Liu Bang's peasant army pressed on toward Xianyang, and forced the abdication of the second Qin emperor.

Xiang Yu then proclaimed himself King of Western Chu, and made Liu Bang King of Han. From 206 BC, Xiang Yu and Liu Bang fought for rule of the empire for nearly four years, in what historians call the "War between Chu and Han". At the beginning of the war, Xiang Yu had an army of 400,000, whereas Liu Bang's forces numbered only 100,000. But Liu Bang won the support of the common people by abolishing the draconian laws and decrees of the Qin Dynasty, and enforcing strict discipline on his troops. In addition, he had the assistance of able officials like Xiao He, Zhang Liang and Han Xin. Occupying the rich and fertile central Shaanxi plain, the Han army led by Liu Bang gradually grew stronger. Xiang Yu, in contrast, was arrogant, and his army was lawless. Wherever they went they lost the support of the people.

In 202 BC, the Han army besieged the Chu army in Gaixia (in today's Anhui Province). Xiang Yu escaped the encirclement with a small force, but was trapped at the Wujiang River (in the northeast of today's Hexian County in Anhui Province), and committed suicide.

Liu Bang then established the Han Dynasty, with Chang'an (in the northwest of today's Xi'an) as the capital.

汉武帝
Emperor Wudi of the Han Dynasty

汉武帝刘彻，公元前140年至公元前87年在位。他当政期间，中国历史上出现了长达50年的盛世景象。

强化中央集权制度　汉初，刘邦分封一些同姓的子弟到全国各地做王，想借此确保刘家的天下。受封的诸侯王的权力很大，他们可以在辖区内拥有军队，征收租税，铸造钱币，任免官吏。后来诸侯王的势力过大，严重影响中央的统治。

汉武帝当政后，准许诸侯王把自己的封地再分给子弟，建立侯国，这就是"推恩令"，一个王国分出许多小侯国，直属的领地就小了，再没有力量对抗中央。后来，汉武帝又陆续夺去大批王、侯的爵位。这样，经过长期斗争，王国对中央的威胁终于解除了，中央集权制度得到加强。

罢黜百家，独尊儒术　汉武帝时期，儒生董仲舒为了适应中央集权政治的需要，对儒家学说进行了发挥。

第一，宣扬天是万物的主宰，皇帝是天的儿子，即天子，代表天统治人民。因此，全国人民都要服从皇帝的统治，诸侯王也要听命于皇帝，这叫做"大一统"。

第二，提出了"罢黜（chù）百家，独尊儒术"的建议。主张只提倡儒家学说，其他各家学说，都禁止传播，以实行思想上的统一，从而巩固政治上的统一。

汉武帝采纳了董仲舒的学说，汉朝政府里就有许多信奉儒家思想的人做了大官。儒家思想逐渐成为封建社会的统治思想。

1. 汉武帝像
   A portrait of Emperor Wudi of the Han Dynasty

Reigned from 140 BC to 87 BC, Liu Che was known as the Emperor Wudi of the Han Dynasty. This half century was a period in which Chinese civilization flourished.

Soon after he founded the Han Dynasty, Liu Bang granted territories in

小资料 Data

秦皇汉武

汉武帝即位后，开拓西部疆域，建立
丰功伟业，使西汉进入鼎盛时期。西
汉帝国的强大，使中原人不再被称为
"秦人"，而通称"汉人"、"汉族"了。
历史上把"秦皇汉武"并称，正是因为
秦始皇和汉武帝先后完成了统一中
国、稳固发展的伟大事业。

Emperor Qinshihuang and Emperor Wudi

Emperor Wudi expanded China's territory in the
west. The Western Han Dynasty was a period of
prosperity. The people of the Central Plains began
to be called the "Han people" instead of the "Qin
people", indicating the might of the Western Han
Dynasty. Like Emperor Qinshihuang, Emperor
Wudi united China and consolidated the central
power.

1. 《漠北之战》绘画 (公元前119年，汉武
帝命大将霍去病、卫青率兵战胜匈
奴。)
   A portrait of the battle at Mobei (In 119 BC,
   Emperor Wudi sent his general Huo Qubing to
   fight the Huns and won.)

strategic parts of the country to nobles of his clan, with the title "king". The kings had their own armies, levied their own taxes, issued currency, and appointed and removed officials within their own jurisdictions.

When Emperor Wudi came to the throne, fearing that the kings were too powerful, he instituted a system whereby the descendants of the kings inherited parts of the kingdoms as marquisates. Thus the kingdoms quickly became divided into smaller and weaker territories, and came under the direct control of the imperial court. Later, Emperor Wudi went even further, depriving many nobles of their titles, and strengthening central rule.

It was during the reign of Emperor Wudi that the Confucian scholar Dong Zhongshu adapted Confucian theory to the needs of centralized politics.

First, he stressed that Heaven dominated everything in the world. The emperor was the Son of Heaven, and he ruled over the people on behalf of Heaven. Therefore, all people, including kings, should abide by the will of the emperor, a concept which was called "grand unification".

Second, Dong Zhongshu advocated suppressing the "Hundred Schools of Thought" and making Confucianism the state ideology. This, he argued, would unify the people's minds, which in turn would consolidate political unity.

Emperor Wudi was impressed by Dong Zhongshu's theories, and filled his administration with Confucian scholars. Confucianism thereby got a foothold as the dominant ideology in China's feudal society.

万里长城
The Great Wall

孟姜女哭长城

千百年来,中国民间流传着这样一个动人的故事:秦朝时候,一个叫孟姜女的姑娘,刚刚结婚,丈夫就被抓去修筑长城了。孟姜女在家日日夜夜地等待,丈夫一直没有回来。冬天到了,天气冷了,孟姜女做好了棉衣,给丈夫送去。她走了很长的路,终于到了长城,却得知丈夫已经死了。孟姜女跪在长城边,哭了几天几夜,竟把一段城墙哭倒了。最后,孟姜女悲痛地投水自杀了。

Meng Jiangnu Weeps Beside the Great Wall

A touching story has been circulating in China for many centuries. It tells how, during the Qin Dynasty, the husband of a woman named Meng Jiangnu was conscripted for forced labor on the Great Wall immediately after their marriage. When winter came, Meng Jiangnu made padded clothes for her husband, and started off on a journey to the Great Wall to deliver them to him. When she finally reached her destination, she learned that her husband had already died. Meng Jiangnu knelt by the Great Wall, and cried for several days. As a result of her wailing, part of the Great Wall collapsed. Finally, Meng Jiangnu drowned herself.

1. 雄伟壮观的万里长城
   The magnificent Great Wall

长城始建于公元前7世纪前后的春秋战国时期。秦始皇统一六国后,将原来秦、赵、燕等国修建的防御性长城扩建修葺(qì),连接成为东起辽东,西到临洮(táo)(今甘肃境内)绵延五千多千米的巨大军事防御工事。这就是举世闻名的万里长城。此后许多朝代都进行过修整。明朝初年大规模修筑长城,约200年后完成,东部主要为砖石结构。

历史上的长城东起鸭绿江,西到嘉峪(yù)关,横穿中国北方8个省、自治区和直辖市(辽宁、河北、北京、山西、内蒙古、宁夏、陕西、甘肃),全长6,700多千米(约13,000华里)的长城,成为世界的著名奇迹之一。

长城由千百座关隘(ài)、城堡、堞楼和高大的城墙组成。遇有敌情,士兵会在长城北侧沿线的烽火台上点燃烟火,将情报传递到附近的城市直至皇帝的都城。

位于北京的八达岭长城、慕田峪长城、司马台长城都是明代修筑的。这里的长城依山而建,高大坚固,绵延起伏,城顶的通道可以容纳五六匹马并排前进,充分展现了万里长城的建筑风格和雄伟气魄。现今是著名的旅游胜地。

1

The origin of the Great Wall can be traced to defensive walls erected by various states during the Spring and Autumn and Warring States periods (around the seventh century BC). After Qinshihuang united the country, he repaired, linked up and extended the walls built by the former states of Qin, Zhao, Yan and others into huge military defense works which started from the Liaodong Peninsula in the east and ended at Lintao (in today's Gansu Province) in the west — a distance of more than 5,000 km. This is the world-famous Great Wall. The Wall was repaired and maintained over the course of many dynasties, especially during the Ming Dynasty, when the work continued for some 200 years.

Nowadays, the Great Wall crosses five provinces (Liaoning, Hebei, Shanxi, Shaanxi and Gansu), two autonomous regions (Inner Mongolia and Ningxia) and one municipality (Beijing) in north China, with a total length of over 6,700 km. It is one of the foremost wonders of the world.

The Great Wall is composed of hundreds of passes, fortresses, towers and stretches of wall. Beacon towers are situated at suitable intervals to give the alarm if an enemy approached.

The parts of the Great Wall located at Badaling, Mutianyu and Simatai in Beijing were all constructed during the Ming Dynasty. These parts of the Wall were built along mountain ridges. On many parts of the Wall five or six horsemen could ride side by side. Parts of the Wall renovated in modern times are popular tourist attractions.

1. 云海中的金山岭长城
   Jinshanling Great Wall in a sea of clouds
2. 嘉峪关。万里长城西端的关隘，位于
   河西走廊的西部，建于公元1372年，
   是丝绸之路的必经要地，被称为"天下
   雄关"
   The Jiayu Pass, marking the western end of the
   Great Wall, is located in the western part of the
   Hexi Corridor, in Gansu Province. It was built in
   1372, and was an important communication
   point on the Silk Road.
3. 长城东端的山海关
   Shanhai Pass is located at the eastern Great
   Wall.

昭君出塞
Zhaojun Goes Beyond the Great Wall as a Bride

在中国古代，汉族统治者与少数民族首领之间，有时为一定的政治目的而通婚，被称为"和亲"。秦汉之际，中国北方古老的游牧民族匈奴势力强大，多次南下威胁中原。汉初国力不强，无法与匈奴对抗，便也采取了和亲政策，求得相对的和平。随着汉朝经济、军事力量的增强，反击匈奴的条件成熟了。到汉武帝时，便放弃了和亲政策，对匈奴采取了攻势。从此，西汉与匈奴80年没和亲。

汉宣帝时，匈奴的势力衰落了。此时，匈奴内部出现了两个单于 (chányú匈奴君主的称号) 对抗的局面。其中呼韩邪 (hūhányé) 单于想借助汉朝的支持，统一整个匈奴，于是决心归依汉朝。他两次到长安见汉朝皇帝，受到隆重的欢迎，他也表示愿协助汉朝政府保护边境。公元前36年，汉朝派兵攻打了另一个单于，呼韩邪统一匈奴。公元前33年，他第三次到长安，向当时的汉元帝提出，愿意当汉家的女婿，再恢复和亲。元帝立即答应，并在宫女中进行选拔。有一个叫王昭君的宫女主动提出要去和亲。王昭君又美丽又聪明，很受呼韩邪的喜爱，被封为"宁胡阏氏" (yānzhī)，意思是将与汉朝建立和平友好的关系。

王昭君出塞以后，生活在匈奴游牧地区几十年。在她的影响下，她的子女及周围的人，都努力维护匈奴与汉的友好关系，使北方边境出现了少有的安定景象。

In ancient China, the ruling families of the Han people sometimes intermarried with rulers of minority ethnic groups in the border areas for political purposes. This was called *heqin* (peace through marriage ties). During the Qin and Han dynasties, the Hun nomads became a threat to the people of the Central Plains, launching numerous southward invasions. In its early years, the Han Dynasty was not strong enough to repel the Huns, so the Han rulers resorted to the policy of *heqin* to pacify the borders. With the strengthening of the economic and military forces of the Han Dynasty, the policy of appeasement was replaced by one of military pacification. By the end of the reign of Emperor Wudi, the Han Dynasty had not intermarried with the Huns for 80 years.

During the reign of Emperor Xuandi (74 -49 BC), the power of the Huns had declined drastically. At that time, two men contended for the title of khan, or paramount chief, of the Huns. One of them, Huhanye by name, sought the help of the Han Dynasty. He visited Chang'an twice, and pledged his allegiance to the emperor. He also expressed his willingness to help the Han Dynasty guard the border areas. In 36 BC, Emperor Yuandi, Emperor Xuandi's successor, dispatched troops, which ensured Huhanye's victory. In 33 BC,

2

Huhanye went to Chang'an for the third time, and offered to restore the *heqin* system by marrying a Han princess. Emperor Yuandi agreed immediately, and set about selecting a woman from his palace to marry Huhanye. A palace maid named Wang Zhaojun volunteered to marry Huhanye. The latter gave her the title "Ninghuyanzhi", which signified that the Huns would build peaceful and friendly relations with the Han Dynasty.

Wang Zhaojun lived in the Huns' encampments for many years. Under her influence, her children and the people around her all did their best to maintain the good relations between the Huns and the Han Dynasty, which brought a rare period of stability to the northern border areas.

1. 湖北兴山县昭君故里的昭君像
   The sculpture of Zhaojun, Xingshan County, Hubei Province
2. 昭君出塞画像
   A portrait of Zhaojun leaving hometown to marry the chief of the Huns
3. 陕西茂陵霍去病墓
   Huo Qubing Mausoleum, Maoling, Shaanxi Province

小资料 Data

霍去病忘家为国

汉代像王昭君这样勇于为国奉献的人有很多，其中一位就是赶走匈奴的大将霍去病。公元前120年前后几年间，霍去病带兵打仗，招降了大量匈奴军队。汉武帝很喜欢他，为他建了很好的房子，他却说，匈奴还没有消灭，怎么能有自己的家呢？

Huo Qubing Abandons His Home for the Sake of His Country

In the Han Dynasty, there were many people who sacrificed their personal interests for their country just like Wang Zhaojun. One of them was Huo Qubing, a general who was successful in his campaigns against the Huns. Around 120 BC, Huo Qubing's army subdued and recruited large numbers of Huns. Emperor Wudi wanted to build a luxurious mansion for him, but Huo Qubing said, "How can I attend to my own house before I wipe out the Huns?"

3

丝绸之路
The Silk Road

张骞通西域及丝绸之路图
Sketch Map of Zhang Qian's Journeys to the Western Regions and the Overland Silk Road

汉代，中国通过"丝绸之路"与域外各民族建立了广泛的交往。这条线路的开辟，首先要归功于张骞（qiān）。

汉武帝时，北方匈奴常常袭扰汉朝边境，还控制了当时西域的几十个小国。公元前138年，汉武帝派张骞带100多人出使西域，联络大月氏（zhī），准备左右夹攻匈奴。没想到刚出边境，张骞就被匈奴抓住了。

在被扣留期间，他学会了匈奴语，掌握了匈奴的地形。10多年后，张骞逃了出来，找到了已经西迁的大月氏。张骞在当地呆了一年，熟悉了西域的环境。后来，见大月氏国王不想报仇，他只好回国。当年与他同去的100多人，只剩下两人回到长安。

公元前119年，汉武帝再次派张骞出使西域，这次随行的有300多人，带去了上万头牛羊和货物。他们访问了许多国家，这些国家也派了使臣带着礼物回访。从此以后，汉朝和西域的往来越来越多。后来，汉还在今天新疆地区设了西域都护府，归

1

中央政府管理。

张骞出使西域后，中西交流的"丝绸之路"开辟了。"丝绸之路"东起长安，向西到地中海东岸，转至罗马帝国。汉朝的商队，运着大量的丝织品同波斯人、印度人、希腊人交换商品，同时带回了外国的核桃、葡萄、胡萝卜等。此后的许多世纪，以丝绸贸易为主的中西交流大多经过"丝绸之路"进行。

1. 新疆吐鲁番高昌故城（丝绸之路遗址）
   Gaochang ancient city, Turpan, Xinjiang (Ruins of the Silk Road)
2. 陕西西安丝绸之路雕像
   The Silk Road sculptures in Xi'an, Shaanxi Province
3. 湖南长沙马王堆西汉墓出土的丝织品
   The silk goods excavated from the Western Han Mausoleum, Mawangdui, Changsha, Hunan Province

In the Han Dynasty, China established wide contacts with various nationalities and kingdoms outside its domain through the Silk Road. Zhang Qian pioneered this route.

In 138 BC, Emperor Wudi sent Zhang Qian with a delegation of over 100 people on a diplomatic mission to the Western Regions to seek allies against the Huns. Zhang Qian was captured by the Huns just as he left Han territory, and was held prisoner for a dozen years. During this period, he learned the Hun language, and got to know well the geography of their territory. Escaping from the Hun encampment, Zhang Qian made his way back to Chang'an, with only one companion left of the 100 who had set out.

In 119 BC, Emperor Wudi sent Zhang Qian on a second diplomatic mission to the Western Regions. This time, he had an entourage of 300, with thousands of head of cattle and sheep and a large amount of gifts. They visited many countries, and these countries sent envoys with tribute to the Han court. From then on, the Han Dynasty had frequent contacts with the countries in the Western Regions, later setting up a Western Regions Frontier Command in today's Xinjiang Uygur Autonomous Region, which was under the administration of the central government.

The Silk Road was another outcome of Zhang Qian's journeys. The Silk Road started from Chang'an in the east and stretched westward to reach the eastern shore of the Mediterranean Sea and the Roman Empire. Trade caravans from China carrying large amounts of silk fabrics exchanged merchandise with traders from Persia, India and Greece, and brought home walnuts, grapes and carrots from abroad. In the following several centuries, Sino-Western exchanges mainly characterized by the silk trade were mostly carried on through the Silk Road.

小资料 Data

海上"丝绸之路"

汉代，海上也有一条"丝绸之路"。它从今天广东沿海港口出发，经10个多月的航行，到达泰国和印度。汉代使者带去丝绸、黄金，换回那儿著名的蓝宝石。东汉时，中国的远洋帆船甚至可到达非洲，由于那里由罗马管理，所以也与罗马帝国建立了直接的交往。

The Maritime Silk Road

There was also a Silk Road on the sea during the Han Dynasty. It started from coastal ports in today's Guangdong Province, and ended in India by way of Thailand after a 10-month voyage. The Han merchants took with them silk and gold, and exchanged them for sapphires. In the Eastern Han Dynasty, Chinese sailing ships reached as far as Africa.

司马迁与《史记》
Sima Qian and His *Records of the Historian*

《史记》的作者司马迁(前145年～?），生于陕西。受父亲影响，他少年时就阅读古人的书籍。20岁时，他到各处去游历，搜集了很多古代名人的资料。后来，他被任命为郎中，可以常随皇帝出游。这些游历，为他以后写《史记》作了准备。

父亲死后不久，司马迁接替他的职务做了太史令，有机会翻阅了很多图书，做了大量笔记。公元前104年，他正式开始写作《史记》。他在写作过程中，因为得罪了皇帝，被判重刑。司马迁因此想到了自杀，但想到自己的书还没有写完，就忍受痛苦，发愤编写，终于完成了《史记》。

《史记》全书130篇，从传说中的黄帝，写到汉武帝时代，跨越了3,000年的历史。这是中国第一部纪传体通史，内容涉及到了政治、经济、文化、军事等各个方面。其文字简洁通俗，生动传神，既是一部有价值的史学著作，也是一部杰出的文学著作。

The author of *Records of the Historian* is Sima Qian (145 BC-?), who was born in what is now Shaanxi Province. Encouraged by his father, he began to read ancient books when he was still very young. At the age of 20 he started to travel extensively, and gathered a great deal of material on ancient celebrities. Later, he was appointed to an official post, and often went on tours with the emperor.

Not long after his father's death, Sima Qian succeeded to his position as the official in charge of historical records. Thus he had the opportunity to read many books and made a great many notes. In 104 BC, Sima Qian commenced his *Records of the Historian*. Falling foul of the emperor, he was punished and dismissed from office. From that time on, he devoted all his time to his life's work.

Records of the Historian is composed of 130 chapters. It starts from the legendary Yellow Emperor (Huangdi), and ends with the reign of Emperor Wudi of the Han Dynasty, spanning 3,000 years. It was the first comprehensive biographical history book to appear in China. It covers a wide range of subjects, political, economic, cultural, military, etc. Its language is terse and lively, and easy to understand. *Records of the Historian* is not only a valuable historical work, but also an outstanding work of literature.

1. 司马迁像
   A portrait of Sima Qian
2. 西汉司马迁编著的《史记》，是中国第一部纪传体通史
   Sima Qian's *Records of the Historian* was the first comprehensive biographical history book in China.
3. 陕西韩城司马迁墓
   Mausoleum of Sima Qian, Hancheng, Shaanxi Province

3

 小资料 Data

班固与《汉书》

班固是东汉时著名的史学家、文学家。从公元64年开始，他奉皇帝的命令开始写西汉的历史，20年后完成了大部分。这是继《史记》后第二部著名的历史书，也是中国第一部纪传体断代史，共100篇，80多万字，记录了汉代200多年的历史。

Ban Gu and the History of the Western Han Dynasty (Han Shu)

Ban Gu, of the Eastern Han Dynasty, began to write the history of the Western Han Dynasty in 64 AD at the order of the emperor, and finished the greater part of it over a period of 20 years. The *History of the Western Han Dynasty* is second only to *Records of the Historian* in historical importance, and was the first dynastic record to emerge in China. It is composed of 100 chapters, totalling over 800,000 characters. It covers the 200 years of the Western Han Dynasty.

科学家张衡
Zhang Heng, a Pioneering Scientist

张衡(公元78~140年)，河南南阳人，东汉杰出的科学家，也是世界上最早的天文学家之一。他特别爱好数学和天文学。朝廷听说他有学问，就让他担任了太史令，掌管历史和历法，负责观察天文。

经过多年的观察，他研制了一架"浑天仪"。凡是知道的重要天文现象，都刻在"浑天仪"上了。

东汉时期，地震很活跃。当时的人们不懂科学，以为地震是鬼神发怒。张衡认为地震是一种自然灾害，他根据自己对于地震现象的观测，在公元132年发明了"候风地动仪"，这台仪器成为世界上第一台观测地震方向的仪器。地动仪制好后，放在洛阳的灵台。公元138年2月的一天，地动仪朝西的龙嘴吐出铜球，掉到了蛤蟆嘴里，这说明西北方向发生了地震。但是洛阳一点也没有地震的感觉，因此，大伙都说张衡的地动仪是骗人的。过了几天甘肃

👉 小资料 Data

地动仪是怎么工作的？

地动仪是用青铜制造的，仪器内部竖着一根铜柱，周围有8根杆子连接外面。外面有8条龙，分别朝着8个方向，每条龙的嘴里各含着一粒小铜球。哪个方向地震，柱子就倒向那个方向，触动杆子，那个方向的龙嘴就张开，吐出铜球，落在下面仰头张嘴的小铜蛤蟆（hámá）口中，这样，人们就知道那里发生了地震。

Zhang Heng's Seismograph

The seismograph was made entirely of bronze. Inside, there was a balanced post and eight rods connected to eight dragon's heads on the outside. When an earthquake occurred, the balanced post would tilt in the direction of the quake, push a rod, and cause the corresponding dragon's head to disgorge a bronze ball, which would then fall into the mouth of a bronze toad below.

东南部有人来报告说，那里前几天发生了大地震，人们这才相信。

这是人类历史上第一次用仪器来观测地震方向。中国以外，直到公元13世纪，才有类似的仪器出现。

1. 地动仪模型 (地动仪是世界上第一部测定地震方向的仪器，由张衡创制。)
   A model of Zhang Heng's seismograph (The world's first instrument to identify and ascertain the direction of earthquakes.)
2. 北京古观象台
   Beijing Ancient Observatory
3. 张衡研制地动仪
   A portrait of Zhang Heng inventing the seismograph

Zhang Heng (78-140 AD) was born in Nanyang, Henan Province. He was one of the world's first astronomers. He was also a learned mathematician. He was appointed official with historiographic duties, and was also in charge of drawing up the calendar and observing astronomical phenomena.

He developed an armillary sphere, on which were carved all the astronomical phenomena known at that time.

Contrary to the popular belief at that time, Zhang Heng maintained that earthquakes were not signs of Heaven's anger but natural disasters. As a result of careful observations of earthquakes, he invented a seismograph in 132, which was the world's first instrument to identify and ascertain the direction of earthquakes. When an earthquake occurred, even if it could not be felt in Luoyang, the capital, a bronze ball would fall from the mouth of one of the carved dragon's heads on the instrument facing the direction of the epicenter of the earthquake into the mouth of a bronze toad below. It was not until the 13th century that similar instruments appeared outside China.

"医圣"张仲景与
"外科鼻祖"华佗

Zhang Zhongjing and Hua Tuo, founders of Medical Science

汉代有两位名医，一位是被尊称为"医圣"的张仲景，另一位是被尊称为"外科鼻祖"的华佗。

张仲景(约公元150～219年)是东汉末年河南南阳人。那时瘟疫(wēnyì)流行，他的家人不到10年，因为伤寒死了三分之二。他精心研究古代医学，广泛收集民间秘方，写成了《伤寒杂病论》十六卷。在他的书里，不仅有大量内服药方，还介绍了中医理论，奠定了中医治疗学的基础。

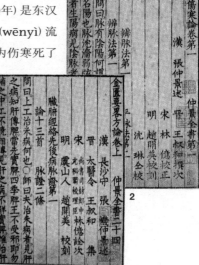

华佗(约公元141—208年)安徽亳(bó)州人，生活在东汉末年。他在内科、外科、妇科、小儿科方面都很精通。华佗的外科技术很高超，他制成了一种麻醉药，叫做"麻沸散"。他曾让患了阑尾炎的病人用酒服"麻沸散"，等病人全身麻醉后，他便开始动手术，最后在伤口上敷上有消毒作用的膏药，一个月以后，病人完全恢复了健康。华佗是世界上第一个应用全身麻醉技术的医生。

此外，华佗还精通针灸(jiǔ)技术。当时丞相曹操得了神经性头痛，就派人请华佗来为自己治病。华佗给曹操针灸，一针下去，曹操的头就不疼了。

华佗重视治疗，更重视疾病的预防。他模仿虎、鹿、熊、猿、鸟五种动物，独创了一套名为"五禽戏"的体操，用来增强体魄。

Zhang Zhongjing (c.150-219 AD) was born in Nanyang, Henan Province. He devoted himself to the study of medicine after typhoid fever decimated most of his family. He gathered folk remedies, and compiled a work titled *Febrile and other Diseases* in 16 volumes. This medical classic also expounds the theories of traditional Chinese medicine.

Hua Tuo (c.141-208 AD) was born in Bozhou, Anhui Province. He was proficient in internal medicine, surgery, gynecology and pediatrics. He is credited with being the first surgeon in the world to use the technique of general anesthesia, using a concoction called *mafeisan* to operate on appendicitis patients. He was also an expert acupuncturist, and once cured Cao Cao, the renowned prime minister at the end of the Eastern Han Dynasty, of a disease using this technique.

Hua Tuo attached importance to therapy. He also emphasized prevention. He devised a set of exercises, known as the Five-Animal Exercise, to strengthen the physique, imitating the actions of the tiger, deer, bear, ape and bird.

1. 张仲景塑像
   A sculpture of Zhang Zhongjing
2. 张仲景所著的《伤寒论》和《金匮要略》
   Zhang Zhongjing's *Febrile Diseases* and *Synopsis of the Golden Chamber*
3. 华佗像
   A portrait of Hua Tuo
4. 河南南阳张仲景祠
   Temple of Zhang Zhongjing, Nanyang, Henan Province
5. 刮骨疗伤图（据说东汉末年蜀将关羽被毒箭射中，华佗为他刮骨疗伤。）
   A portrait of Hua Tuo treating General Guan Yu for an arrow wound

 小资料 Data

汉代还有哪些医学成就？

汉代的医学很发达。除了张仲景和华佗以外，西汉初年的大夫淳于意留下了中国最早的病历。公元前31年诞生了中国最早的药物学专著《神农本草经》。

Other Han Dynasty Medical Achievements

The science of medicine made great strides in the Han Dynasty. Chun Yuyi, a doctor in the early Western Han Dynasty, wrote the earliest medical record in China. In 31 BC, there appeared the *Materia Medica of Shennong (Shennong Bencao Jing)*, the earliest work of materia medica in China.

概述
Introduction

　　三国、两晋、南北朝，又称魏晋南北朝，从公元220年曹丕称帝开始，到589年隋灭陈统一全国结束，共经历了360多年。

　　220年曹丕建立魏国，221年刘备建立蜀国，222年孙权建立吴国，形成了魏、蜀、吴三国鼎立的局面。三国的都城分别在今天的洛阳、成都、南京。

　　263年，魏国灭蜀国，265年魏国大臣司马炎夺取魏的政权称帝，建立晋朝，定都洛阳，历史上称西晋。280年，司马炎灭吴，结束三国分裂局面。西晋的统一局面十分短暂，316年被少数民族政权所灭，中国又陷入分裂割据局面。

　　317年，晋王室的司马睿(ruì)称帝，建立了东晋王朝，都城在今天的南京。同时，迁居到黄河流域的几个少数民族，先后建立了许多国家。北方处于长达130多年的分裂割据时期，历史上称为"十六国"时期。

　　439年，少数民族建立的北魏政权统一了北方。后来，北魏孝文帝进行改革，规定少数民族学习汉族的制度、语言、服饰，促进了

封建国家的分裂和民族大融合时期——

三国、两晋、南北朝

The Division of China Once More and the Intermingling of Ethnic Groups — The Three Kingdoms, the Two Jin Dynasties and the Southern and Northern Dynasties

北方民族的大融合。后来北魏政权分裂为东魏和西魏，接着北齐取代东魏，北周取代西魏。历史上把上述北方五个朝代，总称为北朝。东晋以后，南方在420年至589年的170年里，经历了宋、齐、梁、陈四个朝代，都城都在今天的南京，历史上称之为南朝。南朝和北朝并存时期，史称南北朝时期。

三国鼎立时期，政治、经济、外交各具特色，充满生机，涌现出曹操、诸葛亮等一批杰出的政治家。三国两晋南北朝时期，出现了许多著名的思想家、军事家、科学家、文学家、画家、书法家，还有许多对社会科学和自然科学产生积极影响的名著。这些科学、文化成就，至今仍是中国文化遗产中的瑰宝。

三国两晋南北朝时期，欧洲强大的罗马帝国分裂，西罗马帝国灭亡，日耳曼人的王国在西欧建立，欧洲开始进入封建社会。

The period of the Three Kingdoms, the Western and Eastern Jin dynasties and the Southern and Northern dynasties is also called the period of Wei, Jin and the Southern and Northern dynasties. It started in 220 AD, when Cao Pi claimed himself emperor of the Kingdom of Wei, and ended in 589, when the Sui Dynasty wiped out Chen and united the whole country once more.

In 221, the year after the setting up of the Kingdom of Wei, Liu Bei established the Kingdom of Shu, and in 222

概述
Introduction

Sun Quan founded the Kingdom of Wu, which formed a situation of tripartite confrontation. The capitals of these three kingdoms were located in today's Luoyang, Chengdu and Nanjing, respectively.

In 263, Wei wiped out Shu. In 265, Sima Yan, a Wei minister, seized the throne of Wei, declared founding of the Jin Dynasty and chose Luoyang as his capital. This is known as the Western Jin Dynasty. In 280, Sima Yan conquered Wu, ending the Three Kingdoms Period, but the Jin Dynasty itself was overrun by nomadic people in 316.

In 317, Sima Rui, a descendant of the royal family of the Jin Dynasty, proclaimed himself emperor of the Eastern Jin Dynasty, whose capital was today's Nanjing. At the same time, several minority ethnic groups in the Yellow River basin also established many states. For more than 130 years, northern China was chaotically divided, in a period called the "era of the sixteen states".

In 439, Northern Wei, established by a minority people, united the north. Emperor Xiaowen of Northern Wei effected reforms, decreeing the adoption of native Chinese institutions, language and costume. This resulted in a great intermixing of different ethnic groups in the north. Later, Northern Wei split into Eastern and Western Wei, and then Northern Qi replaced Eastern Wei, and Northern Zhou replaced Western Wei. The above five northern dynasties are known as the Northern Dynasties. During the 170 years from 420 to 589 AD, following the fall of Eastern Jin, there appeared four dynasties in succession, namely, Song, Qi, Liang and Chen, whose capitals were all situated in today's Nanjing. These four dynasties are called the Southern dynasties. The period when the Southern dynasties and the Northern Dynasties co-existed is called the Southern and Northern dynasties.

During the Three Kingdoms Period there emerged a great number of outstanding statesmen and generals, the foremost of whom were Cao Cao and Zhuge Liang. And the two Jin dynasties and the Northern and Southern dynasties produced many famous strategists, scientists, literary figures, painters and calligraphers. Also, a large number of famous works were produced which had a positive influence on the development of the social and natural sciences. These scientific and cultural achievements are gems of the Chinese cultural heritage.

1. 蜀主刘备在长江边的白帝城病逝
Liu Bei, who established the Kingdom of Shu, passed away in the Baidi City near Yangtze River.

曹操
Cao Cao

1. 曹操像
   A portrait of Cao Cao
2. 曹操生平的事迹经常成为民间工艺的素材
   The life of Cao Cao is often a common theme in folk art.

曹操是东汉末年一位杰出的政治家、军事家、文学家。

曹操（公元155～220年），字孟德，安徽人。东汉末年，曹操在镇压农民起义的过程中，建立起一支强大的军队。

作为一个军事家，他喜爱研究兵书，认为打仗要随机应变。在官渡之战中，曹操仅有2万军队，他正确分析了敌我形势，以少胜多，打败了袁绍的10万大军，壮大了自己的军队。军队壮大了，就需要更多的粮食。曹操便让士兵们在不打仗的时候进行耕作，这种"屯田"的办法，不仅解决了军粮，而且使北方社会的经济逐步好转。

在政治上，曹操看到豪强地主势力的发展，造成了东汉末年的分裂局面，因此，他很注意控制豪强地主的势力。他曾在官府门前设立一些大棒，专门打击那些以强欺弱的人，还让敢打击豪强地主

小资料 Data

挟 (xié) 天子以令诸侯

"挟",挟持;"天子"即皇帝;"诸侯",即割据各地的军阀势力。汉朝末年,皇室力量衰弱。公元196年,曹操将汉献帝迎往许都(今河南许昌)。曹操凭借自己强大的军事势力,控制了朝政大权,常用皇帝的名义向其他割据势力发号施令,以获得政治上的主动权,被当时的人称为"挟天子以令诸侯"。

Controlling the Emperor and Commanding the Nobles

Toward the end of the Han Dynasty, the imperial family was very weak. In 196, Cao Cao invited Emperor Xiandi to his headquarters at Xudu (today's Xuchang, Henan Province), where he was put under the protection of Cao Cao's army. From then on, Cao Cao effectively controlled the state power, and issued orders to the other nobles in the name of the emperor.

1. **曹操形象深入民心,这是民间制作的曹操泥塑**
   A clay statue of Cao Cao

1

的人做官。这些做法,有利于巩固统治。

在用人方面,曹操提出"唯才是举"的方针,也就是只要有真才实学,不管出身怎样,都被录用。因此,在他当权的时候,很多有才华的人都受到了重用。这些人为曹操统一北方出了不少力。

由于这些优势,再加上他控制了汉献帝,所以从公元200年官渡之战后,曹操先后消灭了北方各种军阀势力,结束了北方分裂状态。这不仅有利于中原地区社会经济的恢复,也为后来西晋统一全国打下基础。

此外,曹操还很重视文化,他多才多艺,他的两个儿子曹丕 (pī)、曹植也都是有名的文学家。

Cao Cao (155-220 AD) was an outstanding statesman, strategist and man of letters of the late Eastern Han Dynasty.

He was born in today's Anhui Province. He built up a powerful army in the course of suppressing peasant uprisings.

Devoted to the theory of military strategy, Cao Cao had some resounding successes in warfare. At the Battle of Guandu, with only 20,000 men, he soundly defeated Yuan Shao's force of 100,000. A strong army needed more food. Between campaigns, Cao Cao made his soldiers cultivate the land to supply themselves with food. This not only solved the army's food supply problem, it also improved the economy in the north.

On the political stage, Cao Cao saw the rise of powerful landlords in the late Eastern Han Dynasty as a threat to the unity of the country. Therefore, he encouraged the local authorities to punish magnates who bullied the weak, and gave government posts to anti-landlord elements. In fact, Cao Cao insisted on promoting any person of talent, no matter what his background was.

Because of these advantages, added to the fact that he had the Han emperor under his control, Cao Cao put down all the warlords one after another in the north after the Battle of Guandu in 200.

Cao Cao was not just a statesman and general; he was a man of cultured tastes too, as were his two sons Cao Pi and Cao Zhi.

诸葛亮
Zhuge Liang

1. 四川成都武侯祠诸葛亮像
   The statue of Zhuge Liang in the Wuhou Temple, Chengdu, Sichuan Province

诸葛亮是一位杰出的政治家、军事家。

诸葛亮（公元181～234年），字孔明，山东人。后来定居在湖北襄阳城西的隆中。在那儿，他阅读了大量书籍，增长了见识。

曹操统一北方后，准备南下统一中国。当时孙权占据长江中下游。刘备借驻荆州，他的势力最弱。他三顾茅庐，请诸葛亮帮助他。诸葛亮为刘备详细分析了天下的形势，提出了联合孙权抗击曹操的办法。刘备采取了诸葛亮的建议，在赤壁之战中获胜，势力由弱转强。

刘备称帝后不久，病死在白帝城，临死前将蜀国的大权都交给了诸葛亮。诸葛亮一心帮助刘备的儿子新国君刘禅。此时西南少数民族乘机起兵，公元225年，诸葛亮亲自带军南下，用计谋和平地解决了矛盾，并获得了当地少数民族首领孟获的信任。此后，诸葛亮就任用少数民族首领管理当地人，蜀政权与少数民族关系大大改

善。同时，他还大力进行了内部的改革，任用有才能的人，注意农业生产和水利建设，加强部队纪律，使蜀国很快摆脱了危机。

后来，为了国家的统一，他六次北上攻打曹魏，但都失败了。在最后一次北伐中，他由于过度劳累，病死在军营中。

Zhuge Liang (181-234 AD) was an outstanding statesman and strategist.

He was born in what is now Shandong Province, and later settled in Longzhong, to the west of Xiangyang, Hubei Province. Leading a hermit's existence, Zhuge Liang devoted himself to acquiring knowledge, and his reputation for wisdom spread far and wide.

Meanwhile, after uniting the north, Cao Cao prepared to march south. At that time, Sun Quan controlled the middle and lower reaches of the Yangtze, and Liu Bei, the weakest of the three antagonists, was stationed in Jingzhou. Liu Bei went to visit Zhuge Liang three times to ask for the latter's assistance. Zhuge Liang analyzed the situation in the country in detail for Liu Bei, and recommended that he ally with Sun Quan against Cao Cao. Liu Bei adopted Zhuge Liang's suggestion and defeated Cao Cao in the Battle of the Red Cliff,

his forces emerging as a much stronger power.

Not long after he proclaimed himself emperor, Liu Bei died of illness in Baidicheng. Before he died, he handed over the state power of Shu to Zhuge Liang, to be wielded on behalf of Liu Bei's son, Liu Chan. In 225, Zhuge Liang led an army south, and pacified the rebellious tribes there. His strategy was to govern through the local chieftains, which greatly improved relations between the Shu government and the minority peoples. Meanwhile, he also carried out far-reaching internal reforms — employing people with ability, stressing agricultural production and construction of irrigation works, and strengthening discipline in the army, which helped Shu quickly overcome a series of crises.

Later, Zhuge Liang launched six expeditions northward aimed at overthrowing Wei and unifying the country, but failed. On his last northern expedition, he died of illness.

1. 刘备三顾草庐，邀请诸葛亮辅政
   In need of a brilliant military strategist, Liu Bei paid three visits to Zhuge Liang's thatched cottage to seek his assistance.
2. 纪念诸葛亮的陕西勉县武侯祠
   Wuhou Temple, Mian County, Shaanxi Province (In memorial of Zhuge Liang)

赤壁之战
The Battle of the Red Cliff

1

曹操统一了北方之后，剩下能与他对抗的，就只有在长江一带的孙权和在湖北一带的刘备了。

公元208年，曹操带了20万大军（对外号称80万）南下。刘备退守湖北武昌，此时他只有军士2万多人。在军师诸葛亮的建议下，他决定与孙权共同抗曹。诸葛亮向孙权指出，曹操虽然人多，但其中有七八万是刚投降的荆州士兵，这些人主要是水军，是作战的主力，但他们不一定真心服从曹操。而北方的曹操士兵，不善于水战，长途而来生病的也很多。这些分析使孙权看清了形势，同意派大将周瑜带领3万军士与刘备一起战斗。

曹军驻扎在赤壁（今湖北赤壁市，又一说在今湖北嘉鱼县东北），曹操下令用铁索把战船锁在一起，以便

三国鼎立形势图
Sketch Map of the Triangular Balance of Power between the Three Kingdoms

1. 江西九江甘棠湖。相传为三国时期东吴都督周瑜的点将台旧址
Gantang Lake, Jiujiang, Jiangxi Province (Legend has it that this was where the military governor Zhou Yu of the Kingdom of Wu appointed commanders for war during the Three Kingdoms Period.)

北方士兵在船上行走。诸葛亮和周瑜都决定用"火攻"的方法进攻曹操。一天夜里，刮起了东南风。周瑜派部下黄盖假装投降曹操，带着十艘战船，船上装着灌了油的柴草，向曹军驶去。接近曹军时，他们同时点火，火船顺风向曹操的战舰驶去，曹军战舰因为锁在一起，一时无法解开，不一会便成了一片火海。火又烧到了岸上，曹军死伤很多。

赤壁之战后，全国形势发生了变化。曹操退回北方。曹操

赤壁之战示意图
Sketch Map of the Battle of the Red Cliff

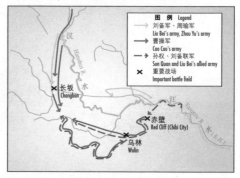

死后，公元220年，他的儿子曹丕废掉汉献帝自立，国号为"魏"，都城为洛阳。刘备乘机占据了荆州大部分地方，又向西发展，在公元221年，也自立为帝，国号为"蜀"，建都成都。孙权则巩固了长江中下游的势力，公元222年称王，国号"吴"，都城为建业（今南京）。三国鼎立的局面，直至公元280年西晋灭吴才结束。

1. 湖北赤壁山
   The site of the Battle of the Red Cliff, Hubei Province
2. 湖北东吴水寨故址
   The site of Kingdom of Wu's water village, Hubei Province
3. 湖北周瑜塑像
   A statue of Zhou Yu, Hubei province

After Cao Cao united north China, he had only two rivals — Sun Quan in the middle and lower reaches of the Yangtze and Liu Bei in what is now the area of Hubei Province.

In 208 AD, Cao Cao led an army of 200,000 men south against Liu Bei and Sun Quan, who had only about 100,000 men

3

between them. Cao Cao embarked his men on ships, and the fleet sailed up the Yangtze River, and anchored at a place called the Red Cliff (in today's Chibi City, Hubei Province, although it has been alternately located in the northeast of today's Jiayu County in Hubei). The ships were chained together. One night, when the wind was favorable, Zhuge Liang dispatched a general with 10 ships to sail toward the enemy, pretending to be surrendering. The ships were loaded with firewood soaked in oil. When they were near enough to Cao Cao's fleet, they were set on fire and left to drift into the enemy ships, which were totally destroyed.

This was a disaster for Cao Cao, who retreated back to the north. In 220, after Cao Cao's death, his son Cao Pi dethroned Emperor Xiandi of the Han Dynasty and proclaimed himself emperor, renaming his territory Wei, with Luoyang as its capital. Following his victory in the Battle of the Red Cliff, Liu Bei occupied most of Jingzhou, and then spread his power to the west. In 221, he also proclaimed himself emperor, and named his state Shu, with the capital in Chengdu. Sun Quan consolidated his power in the middle and lower reaches of the Yangtze, and proclaimed himself emperor in 222. He named his state Wu, and made Jianye (today's Nanjing) his capital. The struggle between the three kingdoms lasted until 280, when the Western Jin Dynasty wiped out Wu.

小资料 **Data**

孙权称霸江东

孙权(约公元182～252年),字仲谋,今浙江人。他在哥哥孙策死后,接管了长江中下游的军政大权。当时有人很轻视他,公开反叛,孙权迅速调来军队,把反叛的人杀了。大家见他这样有胆量,都很佩服他。后来,曹操要孙权送一个儿子去做人质,保证双方友好。孙权听从了周瑜的意见,决定不服从曹操,利用江东的地理优势,自己开创霸业,于是才有后来三国鼎立的出现。

Sun Quan Rules the Roost in Jiangdong

Sun Quan (c.182-252 AD) was born in today's Zhejiang Province. After his elder brother Sun Ce's death, he took over his rule over the middle and lower reaches of the Yangtze River area. At that time, there were people who looked down on him and rebelled against him publicly. Sun Quan dispatched troops quickly and killed the rebels. Seeing him so courageous and resourceful, people all admired him very much. Later, Cao Cao proposed that as long as Sun Quan sent one of his sons to Cao Cao as hostage, Cao Cao would promise to keep good relations with Sun Quan. Adopting Zhou Yu's advice, Sun Quan did not listen to Cao Cao's proposal. Instead, he developed and expanded his own power relying on the geographical advantages in Jiangdong (roughly areas south of the Yangtze River), which finally led to the situation of tripartite confrontation.

淝水之战
The Battle of Feishui

公元4世纪下半期，前秦皇帝苻 (fú) 坚统一了北方黄河流域。公元383年5月，苻坚征集了80多万人的军队开始进攻东晋。

面对前秦的进攻，东晋上下决心同心协力抗敌。当时，晋军将领是谢石、谢玄和刘牢之，总数只有8万人。10月，前秦军队攻占寿阳(今安徽寿县)，苻坚派被俘的东晋将军朱序到晋军中去劝降。朱序到了晋营，趁机告诉谢石，前秦军队到达前线的只有25万军士，建议先发起进攻。

11月，刘牢之带精兵5,000人进攻，消灭了秦军5万人。谢石等随后乘胜前进，在淝 (féi) 水与前秦军隔水对阵。一天，谢玄以隔水不方便打仗为理由，请秦军后退。苻坚想乘晋军渡河时用骑兵猛冲，消灭晋军，于是命令秦军后退。可是，前秦士兵不明白后退的意思，以为秦军已战败了。此时，朱序又乘机大喊："秦军败了！秦军败了！"前秦军队顿时大乱。晋军乘机渡过了淝水，秦兵拼命逃跑，苻坚被箭射伤，只带了10多万人逃回长安。

这是历史上有名的以少胜多的淝水之战。淝水之战后，前秦瓦解，北方又重新分裂。

东晋和十六国形势图
Sketch Map of Eastern Jin and the Sixteen States of North China

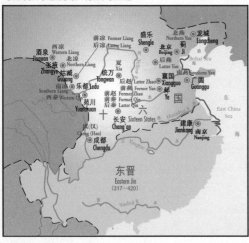

In the latter half of the fourth century, Fu Jian, ruler of the Former Qin Dynasty, united the Yellow River Valley area. In the fifth lunar month of 383, Fu Jian led an army of over 800,000 men against Eastern Jin.

Facing the attack of Fu Jian's army, the Eastern Jin Dynasty decided to make concerted efforts to fight against the enemy. At that time, leaders of the Jin army were Xie Shi, Xie Xuan and Liu Laozhi. They had an army of only 80,000 men. In the 10th lunar month Fu Jian's army captured Shouyang (today's Shouxian County, Anhui Province). Fu Jian sent Zhu Xu, a Jin general captured by the Former Qin army, to the Jin army, to induce them to capitulate. Seizing the chance of going to the Jin camp, Zhu Xu told Xie Shi that there were only 250,000 Former Qin soldiers in the front, and he suggested the Jin army launch an attack first.

In the 11th month, Liu Laozhi attacked the Former Qin army with 5,000 crack soldiers and wiped out 50,000 Former Qin soldiers. Xie Shi and other generals advanced on the crest of the victory and confronted the Former Qin army with each army on one side of the Feishui River. One day, Xie Xuan proposed that it was not convenient for the two belligerent parties to fight on different sides of the river and asked the Former Qin army to draw back. Fu Jian had planned to attack the Jin army when they crossed the river, so he ordered his army to retreat. However, his soldiers did not know the real meaning of the retreat, and many of them thought that they had lost the battle. Just at that time, Zhu Xu shouted loudly, "Fu Jian's army has lost the battle! Fu Jian's army has lost the battle!" This threw the Former Qin soldiers into great confusion at once. The Jin army took advantage of the occasion and crossed the Feishui River. Fu Jian's soldiers fled desperately and Fu Jian himself got wounded by an arrow. At last, Fu Jian returned to Chang'an with only a little more than 100,000 soldiers.

This was the famous Battle of Feishui in history, in which a small army defeated a big one. After the Battle of Feishui, the Former Qin Dynasty fell down and north China was again rent by independent regimes.

泚水之战图
Sketch Map of the Battle of the Feishui

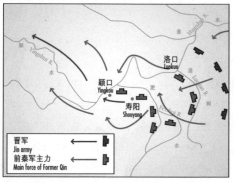

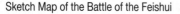

小资料 Data

"草木皆兵"的来历

泚水之战时，前秦军队与晋军隔水对阵。一天，符坚登上寿阳城头观察，望见东晋的部队很严整，又远远望见对面八公山上草木摇动，以为那也是晋兵。他对身旁的弟弟说道，这是很厉害的敌人，怎么能说他们弱呢。说完脸上露出害怕的神情。这就是成语"草木皆兵"的来历，用来形容人在非常害怕的时候，听到一点点动静，就很紧张。

The Origin of "Every Bush and Tree Looks like an Enemy"

Besieged in Shouyang, Fu Jian, commander of the army of Former Qin, was so nervous that he thought that every time a bush or tree moved on the mountain opposite was an enemy soldier. This is the origin of the Chinese idiom "Every bush and tree looks like an enemy", which is a metaphor for extreme timidity.

1.　泚水之战图
　　A portrait of the Batttle of Feishui

"书圣"王羲之与
"画绝"顾恺之
Wang Xizhi, the Saint of Calligraphy, and Gu Kaizhi, the Matchless Painter

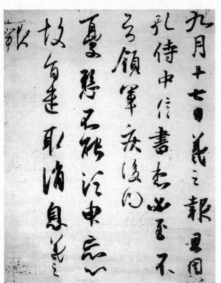

1

王羲 (xī) 之 (约公元303~约361年)，山东人，东晋大书法家，后人尊称他为"书圣"。

王羲之年轻时跟卫夫人学习书法，后来又游历名山大川，观察、学习了前辈书法家们的碑刻。他练习书法十分刻苦，据说，他曾在浙江绍兴兰亭的池塘边日夜练习，竟使一池清水变成了黑色。在休息的时候，他还常常想着字的结构，手指就在衣服上画，时间一长，连衣服也写破了。最后，他终于形成了自己独特的风格。王羲之的行、草书对后人影响很大，他有名的碑帖有《兰亭集序》、《快雪时晴帖》等。唐太宗对王羲之的书法非常重视，特别选取了他书法作品中的1,000个字，编成《古千字文》一书，让学生们学习。

顾恺 (kǎi) 之 (约345~406年)，东晋杰出画家，后人把他和陆探微、张僧繇 (yáo)、吴道子并称为"画家四祖"。他曾遍游中国南方，为绘画创作积累了丰富的素材。

顾恺之的人物画特别出色，他强调"以形写神"，主张通过人物的眼睛看见心灵的秘密。他曾在一座寺庙里作壁画，画完人物后不点眼珠，等到参观的时候，他当场点画眼珠，人像顿时精神焕发，仿佛真人一样。顾恺之的绘画真迹早已失传，现在保存的有古人的摹 (mó) 本《女史箴 (zhēn) 图卷》、《洛神赋图卷》、《列女仁智图卷》。

Wang Xizhi (c.303-c.361 AD) was born in today's Shandong Province. He was a great calligrapher of the Eastern Jin Dynasty, and was called by later generations the Saint of Calligraphy.

Wang Xizhi studied calligraphy under the calligraphy master Madame Wei in his youth. Then he traveled widely to study tablet inscriptions executed by famous calligraphers of older generations. It is said that he used to practice calligraphy by the pond beside Lan (Orchid) Pavilion in Shaoxing, in today's Zhejiang Province, day and night, until the clear pond water turned black from his dipping his inky brush into it so many times. When he took a rest, he still thought of the structure of characters, and his fingers would trace them on his garments. As a result, his clothes soon became worn out. Wang Xizhi's unique style in both running hand and cursive script had a great influence on later generations of calligraphers. His famous

1. 王羲之《孔侍中帖》
   Wang Xizhi's calligraphy

2. 王羲之《兰亭集序》
   Wang Xizhi's most celebrated piece of calligraphy: *The Preface of the Orchid Pavillion*

3. 浙江绍兴兰亭。传"鹅池"二字为王羲之所书
   It is said that the tablet inscription at the Orchid Pavilion in Shaoxing, Zhejiang Province, was written by Wang Xizhi.

1. 《女史箴图卷》(顾恺之画，长349厘米，高25厘米。)
   Gu Kaizhi's *Picture Scroll of Female Scholars* (349cm long, 25cm wide)

rubbings of stone inscriptions include the *Preface to Orchid Pavilion* and the *Kuaixueshiqing Rubbing*. Emperor Taizong of the Tang Dynasty admired Wang Xizhi's calligraphy, and chose 1,000 characters written by him, which he included in a book titled *Ancient 1,000-Character Text* to be used as a guide for students of calligraphy.

Gu Kaizhi (c.345-406 AD) was an outstanding painter in the Eastern Jin Dynasty. Later generations grouped him together with Lu Tanwei, Zhang Sengyao and Wu Daozi, and called them the "Four Ancestors of Painting". Gu traveled all over south China accumulating rich materials for his paintings.

Gu Kaizhi was especially good at figure painting. He maintained that a subject's heart could be read through looking deep into his or her eyes. He painted the eyes last, and viewers said that only then did the subject come to life. Gu Kaizhi's works have long been lost; what remain nowadays are only facsimiles of his *Picture Scroll of Female Scholars*, *Picture Scroll of the Luoshui River Nymph* and *Picture Scroll of Virtuous Ladies*.

数学家祖冲之
Zu Chongzhi, the Remarkable Mathematician

1. 祖冲之像
A statue of Zu Chongzhi

祖冲之（公元429～500年），南朝宋齐时期人。他年轻时就学问渊博，尤其喜爱数学。

祖冲之在数学方面的成就，是求出了比较精确的圆周率。圆周率是圆的周长和直径之间的比例，中国古代很早就知道这个概念，但不太准确。祖冲之总结前人经验，决定利用三国时候刘徽（huī）的"割圆术"来求圆周率。可是，那时运算的工具是竹棍，对于九位数的运算，要经过130次以上的反复计算，而且又容易出错。祖冲之每算一次，至少重复两遍，直到几次的结果完全相同才行。经过刻苦运算，他一直算到了12,288边形和24,576边形，终于得出圆周率大于3.1415926，小于3.1415927的结论。

祖冲之是世界上第一个把圆周率算到小数点后7位数字的科学家，900年后，一位中亚的数学家推算到小数点后16位，才超过了他。除此之外，祖冲之编写过一部《缀（zhuì）术》，收集了他研究数学的主要著作。唐朝时把《缀术》列为数学课的主要教科书。

Zu Chongzhi (429-500 AD) lived in the period of Song and Qi of the Southern dynasties. He devoted himself to study in his youth, being especially fond of mathematics.

Zu calculated the ratio of the circumference of a circle to its diameter at between 3.1415926 and 3.1415927, a figure which was not surpassed in accuracy until 900 years later. In fact, Chinese scientists of previous dynasties had already made their own rough calculations of the ratio. Zu Chongzhi compiled his major achievements in mathematics into a book called *Zhuishu*, which became the main textbook on mathematics in China during the Tang Dynasty.

小资料 Data

中国古代对圆周率的推算表

从西汉开始到祖冲之，历代都有人对圆周率进行了推算，可从下表看出：
Calculation Graph of the ratio of the circumference of a circle to its diameter from Liu Xin of the Western Han Dynasty to Zu Chongzhi.

时代 Period	科学家 Name of the scientist	圆周率（π） Ratio
西汉 Western Dynasty Han	刘歆 Liu Xin	3.1547
三国魏晋 Three Kingdoms and Wei and Jin Dynasties	刘徽 Liu Hui	3.14159
南朝宋 Song of the Southern Dynasties	何承天 He Chengtian	3.1428
南朝宋齐 Song and Qi of the Southern Dynasties	祖冲之 Zu Chongzhi	3.1415926～3.1415927

花木兰与《木兰辞》
Hua Mulan and *The Ballad of Mulan*

"唧 (jī) 唧复唧唧，木兰当户织，不闻机杼 (zhù) 声，唯闻女叹息……"这是一首流传很广的北方民歌《木兰辞》的开头，这首民歌的主角是一位英勇的北方女性，叫花木兰，这首长篇叙事诗讲述了花木兰女扮男装替父从军的传奇故事。

据说花木兰是北魏人，北方人喜欢练武。花木兰的父亲以前是一位军人，从小就把木兰当男孩来培养。木兰十来岁时，他就常带木兰到村外小河边练武，骑马，射箭，舞刀，使棒。空余时间，木兰还喜欢看父亲的旧兵书。

北魏经过孝文帝的改革，社会经济得到了发展，人民生活较为安定。但是，当时北方游牧民族柔然族不断南下骚扰，北魏政府规定每家出一名男子上前线。木兰的父亲年纪大了，哪能上战场呢？家里的弟弟年纪又小，于是木兰决定替父从军，从此开始了她长达12年的军队生活。去边关打仗，对于很多男人来说都是艰苦的事情，更不要说木兰又要隐瞒身份，又要与伙伴们一起杀敌。但是花木兰最后完成了自己的使命，12年后胜利还家。皇帝因为她的功劳，想请她做大官，不过被花木兰拒绝了。

千百年来，花木兰一直是受中国人尊敬的一位女性，因为她既勇敢又纯朴。1998年，迪士尼将花木兰的故事改编成了动画片，受到了全世界的欢迎。

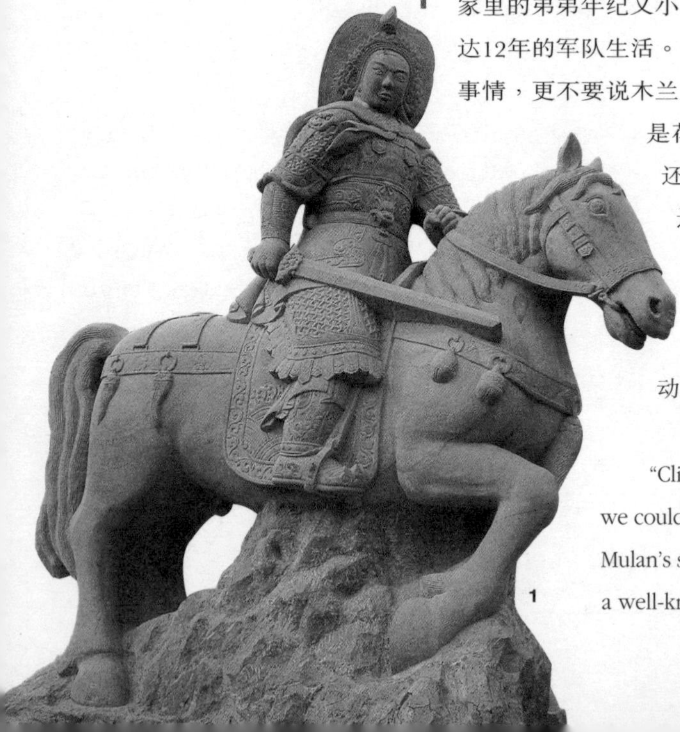

"Click, click, click. Mulan wove cloth in the house. Yet we could not hear the sound of the shuttle, but the sound of Mulan's sighs..." This is the opening of *The Ballad of Mulan*, a well-known folk song in north China. The heroine of this

1

ballad was a heroic woman of Northern Wei named Hua Mulan. The song tells how Hua Mulan disguised herself as a man, and joined the army in place of her father.

Mulan's father, and ex-soldier, taught his daughter military skills, including horse riding, archery and swordsmanship. Hua Mulan also read her father's books on military science.

To ward off incursions by the Rouran nomads, the ruler of Northern Wei ordered that every household provide a man to join an expedition against them. Mulan's father was old then, and her younger brother was too young to go and fight. So Mulan decided to join the army instead of her father. For 12 years, Mulan fought the invaders, successfully maintaining her disguise. In view of her exploits on the battlefield, the ruler of Northern Wei offered Mulan a high official position, but she refused it.

Hua Mulan has been highly respected as a filial daughter by the Chinese people for hundreds of years, even though her story might be no more than a legend. In 1998, her story was adapted for an animated cartoon in a Disney amusement center in the United States, to the acclaim of visitors young and old.

1. 陕西万花山花木兰墓前的木兰从军塑像
   A sculpture of Hua Mulan in front of her mausoleum at Mt. Wanhua, Shaanxi Province
2. 中国发行的花木兰邮票
   The stamp collection of Hua Mulan
3. 木兰从军年画
   A portrait of Hua Mulan

小资料 Data

北魏孝文帝改革

孝文帝拓跋宏(tuòbáhóng)的祖母是汉族人，在其影响下，他学了很多汉族文化知识。为了接受汉族的先进文化，同时解决粮食问题，公元493年，他还把首都迁到了洛阳。此后，他还要求贵族说汉话，改穿汉族服装，又把鲜卑的姓改为汉姓，并带头把自己的姓改为"元"。他还娶了汉族大户人家的女儿为皇后和妃子。他还极力提倡佛教，闻名中外的洛阳龙门石窟，就是从他在位时开始修建的。

The Reforms of Emperor Xiaowen of Northern Wei

Northern Wei was founded by the Tuoba clan of the Xianbei people, but under the rule of Emperor Xiaowen they became completely sinicized. In 493, he moved the capital to Luoyang in order to better absorb the advanced Han culture. The Han language and costume were adopted universally, as were Han surnames. The emperor himself changed his surname to Yuan, and took daughters of rich and influential Han families as his empress and imperial concubines. He also actively promoted Buddhism. The world-famous Longmen Grottoes were carved out during his reign.

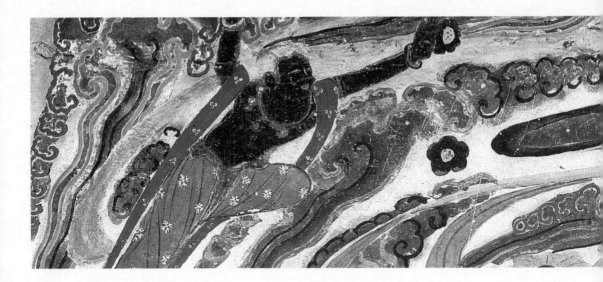

概述
Introduction

　　公元6至10世纪，在中华大地上出现了全国大统一的隋 (suí)、唐王朝。公元581年，杨坚夺取北周政权，建立隋朝。杨坚就是隋文帝。589年，隋灭陈，重新统一南北。618年，隋炀 (yáng) 帝在农民大起义中被部下杀死，不久，隋朝灭亡。在这场农民大起义中，隋朝大官僚李渊父子，乘机起兵，建立唐朝。从唐太宗、武则天到唐玄宗前期，唐朝先后出现过"贞观之治"和"开元盛世"。唐朝的疆域空前辽阔，东到大海，南及南海诸岛，西越巴尔喀什湖，东北到外兴安岭一带，边疆少数民族地区逐步得到开发，国势十分强盛。

　　隋唐时期，经济空前繁荣，对外交往频繁，科技文化成就辉煌灿烂。唐代的书法、绘画、雕刻等成就都很高；唐诗在中国古代诗歌史上发展到了最高峰，李白、杜甫是唐朝最伟大的诗人；唐代散文也有很大成就，韩愈和柳宗元是杰出的代表。唐朝不仅是中国古代强大的王朝，而且也是当时世界上最繁荣富强的国家之一。

　　隋唐时期，西欧国家分裂，政局混乱，工商业衰落，文化处于黑暗的低潮时期。与之相反，亚洲则生机勃勃。唐朝与亚洲各国之间的经济文化交往出现了前所未有的盛况。隋唐政治、经济、文化的发展，影响了亚洲，尤其是东亚的许多国家。唐都长安，不仅是当时的政治中心，而且是亚洲各国经济文化交流的中心之一。因为唐朝在国际上的影响巨大而深远，国外称中国人为"唐人"。

封建社会的繁荣时期——隋、唐

The Heyday of Feudal Society — The Sui and Tang Dynasties

From the 6th to the 10th centuries, China was once more united, under the Sui and Tang dynasties. In 581, Yang Jian usurped the throne of Northern Zhou, and established the Sui Dynasty. Yang Jian reigned as Emperor Wendi of Sui. In 589, Sui conquered the Chen Dynasty, and reunified the northern and southern parts of the country. In 618, a peasant uprising brought about the end of Sui, with the death of Emperor Yangdi. Li Yuan, a powerful Sui official, and his sons, established the Tang Dynasty. The period from the reign of Emperor Taizong (r. 627-649 AD) to the early part of the reign of Emperor Xuanzong (r. 712-756 AD) is called the time of the "Benign Administration of the Zhenguan Reign Period", and the "Flourishing Kaiyuan Reign Period", Zhenguan and Kaiyuan being the reign titles of emperors Taizong and Xuanzong, respectively. The territory ruled by the Tang Dynasty was broader than that of any of the previous dynasties. It reached the East China Sea in the east, extended to the islands in the South China Sea in the south, bordered Lake Balkhash in today's Kazakhstan in the west and extended as far as the Outer Hinggan Mountains in the northeast.

During the Sui and Tang dynasties, the economy of China prospered, exchanges with the outside world were frequent, and glorious scientific and cultural achievements appeared. Calligraphy, painting and sculpture flourished in the Tang Dynasty. In particular, Tang Dynasty poetry is regarded as the acme of this genre, represented by the poets Li Bai and Du Fu. In the field of prose literature, Han Yu and Liu Zongyuan were outstanding. Tang was one of the richest and most powerful countries in the world at that time.

The burgeoning economy and culture of the Sui and Tang dynasties influenced the whole of Asia, especially the countries in East Asia. Chang'an, the capital city of the Tang Dynasty, was not only the political center of China at that time, it was also one of the centers for economic and cultural exchanges in the whole Asian region. Because of the Tang Dynasty's enormous international influence, Chinese people were called the "people of Tang" by their neighbors.

隋朝大运河
The Grand Canal

中国的大河如黄河、长江等，大多数是从西向东奔流入海。南北之间要有一条畅通的河流，只能靠人力开凿(záo)。中国古代劳动人民开凿过不少人工河道，其中最著名的就是大运河。

公元605至610年，隋炀帝为了加强对南北方的控制，活跃南北物资的交流，动用几百万民工，花费了约6年的时间，开凿了这条运河。其中有些河段，是把以前挖好的运河修复、增宽、加深，中间也利用一些天然河、湖与运河相连接。隋代大运河全长2,000多千米，水面宽30到70米不等，北通涿郡(今北京)，南达余杭(今杭州)，它沟通了海河、黄河、淮河、长江、钱塘江等大河流，经过今天的河北、山东、河南、安徽、江苏和浙江等广大地区。大运河的开通，对于促进南北经济、文化的交流和发展，维护国家的统一，起到了非常重要的作用。隋炀帝南下游玩就利用了运河，随行的船有几千艘（sōu），在大运河中船头船尾相连，竟有两百多里长。

元朝在疏通旧河道的基础上又开凿了山东运河和通惠河，形成一条北起北京、南达杭州的京杭直通大运河，使它成为中国南北交通的重要水路。

中国今日又计划修复大运河，目的不仅是为方便南北的联系，更主要是使南水北调，解决北方缺水的问题。

China's major rivers, such as the Yellow River and the Yangtze River, all flow from west to east into the ocean. There was long felt a need for a waterway to facilitate transport from north to south and vice versa. Several attempts to build a north-south canal had been made, but had been only partially successful. Finally, the stretches of the canals that had been dug earlier were joined up, and the Grand Canal came into existence.

The work was started by Emperor Yangdi (605-618 AD) of the Sui Dynasty. The Grand Canal took several million workers about six years to complete. Some natural rivers and lakes were also included in the project. The Grand Canal was originally some 2,000 km long, and the width of the water surface was from 30 to 70 m. The canal reached Zhuojun County (in today's Beijing) in the north, and extended to Yuhang (today's Hangzhou) in the south. It was connected with big rivers like the Haihe, the Yellow River, the Huaihe, the Yangtze River and the Qiantang. The canal flows through Hebei, Shandong, Henan, Anhui, Jiangsu and Zhejiang provinces. The opening of the Grand Canal played a very important role in promoting the economic and cultural development of the whole country and in maintaining political unity. Emperor Yangdi traveled to the south along the canal, accompanied by a vast fleet of ships some 100 km long.

In the Yuan Dynasty (1271-1368 AD), the canal was further dredged and extended to become the main north-south communication waterway.

Today, China is planning to restore the Grand Canal, not only for the convenience of transportation between the north and the south, but also to transfer water from the south to the north to solve the problem of water shortage in the north.

1. 京杭大运河——杭州段
   The Hangzhou section of the Beijing-Hangzhou Grand Canal
2. 江苏扬州古运河遗址
   The ruin of ancient canal, Yangzhou, Jiangsu Province

贞观之治
The Benign Administration of the Zhenguan Reign Period

唐太宗李世民当皇帝时，年号是贞 (zhēn) 观。贞观年间 (公元627～649年)，唐太宗吸取隋朝灭亡的教训，用心治理国家，实行了很多开明的政策和利国利民的措施，使唐朝政权得到巩固，社会经济得到恢复和发展，从而出现了一个比较安定祥和的社会环境。历史学家把这一时期称为"贞观之治"。

唐太宗知道要做到政治清明，就要善于用人，还要广泛听取意见。因此只要有才能的人，不管出身贵贱 (jiàn)，都能够得到他的重用。魏征敢向太宗直接提意见，即使太宗生气，也不退让。魏征病死，太宗痛哭着说，用铜作镜子，可以整理衣帽；用历史作镜子，可以了解兴亡；用人作镜子，可以明白对错，魏征死了，我失去了一面镜子。

唐太宗采取了许多措施，如合并州县，节省开支；让农民拥有一定的土地；减轻劳役负担，让农民的生产时间得到保证等。这些措施很得民心，唐太宗引用古人的话说，皇帝是船，人民是水；水能载船，也能覆 (fù) 船。

唐太宗采用较为开明的民族政策，赢得各民族的拥护。北方各族尊称他为"大可汗"。唐太宗还将文成公主嫁给土蕃 (bō) 的王，使汉藏民族关系更加友好亲密，对中国多民族国家的稳定作出了贡献。

The reign period (627-649 AD) of the second emperor of the Tang Dynasty, Emperor Taizong, was known as Zhenguan. Drawing lessons from the downfall of the Sui Dynasty, Emperor Taizong carried out many enlightened policies and measures beneficial to the country and the people, which consolidated the state power of the Tang Dynasty, restored social stability and boosted the economy. Therefore, the reign was termed the

1. 唐太宗像
   A portrait of Emperor Taizong
2. 唐阎立本《步辇图》(唐太宗会见吐蕃王松赞干布派来求婚的使者)
   A portrait of the formal meeting between Emperor Taizong and the messengers (of King of Tubo — Songtsen Gampo) presenting a marriage proposal
3. 唐三彩乐伎俑
   The Tang tricolor pottery model of a musical group

小资料 Data

唐三彩

唐代一种涂了黄、绿、褐、蓝、黑、白等多种釉彩的陶器。"三彩"就是多种颜色的意思。中国古代陶器分为素陶和彩陶两种。唐代以前，彩陶多是单色陶。到了唐代，三彩陶发展很快，它吸收了绘画、石刻、雕塑等艺术的优点，采用了多种形式的装饰图案，创立了唐代彩色塑陶艺术的独特风格，艺术地再现了"盛唐景象"。

Tang Tricolor Pottery

Tang Tricolor refers to a kind of glazed pottery painted with the colors yellow, green, brown, blue, black and white. "Tricolor" simply means a lot of colors. Ancient Chinese pottery was divided into the plain type and the colored type. Colored pottery before the Tang Dynasty was mostly monochrome. During the Tang Dynasty, tricolor pottery developed very quickly, drawing on the strong points of painting, stone carving, sculpture and other artistic modes. This kind of pottery reflects the colorful prosperity of the Tang Dynasty itself.

"Benign Administration of the Zhenguan Reign Period" by historians.

Emperor Taizong knew that a well-ordered administration needed capable people and a wide range of expert opinions. So he made good use of capable people no matter what their backgrounds were. He once said that using a bronze mirror, one could tidy one's clothes; using history as a mirror, one could know the way of governing a country; using people as a mirror, one could tell right from wrong.

Emperor Taizong implemented many measures that enjoyed the support of the people, such as joining counties and prefectures together to reduce expenditure; letting peasants have a certain amount of land; and reducing the burden of corvee labor to ensure that peasants had time to work on their land. Citing an ancient saying, Emperor Taizong said that the emperor was like a boat and the people were like water; water could carry the boat, but it could also capsize it.

Emperor Taizong won the support of all minority peoples by adopting relatively enlightened policies toward them. The ethnic groups in the north called him "Great Khan". The emperor sent Princess Wencheng to the king of Tubo, in Tibet, which made the relations between the Han and Tibetan peoples closer, and contributed to the stability of China as a multi-ethnic country.

女皇帝武则天
Wu Zetian, China's First Female Monarch

1. 武则天故乡四川广元皇泽寺内的武则天像
   A statue of Wu Zetian in the Huangze Temple, Guangyuan (Wu's hometown), Sichuan Province
2. 武后行从图
   A portrait of Empress Wu Zetian and her team of servants
3. 皇泽寺是四川广元人为纪念武则天而修建的祠院，已有千多年历史
   The 1,200-year old Huangze Temple was built by the Guangyuan people of Sichuan Province in memorial of Wu Zetian.
4. 陕西乾陵，唐高宗李治与武则天合葬于此
   Qian Mausoleum of Shaanxi Province is where Emperor Gaozong and Wu Zetian were buried.

武则天（公元624～705年）是中国历史上杰出的女皇帝和政治家。

武则天从小聪明果断，通文史，长得又漂亮，14岁那年被唐太宗召进皇宫，成为才人。太宗死后，武则天被送进寺院做尼姑。太宗的儿子高宗当太子时就看中了武则天，他当上皇帝两年后，就把武则天从尼姑庵（ān）里接了出来。后来又废掉皇后，立武则天为皇后。

武则天当上皇后以后，帮高宗处理朝廷事务，并趁（chèn）机除掉了一些反对她的大臣。唐高宗身体不好，他看武则天十分能干，有时就把朝政大事交给她去处理，武则天的权力因此越来越大。当时高宗与武则天被称为"二圣"，就是两个皇帝的意思。

公元683年，高宗死后，武则天就以太后的名义管理朝政。公元690年，武则天改国号为周，正式做了皇帝。此后，武则天继续推行唐太宗发展生产的政策，还破格提拔许多有才能的人。唐朝的政治经济在武则天时又得到发展。当然，她统治时期重用武氏家族、大建寺院、过分崇佛等，也给老百姓增加了负担。武则天去世前在大臣的逼迫下将皇位传给了儿子，又恢复了唐朝的统治。

Wu Zetian (624-705 AD) was an outstanding stateswoman in Chinese history.

At the age of 14, she was taken into the imperial palace by Emperor Taizong as a concubine. After

Emperor Taizong died, she was sent to a temple, and became a nun. Emperor Gaozong, son of Emperor Taizong, was fond of Wu Zetian when he was crown prince, and two years after he succeeded to the throne he had Wu Zetian brought back to the imperial palace. Then he demoted his consort, and made Wu Zetian the empress.

Wu Zetian soon became involved in affairs of state and palace intrigue, including getting rid of officials who opposed her. Gaozong, not being in good health, often let her handle his duties for him. At that time, Emperor Gaozong and Wu Zetian were called the "Two Saints" by the people, which meant they had two emperors.

When Emperor Gaozong died in 683, Wu Zetian administered the country as the Empress Dowager. In 690, Wu Zetian changed the name of the dynasty to Zhou, and became empress herself. She carried on the policy of developing production initiated by Emperor Taizong. She also promoted many talented people in defiance of protocol, especially members of her own clan. She was a devout Buddhist, and spent money lavishly on the construction of temples. Eventually, Wu Zetian was forced by her senior ministers to hand over power to her son, and the country returned to the control of the Tang Dynasty.

小资料 Data

武则天小故事

武则天当皇帝时，一个叫骆宾王的诗人参加了反对武则天的军队，还写文章骂她。武则天看了那篇文章以后，没有给骆宾王定罪，反而夸他文章写得有文采，责怪宰相没发现这一人才。

Wu Zetian and the Poet

A poet named Luo Binwang was a member of the court faction that opposed Wu Zetian's exercise of power. He wrote an essay criticizing her, but failed to arouse her anger. Instead, the empress expressed admiration for his literary grace as manifested in the essay, and censured her prime minister for not discovering such a talented person.

开元盛世
The Flourishing Kaiyuan Reign Period

1. 唐玄宗像
   A portrait of Emperor Xuanzong
2. 唐玄宗曾到五岳之首的泰山封禅祭天。图为泰山摩崖石刻
   The carving on the cliffs of Mt. Taishan. Emperor Xuanzong was here once to worship Heaven.
3. 唐开元通宝 (开元通宝是唐代流行时间最长、最重要的货币)
   Kaiyuantongbao coins — the longest-lasting and most important form of currency used during the Tang Dynasty
4. 杨贵妃深受唐玄宗宠幸,但最后被缢死于马嵬坡。图为杨贵妃墓
   Mausoleum of Lady Yang. Although she was the favorite concubine of Emperor Xuanzong, she was hung to death on Mawei Hill during the revolt of An Lushan.

开元 (公元713～741年) 是唐玄 (xuán) 宗李隆基统治前期的年号。从唐太宗贞观初年到开元末年,经过100多年的积累,唐朝出现了全面繁荣的景象,历史上叫做"开元盛世"。

唐玄宗又称唐明皇,是武则天的孙子,他当上皇帝后,立志继承唐太宗的事业,任用有才能的人,接受大臣的正确意见,精心治理国家。有一年河南等地发生很严重的蝗 (huáng) 虫灾害。蝗虫飞过时,黑压压的一大片,连太阳都遮没了。田里的庄稼都被蝗虫吃光了。许多人都认为这是上天降给人们的灾难,没有办法。但唐玄宗听从当时宰相 (中国古代帮助皇帝治理国家的最高官员) 的意见,认为蝗虫只不过是一种害虫,没有什么可怕的,应坚决消灭它。由于采取了有效的措施,各地的虫灾都得到了治理。

唐玄宗在位最初20年里,唐朝出现了兴盛的景象。大诗人杜甫在《忆昔 (xī)》诗中这样描述:"忆昔开元全盛日,小邑 (yì) 犹藏万家室。稻米流脂粟米白,公私仓廪 (lǐn) 俱丰实。"诗句的意思是开元全盛时期,连小县城都有上万户人家。农业连年获得丰收,粮食装满了公家和私人的仓库,人民生活十分富裕。

开元年间,社会安定,天下太平,商业和交通也十分发达。扬州位于大运河和长江交汇 (huì) 处,中外商人汇集,

城市特别繁华。唐都长安城里更是热闹非凡，世界上很多国家的使臣、商人、学者、工匠都争相前往唐朝进行友好交往，开展贸（mào）易，学习文化、技术。中国封建社会出现了前所未有的盛世景象，这就是历史上有名的"开元盛世"。

3

Kaiyuan (713-741 AD) was the earlier reign period of Li Longji, Emperor Xuanzong (r.712-756 AD). The unprecedented prosperity of these years earned them the description "The Prosperous Kaiyuan Period".

Emperor Xuanzong was the grandson of Wu Zetian, but he modeled his rule on that of Emperor Taizong. He made use of capable people, listened to his ministers' advice and devoted himself to affairs of state. He demonstrated his capability with prompt measures one year to combat a plague of locusts in northern China, and saved the people from starvation.

The renowned poet Du Fu described the prosperity of that time in his poem "Remembering the Past": "I remember the good old Kaiyuan days/ When even a small county had ten thousand households/The rice shone and the corn was white/And granaries of state and people burst with grain alike."

4

During the Kaiyuan Period, the society was stable and peaceful, and commerce and transportation were highly developed. Yangzhou, located where the Grand Canal meets the Yangtze River, was a bustling city where merchants from all over China and abroad converged. Chang'an, the capital of the Tang Dynasty, was then one of the world's great metropolises. Envoys, merchants, scholars and artisans of many countries flocked to Chang'an to trade, and to study the advanced culture and technology of the Tang Dynasty.

小资料 Data

安史之乱

安史之乱是安禄山和史思明发动的叛乱战争。天宝年间，唐玄宗宠幸杨贵妃，不理朝政。国家政治腐败，军队战斗力锐减。安禄山（703～757年）骗取了唐玄宗的信任，掌管10多万人的兵权。天宝十四年（755年），安禄山以讨伐杨国忠为名，发兵15万，在范阳发动叛乱。叛军很快攻占东都洛阳，直抵京城长安东边的大门——潼关。接着，安禄山在洛阳自称"大燕皇帝"，建立起一个割据政权。安禄山死后，他的部将史思明继任叛军首领。762年叛乱得以平息。这场叛乱使中国北方经济遭受严重摧残，唐朝从此走向衰落。这以后中国的经济中心逐渐南移。

The Revolt of An Lushan and Shi Siming

In the second half of his reign, the Tianbao years (742-756 AD), Emperor Xuanzong was obsessed by his favorite concubine, Lady Yang, and neglected his duties. The court was corrupt, and the army weak. An Lushan (703-757 AD) wormed his way into Emperor Xuanzong's confidence, and took command of a great part of the dynasty's armed forces. In the 14th year of the Tianbao Period (755 AD), An Lushan staged a revolt in Fanyang with an army of 150,000, under the pretext of punishing Yang Guozhong, Lady Yang's brother, who was seen as having too much power. The rebels quickly captured Luoyang, the eastern capital, where An Lushan proclaimed himself "Emperor of Great Yan". He died soon afterward, and was succeeded by his subordinate Shi Siming. In 762, the revolt was suppressed. This revolt did serious damage to the economy of north China, and marked the decline of the Tang Dynasty. China's economic center began to move gradually southward.

繁盛的长安城
The Heyday of Chang'an

唐代的都城长安，今名西安。长安城建于隋代，叫大兴城，唐代改称长安城，经过近100年的建设，规模宏大的长安城才最后建成。唐代的长安城比现在的西安旧城要大近十倍，是当时国际性的都市。

唐都长安，有雄伟的宫城，是皇帝居住和处理国家政务的地方。宫城南面的皇城里面有政府的官署。城内街道和住宅设计得像棋盘，布局整齐，东西对称。城里的很多街道宽度都在100米以上，其中朱雀大街最宽。这充分体现出当时国力的强盛和经济的繁华。明清时代的北京城就是仿照唐代长安城修建的。

长安城内有坊，有市。坊为住宅区，市为繁华的商业区，市坊分开。市里开设了许多店铺，叫做"行"，有"肉行"、"鱼行"、"药行"、"绢行"、"铁行"、"金银行"等，据说仅东市就有200多种行业。四面八方的奇珍异宝，在这里都有出售。

长安城还是当时的文化中心，娱乐活动丰富多彩，如音乐、舞蹈、斗鸡、拔河、荡秋千等。唐代最有名的画家、书法家和诗

唐朝长安城平面图
Layout of Chang'an in the Tang Dynasty

人都聚集在长安城中，他们的创作活动给长安城增添了许多光彩。那时日本、新罗（今朝鲜半岛）等许多国家都派人来长安留学，波斯（今伊朗一带）和大食（今中亚一带）的商人也纷纷前来长安城经商。当时，百万人口的长安，长期居住的外国人达万家以上。长安不仅是唐代中国的政治、经济、文化中心，而且已经成为了当时国际上著名的城市。

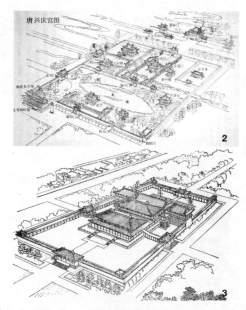

2

3

Chang'an, the capital city of the Tang Dynasty, is now called Xi'an. The city of Chang'an was built in the Sui Dynasty, and called at that time Daxing. The city took nearly 100 years to build. During the Tang Dynasty, Chang'an was almost 11 times as big as today's Xi'an, and was a metropolis of international renown.

There emperor lived and ruled in the imperial palace in Chang'an. To the south of the palace there was the so-called Imperial City, where the government offices were located. The streets and residences of Chang'an were designed like a chessboard, with neat and symmetrical layout of the east and west. The width of many streets and avenues inside the city was over 100 m (Zhuque Avenue was the widest street). The city of Beijing in the Ming and Qing dynasties was modeled on the pattern of Chang'an.

The residential areas and commercial areas inside the city were located separately. In the commercial areas there were many shops: meat shops, fish shops, medicine shops, silk shops, iron shops, gold and silver shops, etc. There were said to be over 200 kinds of shops in the eastern commercial area. All kinds of precious and rare goods were available there.

Chang'an was also the cultural center of China at that time, with rich and colorful recreational activities, such as music, dancing, cock fighting, tug-of-war, swing-playing, etc. The most famous painters, calligraphers and poets of the Tang Dynasty all gathered in Chang'an, and their creative activities added much glory to the city. Students came from Japan and Korea to study in Chang'an, and merchants flocked there from Central Asia. Among the population of around one million in Chang'an, there were over 10,000 foreign households.

1. 今陕西西安市的明代城墙，部分建在唐长安皇城墙基上
   The south gate and the embrasure watchtowers in today's Xi'an (The city wall of today's Xi'an was built on the base of the Imperial City of Chang'an in the Tang Dynasty.)

2. 唐玄宗李隆基的离宫——兴庆宫的复原图
   Recreating the image of Tang Dynasty's Xingqing Palace (Emperor Xuanzong's detached palace)

3. 唐太祖李渊修建的夏宫——大明宫麟德殿的复原图
   Recreating the image of Tang Dynasty's Linde Hall in Daming Palace (Emperor Taizu's summer palace)

 小资料 Data

六大古都

中国古代历史上有"六大古都"，它们分别是陕西西安、河南洛阳、江苏南京、北京、河南开封和浙江杭州。

The Six Major Ancient Capitals

There were six major ancient capitals in Chinese history, namely, Xi'an in Shaanxi Province, Luoyang in Henan Province, Nanjing in Jiangsu Province, Beijing, Kaifeng in Henan Province, and Hangzhou in Zhejiang Province.

松赞干布和文成公主
Songtsen Gampo and Princess Wencheng

　　吐蕃人是藏族的祖先，很早就生活在青藏高原一带，过着农耕和游牧的生活。公元7世纪前期，吐蕃杰出的首领松赞干布统一了那里的许多部落，定都逻 (luó) 些 (今西藏拉萨)。

　　松赞干布非常喜爱唐朝文化，也希望得到先进而强盛的唐朝的支持，他几次向唐求婚，于是，唐太宗把文成公主嫁给了他。

　　公元641年，文成公主在唐朝官员的护送下来到吐蕃，与松赞干布举行盛大的婚礼。吐蕃人民像过节一样，唱歌跳舞，欢迎文成公主入藏。吐蕃人原来住帐篷，据说为了迎接文成公主，特地修建了华丽的王宫，就是今天布达拉宫的前身。

　　文成公主读过许多书，很有才华。她入吐蕃时带去了许多医药、生产技术书籍 (jí) 和谷物、蔬菜的种子，还有唐朝精制的手工艺品。与她一起进藏的还有许多会养蚕、酿 (niàng) 酒、造纸的工匠和会纺织、刺绣的侍女。文成公主信佛教，据说大昭 (zhāo) 寺的基址就是她选定的。先进的汉族文化传入吐蕃，对吐蕃生产和文化的发展起了很大的促进作用。

文成公主在吐蕃生活了40年。她为汉藏两族人民的友谊作出了贡献,一直受到藏族人民的怀念和爱戴。直到现在,西藏拉萨的大昭寺和布达拉宫中,还保存着文成公主的塑像。在藏族人民中间,流传着许多关于文成公主的美好传说。

The Tubo people were the ancestors of the Tibetan people. They appeared on the Qinghai-Tibet Plateau at a very early period. They were farmers and herders. In the early seventh century, Songtsen Gampo united the various Tubo tribes, and made Luoxie (today's Lhasa) the capital of the Tubo kingdom.

Songtsen Gampo admired the culture of the Tang Dynasty, and was eager to form an alliance with that powerful empire. In 641, Emperor Taizong sent Princess Wencheng to him as his bride.

The Tubo people used to live in tents. It is said that a gorgeous palace was built specially for her, which was the predecessor of today's Potala Palace.

Princess Wencheng took with her to Tubo medicines, books on science and technology, grain and vegetable seeds, and exquisite handicrafts of the Tang Dynasty. In addition, people who were proficient in raising silkworms, making wine and paper, and weaving and embroidering accompanied her, to teach these arts to the people of Tibet. Princess Wencheng was an ardent believer in Buddhism. It is said that the location of the Jokhang Temple was chosen by her.

Princess Wencheng lived in Tubo for 40 years, making great contributions to the friendship between the Han and Tibetan peoples. She is still remembered and loved by the Tibetans. Statues of Princess Wencheng are preserved in the Jokhang Temple and Potala Palace. There are many beautiful legends told about Princess Wencheng among the Tibetan people.

小资料 Data

和同为一家

8世纪初,唐中宗接受吐蕃首领赞普尺带珠丹的请求,把金城公主嫁给他。尺带珠丹在写给唐朝皇帝的信中说,吐蕃同唐朝已经"和同为一家"了。

Uniting as One Family

When, at the beginning of the eighth century, Emperor Zhongzong of the Tang Dynasty sent Princess Jincheng to be the bride of the king of Tubo, the king wrote a letter to the emperor, saying that Tubo and the Tang Dynasty had "united as one family".

1. 西藏拉萨布达拉宫
   Potala Palace, Lhasa, Tibet
2. 文成公主像
   A statue of Princess Wencheng
3. 松赞干布像
   A statue of Songtsen Gampo

玄奘西游
Xuanzang's Journey to the West

《西游记》里有个和尚唐僧，他去"西天"，也就是今天的印度半岛取经，带着他的徒弟孙悟空、猪八戒、沙和尚，历尽艰辛，经过"九九八十一难"，终于到达西天，取到了

玄奘西游行程略图
Sketch Map of Xuanzang's Journey to the West

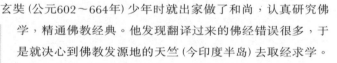

真经。故事里的唐僧，心地善良，却又有些糊涂，这是虚构的神话故事。其实在历史上，还真有这么一个去"西天"取经的唐僧。他的法号叫玄奘（xuánzàng）。

玄奘（公元602～664年）少年时就出家做了和尚，认真研究佛学，精通佛教经典。他发现翻译过来的佛经错误很多，于是就决心到佛教发源地的天竺（今印度半岛）去取经求学。

玄奘于唐贞观元年（公元627年）出发西行。他穿过大片沙漠，克服重重困难，整整走了一年，终于到达天竺（zhú）。

玄奘西行游历了70多个国家，留学天竺达15年之久，他的壮举感动了许多天竺人，有的国王还派人为他抄录经典，他也把当地失传的佛经介绍给他们。他还学会了天竺的语言，参加那儿研究佛学的盛会，发表演讲。玄奘的博学，受到天竺人民的尊敬。

42岁时，玄奘带着650多部佛经回到长安，受到热烈欢迎。回国后，玄奘立即开始大规模的翻译佛经工作，前后翻译佛经74部，约1,300多卷。

作为一名高僧，一位大翻译家，中印人民的友好使

1. 西安大雁塔。玄奘在此翻译从印度带回的佛经
   The Greater Goose Pogoda of Xi'an stores the Buddhist scriptures that Xuanzang brought back from India.
2. 玄奘像
   A portrait of Xuanzang

者，玄奘为中国文化的发展，为中外尤其是中国和印度之间的文化交流作出了巨大的贡献。

In the classic novel *Journey to the West*, a monk, the Tang Priest, goes on a pilgrimage to India to fetch the Buddhist scriptures back to China. Together with his disciples Monkey, Pig and Friar Sand, he overcomes 81 hardships and his mission is successful. The novel is a collection of legends, but in history there really was such a monk. His Buddhist name was Xuanzang.

Xuanzang (602-664 AD) renounced the world, and became a monk. He acquired a good command of the Buddhist classics, and he found that there were a great many errors in the translated Buddhist scriptures. Therefore, he decided to go to Tianzhu (today's Indian Peninsula), the birthplace of Buddhism, to study and bring back the authentic scriptures.

Xuanzang started his journey to the west in the first year (627 AD) of the Zhenguan reign period of the Tang Dynasty. He crossed mountains and deserts, overcoming numerous hardships, and finally reached Tianzhu after a journey of whole year.

During his journey to the west, Xuanzang traveled through over 70 countries, and studied in Tianzhu for 15 years.

At the age of 42, Xuanzang returned to Chang'an, bringing back more than 650 Buddhist scriptures. He then commenced the work of translating the Buddhist scriptures. He translated 74 Buddhist scriptures altogether, amounting to about 1,300 volumes.

Xuanzang was not only an eminent monk, but also a great translator and an envoy for friendship between China and India. He made great contributions to the development of Chinese culture, and for cultural exchanges between China and India and other countries.

2

👉 小资料 Data

《大唐西域记》

玄奘西游回国后还写了《大唐西域记》一书，详细记载了当时称为西域的100多个国家和地区不同的风土人情、物产、气候以及地理、历史、语言、宗教的情况，其中大多数是他西行所见所闻，是今天研究中亚和南亚古代的地理和历史的重要资料。现此书已被译成多种外国文字，成为一部世界名著。

Records on the Western Regions of the Great Tang Empire

After he returned to China, Xuanzang wrote a book titled *Records on the Western Regions of the Great Tang Empire*. The book records in detail the different traditions and customs, products, climates, geographical conditions, histories, languages and religions of over 100 countries and areas in the Western Regions at that time. Most of the contents were what he saw and heard on his journey, which are very important materials for research into the geographical and historical conditions in ancient Central and South Asia. Now this book has been translated into many languages, and enjoys worldwide fame.

鉴真东渡
Jianzhen Crosses the Ocean to Japan

1. 江苏扬州鉴真纪念堂
   Jianzhen Memorial Hall, Yangzhou, Jiangsu Province
2. 欢迎鉴真图（鉴真第六次东渡成功，到日本后受到欢迎的情景。）
   A portrait of Jianzhen receiving a warm welcome in Japan. (He finally reached Japan on his sixth attempt of cossing the hazardous ocean.)
3. 鉴真坐像（现藏于日本奈良唐招提寺"开山堂"）
   A statue of Jianzhen (In Japan's Toshodai Temple)

当玄奘西游取经返回长安差不多100年以后，唐代另一位佛教大师鉴真，决心东渡日本，传播佛法。

鉴真，扬州人，少年时出家当和尚。他学问渊博，有深厚的佛学基础，曾担任扬州大明寺住持。

公元742年，日本天皇派人来到大明寺，请鉴真去日本传播佛法。当时海上交通十分艰险，有人表示疑虑，鉴真果断地说：为了传播佛法，我怎么能怜惜自己的生命呢？但是，鉴真去日本的计划一次又一次受阻。一次出海不久，船只触礁（jiāo），又有一次被官府扣留。当他第五次东渡时，遇上狂风大浪，航向发生偏差，船在海上漂流14天后才获救，这次东渡又没有成功。

不久，鉴真因病而双目失明，但他去日本传播佛法的决心没有丝毫动摇。公元753年，他已经66岁了，又开始了第6次航行。在海

上与风浪搏斗了一个多月，鉴真终于登上日本岛，实现了自己的愿望。跟随鉴真渡海东去的还有23名弟子。他们随身带去许多书籍、佛像、经书和其他珍贵物品。

鉴真居留日本10年，不仅传播了佛法，而且对日本建筑、医学、艺术等方面都有突出贡献。鉴真在奈良设计创建的唐招提寺，被日本人民看作艺术明珠。他的医术在日本也有很大影响，被日本人誉为"医术之祖"。后来他在日本去世。

小资料 Data

遣唐使

唐朝时期，中国是东方最先进的国家，日本先后派了10多批遣唐使到中国学习，人数多时达五六百人。这些遣唐使回国以后，积极传播中国的社会制度和文化，促进了中日友好关系和文化交流。

Envoys Sent to the Tang Empire

During the Tang Dynasty, China was the most advanced country in the East. On a dozen occasions, Japan sent groups of 500 to 600 students at a time to study in China. After these people returned to Japan, they spread knowledge of China's social institutions and culture, which did a great deal to promote the friendly relations and cultural exchanges between China and Japan.

Almost 100 years after Xuanzang's return to Chang'an, Jianzhen, another eminent Buddhist monk of the Tang Dynasty, crossed the ocean eastward to Japan, to spread Buddhism.

Jianzhen was born in Yangzhou. As the abbot of the Daming Temple in that city, he received envoys sent by the ruler of Japan in 742, who requested that teachers of Buddhism be sent to their homeland. Jianzhen decided to go himself. However, the crossing was fraught with hazards, and it was only on his sixth attempt that Jianzhen — by that time 66 and blind — finally reached Japan, in 753, together with 23 disciples.

Jianzhen lived in Japan for 10 years. He not only spread knowledge of Buddhism, he also made prominent contributions to Japan's architecture, medicine and art. He designed the Toshodai Temple in Nara, and he is praised as the "Founder of Medicine" by the Japanese people. Jianzhen died in Japan.

科举制
The Imperial Civil Examination System

1. 宋人科举考试图
   A portrait of the Imperial Civil Examination System
2. 江苏常熟清代状元翁同龢故居的牌匾。翁同龢曾任光绪皇帝的老师
   The signboard inscribed with "Imperial Scholar" is hung over the entrance of Weng Tonghe's old residence, Changshu, Jiangsu Province (Weng topped the imperial civil examination and became the teacher of Emperor Guangxu of the Qing Dynasty.)
3. 清代用于公布殿试结果的大金榜，张贴在皇宫门外。殿试是科举中最高级别的考试。"金榜题名时"是学子的大喜事，但能通过考试的人极少
   Da Jinbang — posted on the wall of the Imperial Palace, this is the list of all successful candidates in the top imperial civil examination of Qing Dynasty. Since only a handful of students who could make the list, it was considered an exceptional honor.
4. 清代殿试试卷封面
   The cover of an examination paper of the palace examination of the Qing Dynasty

科举制也称"开科取士"，就是朝廷开设科目公开考试，然后根据考试成绩来选取人才，分别授予官职的一种制度。科举制产生于隋朝，唐朝继承了这一制度，并进一步完善，成为国家选拔人才的主要方式。

唐朝科举考试分为常科和制科两种。常科每年举行，考试科目有秀才、明经、进士等。在众多科目中考进士科难度很大，往往百人中才取一两名，因此特别受到读书人的重视。进士科考试合格称为"及第"。及第的人要在曲江池参加庆祝宴会，并在长安慈 (cí) 恩寺大雁塔下题名，十分荣耀。制科是皇帝临时诏令设置的科目，名目也很多，通常由皇帝亲自主持，但在士人眼里往往被视为非正途出身，不受重视。

唐代考生有两个来源：一是由学馆选送的学生，称为生徒；二是经州县初考合格后，再进京参加考试，称为乡贡。唐代科举考试一般由礼部主持，考生录取以后，再经吏部复试，根据成绩授予各种官职。

隋唐时期形成的科举制，使普通的读书人获得参加考试然后被选拔做官的机会。这就使封建王朝能在更大的范围内选拔官员。科举制历经隋、唐、宋、元、明、清，一直为历代王朝所采用。但是到了明清时科举制演变成一种刻板、僵 (jiāng) 化的制度，也束缚 (fú) 了中国读书人的思想，对历史发展产生了消极的影响。

Starting in the Sui Dynasty, the imperial government selected its officials from the ranks of the successful candidates in the imperial civil examinations.

The imperial civil examination in the Tang Dynasty was classified into two types: the regular one and the irregular one. The regular examination was held every year. It had many levels, such as *Xiucai, Mingjing* and *Jinshi*. The *Jinshi* degree was the most difficult to attain. Every year hundreds of men took the *Jinshi* examination, but only one or two passed.

Those who passed the *Jinshi* examination would attend a lavish banquet held by the Qujiang Pond, and their names would be announced under the Greater Goose Pagoda in the Ci'en Temple. The irregular examination was set spontaneously by the emperor himself, who acted as the chief examiner. However, it was of less importance than the regular one.

2

There were two kinds of people who took the imperial civil examination. One consisted of students chosen by academies, who were called *shengtu*; the other kind, called *xianggong*, consisted of those who had passed the examinations held by prefectures and counties. The imperial civil examination in the Tang Dynasty was usually presided over by the Board of Rites. Those who passed the examination would be re-examined by the Board of Rites, and then receive various kinds of official positions according to their examination results.

The imperial civil examination system was the method used until the late years of China's last feudal dynasty, the Qing, which fell in 1911, to choose talented men for official positions. However, during the Ming and Qing dynasties, the imperial civil examination system, which stressed knowledge of the Confucian classics exclusively, became a rigid and stultifying institution which kept China from adopting modern scientific methods.

4

小资料 Data

科举考试制度的变化

科举考试的内容有两次比较大的变化。第一次是北宋后期，王安石改革科举考试的内容，不考诗赋，考经义、论、策，这有利于培养和选拔对社会发展有用的人才。第二次是明代，考试内容从可以自由陈述自己意见的散文，变成有严格的格式，不能自由发挥的八股文（有八个严格规定的部分）。这是科举考试形式的一大倒退。

Changes in the Imperial Civil Examination System

The imperial civil examination system underwent two great changes. The first change took place in the late Northern Song Dynasty, when Wang Anshi substituted a politics test for the poetry test. The second change took place in the Ming Dynasty, when all the examination answers had to be in the form of an eight-part essay, with no free expression of opinions.

3

三大石窟
The Three Famous Grottoes

大约公元一世纪前后，佛教从新疆传入内地。进入南北朝以后，统治者为宣扬佛教，在一些地方劈山削崖，开凿石窟 (kū)。隋唐时期，石窟艺术又有很大发展。其中，著名的有山西大同的云冈石窟、河南洛阳的龙门石窟和甘肃敦煌的莫高窟。它们以藏有大量丰富多彩、千姿百态的佛教壁画与雕像塑像闻名于世，被称为艺术的宝库。

山西的云冈石窟在北魏佛教艺术中最有名。它依山开凿，东西长1,000米，雕刻着成千上万大大小小的佛像，最大的佛像高达13.7米。

龙门石窟里最大的洞窟是唐朝时开凿的，佛像的造型和服饰更加东方化，更加真实，体现了唐代社会人们的审美观念。

莫高窟有1,000多个洞窟，又叫千佛洞，现有几百个洞窟，其

乐山大佛

四川乐山的乐山大佛是世界上现存最大的一尊石刻坐佛像，于唐玄宗开元元年（713年）动工兴建，于唐德宗贞元十九年（803年）完工。乐山大佛是弥勒坐像，全身通高70.8米，肩宽24米。完工时的弥勒坐像，全身彩绘，上面盖有宽60米的7层楼阁，这楼阁后来毁于战火。乐山大佛拥有"山是一尊佛，佛是一座山"的美誉。

The Great Statue of Buddha at Leshan, Sichuan Province

The Leshan Buddha is the biggest stone seated statue of Buddha extant. Construction of the statue started in the first year (713 AD) of the Kaiyuan reign period of Emperor Xuanzong of the Tang Dynasty, and it was completed in the 19th year (803 AD) of the Zhenyuan reign period of Emperor Dezong. It is a seated statue of Maitreya (the Buddha of the Future). It is 70.8 m high, and the shoulder width is 24 m. When the statue was completed, it was painted in colors all over, and a seven-story tower 60 m wide was erected above it. This tower was destroyed in a war. There is a saying about the Leshan Buddha: "The mountain is a Buddha, and the Buddha is a mountain."

中十分之六七的洞窟是隋唐时期开凿的。洞窟的四壁和顶上画满了彩色壁画。现存壁画总面积有45,000多平方米，内容表现了佛教故事，不少画面反映出隋唐时期社会的繁荣。莫高窟的塑像共有2,400多尊，隋唐时期占了近一半。这些塑像都富于艺术魅力。

Buddhism spread into the hinterland of China by way of Xinjiang around the first century. In the Southern and Northern dynasties, grottoes were carved in cliffs to house statues of Buddha and sacred murals. In the Sui and Tang dynasties, grotto art made great strides. The three most famous groups of grottoes are the Yungang Grottoes in Datong, Shanxi Province, the Longmen Grottoes in Luoyang, Henan Province, and the Mogao Grottoes in Dunhuang, Gansu Province. They are world-famous for their great number of rich and colorful Buddhist frescos, sculptures and statues.

The Yungang Grottoes are the

1. 洛阳龙门石窟奉先寺北壁塑像
   The Buddhist statues in the Longmen Grottoes in Luoyang
2. 山西大同云冈石窟第20窟雕像
   The Buddhist statues (No.20 Yungang Grottoes at Datong, Shanxi Province)
3. 北周菩萨绘像（甘肃敦煌莫高窟第428窟）
   The portrait of Bodhisattva created during the Northern Zhou (557-581 AD) (No.428 Magao Grottoes at Dunhuang, Gansu Province)

most eminent among the Buddhist artistic works of the Northern Wei Dynasty. They are cut into the foot of a mountain, and stretch 1,000 m from east to west. They contain thousands of Buddhist sculptures of various sizes, among which the biggest one is 13.7 m high.

The largest cave in the Longmen Grottoes was hollowed out during the Tang Dynasty. The Buddhist statues in these grottoes show the influence of the esthetic concepts of the people of India and Central Asia.

The Mogao Grottoes at Dunhuang used to have over 1,000 caves, but nowadays there remain only a few hundred, of which 60-70% were made in the Sui and Tang dynasties. The walls and ceilings of the grottoes are covered with colored frescos, totaling more than 45,000 m². The frescos depict Buddhist stories. Many of them reflect the prosperity of the Tang Dynasty. The Mogao Grottoes boast over 2,400 statues, almost half of which date from the Sui and Tang dynasties.

1. 敦煌莫高窟外观
   Outside of Magao Grottoes
2. 释迦牟尼涅槃像，中唐时期作品 (甘肃敦煌莫高窟第158窟)
   A statue of Sakyamuni's nirvana created during the mid-Tang Dynasty (No.158 Magao Grottoes at Dunhuang, Gansu Province)

大诗人李白、杜甫、白居易
The Great Poets Li Bai, Du Fu and Bai Juyi

1. 李白像
   A portrait of Li Bai
2. 李白《蜀道难》诗意图
   The painting was inspired by Li Bai's poem "The Strenuous Journey to Shu".

　　唐朝是诗人辈出的时代，在为数众多的诗人中有三位大诗人，那就是李白、杜甫和白居易。

　　李白小时候学习刻苦，青年时很想为国家做一番事业。但他不肯迎合世俗的性格，使他的希望一次又一次地破灭。于是他到处游历，饮酒写诗。他写了大量赞美祖国大好河山的诗篇。如他写长江的茫茫无际："孤帆远影碧空尽，唯见长江天际流"；写黄河的一泻千里："黄河之水天上来，奔流到海不复回"；写庐山瀑布的壮丽景象："飞流直下三千尺，疑是银河落九天"；写静夜思乡之情："床前明月光，疑是地上霜。举头望明月，低头思故乡"。李白的诗想像丰富，气势宏大，语言自然，是盛唐时代精神的典型代表。后人尊他为"诗仙"。

　　杜甫生活在唐朝由强盛转向衰落的时代。和李白一样，年轻时杜甫到各地漫游，在洛阳和李白相遇，两人结下了深厚的友谊。他的一生充满了苦难，也没有实现救济天下的大志。杜甫有强烈的爱国情感，把自己和国家的命运联系在一起，十分同情人民的苦难，他用诗

小资料 Data

唐诗和唐诗人知多少

据清代的《全唐诗》及相关的资料统计，唐朝诗人大约有3,700人，唐诗约有53,000余首。由此可见唐代诗歌作者很多，诗篇更多。

Tang Poems and Poets

It is said that the Tang Dynasty produced 3,700 poets, who wrote over 53,000 poems altogether.

1. 杜甫像
   A portrait of Du Fu
2. 杜甫的诗反映了唐朝由强转衰的时代
   Du Fu's poems reflected the gradual decline of the once-great Tang Dynasty.
3. 白居易《琵琶行》诗意图
   The portrait is inspired by Bai Juyi's poem *Song of a Pipa*.
4. 白居易像
   A portrait of Bai Juyi
5. 四川成都杜甫草堂。杜甫为避"安史之乱"，在此居住了9个月，写下了240首诗
   Du Fu Memorial Hall at his thatched cottage near Chengdu, Sichuan Province (To avoid the turmoil of war, Du Fu lived here for nine months and wrote a total of 240 poems.)

歌描写了一个复杂多变的时代，后人称他的诗为"诗史"。如"朱门酒肉臭，路有冻死骨"、"国破山河在，城春草木深"等都已成为千古传诵的名句。他的诗沉郁悲凉，语言精练，达到了很高的艺术水平，以后历代很多诗人都受他的影响。后人尊他为"诗圣"。

白居易十几岁就写下了"离离原上草，一岁一枯荣。野火烧不尽，春风吹又生。"这样的名句。他生活在社会矛盾重重的中唐时期，提倡诗歌反映人民的生活。白居易的诗写得通俗明白，在当时流传很广。据说他写了诗常常先念给老婆婆听，再不断修改，直到老婆婆听懂。他的长诗如《长恨歌》、《琵琶行》写得十分优美动人。

Poets emerged in large numbers in the Tang Dynasty, among whom the three most celebrated were Li Bai, Du Fu and Bai Juyi.

Li Bai studied very hard and had an ambition to serve the country in his youth. But he became disillusioned with the orthodox ladder to success through officialdom. He devoted himself to traveling, drinking and writing poems. Many of his poems eulogize China's scenery. For example, he describes the vastness of the Yangtze as follows: "The lonely sail disappears in the distance, leaving the sky clear and blue/ There remains nothing but the Yangtze flowing to the horizon." Of the Yellow River he writes, "The waters of the Yellow River come down from Heaven/ Rushing to the sea, never to come back". He says of the Lushan waterfall: "Its torrent dashes down three thousand feet from

high/ As if the Milky Way has fallen from the azure sky."
Another poem of his describes his longing for his
hometown in the dead of night: "The bright
moonlight before my bed/ I thought was frost
on the floor/ When I raised my eyes I saw
the moon gleaming/ When I dropped my
head, I thought of my hometown." He was spoken
of as the "poet immortal" by people of his time.

Du Fu lived in the period when the Tang Dynasty had passed its days
of glory and was heading toward decline. Like Li Bai, Du Fu traveled a lot
in his youth. He met Li Bai in Luoyang, and they became good friends. Also

like Li Bai, Du Fu's ambition was thwarted,
and his life was full of suffering. His poems
describe a sophisticated but changing
society. For example, "The fragrance of meat
and wine exudes from rich men's houses/
While the poor die of cold and hunger in
the streets" and "The country has fallen into
the enemy's hands/ Yet the rivers and
mountains are still here/ Spring has come to
the city/ Where trees and grass grow exuberantly". These famous verses
have been remembered and recited for centuries. Du Fu's poems are grave
and melancholy. The succinct language he uses reaches a very high artistic
level, and influenced numerous poets after him. He was called
the "sage poet" by later generations.

When he was just a tcenager, Bai Juyi wrote famous
verses like "The grass on the vast prairie lives and dies every
year/ Fire cannot burn it all/ When the spring wind blows/ It
will grow again". His poems are easy to understand, and were
popular in his lifetime. It is said that after he wrote a poem
he first read it to an old woman. He would amend it until the
old woman could understand it. Of his profuse works, the
most famous are the long narrative poems *The Everlasting
Regret* and *Song of a Pipa* (Lute Player).

概述
Introduction

　　五代、辽、宋、夏、金、元时期，从公元907年后梁建立开始，到1368年元朝灭亡为止，长达460多年。从朱温废掉唐朝皇帝，建立梁朝（史称后梁）以后的50多年里，中国北部先后出现后梁、后唐、后晋、后汉、后周五个朝代，史称五代。南方各地和北方的山西，还先后出现了前蜀、吴、闽、吴越、楚、南汉、南平、后蜀、南唐、北汉等十个割据政权，总称十国。

　　960年，后周大将赵匡胤（yìn）发动陈桥兵变，建立宋朝，都城在今天的开封，历史上称北宋。当时，中国还有辽、西夏等几个少数民族政权。1127年，女真贵族建立的金朝派军队攻入开封，北宋灭亡，继位的皇帝赵构逃往南方，后来在今天的杭州定都，史称南宋，出现了宋、金对峙的局面。1206年，成吉思汗建立了蒙古政权，并统一蒙古，蒙古先后灭西夏、金，并一直打到多瑙河流域。1260年，忽必烈继承汗位，后来定都于今天的北京。1271年，忽必烈正式定国号为元，元军于1276年攻占杭州，1279年消灭了南宋残

封建社会的继续发展和民族政权并立时期——

五代、辽、宋、夏、金、元

The Continued Development of Feudal Society and the Co-existence of Ethnic Regimes — The Five Dynasties, and the Liao, Song, Xia, Jin and Yuan Dynasties

余势力，统一了中国。1368年，朱元璋的军队攻占北京，元朝灭亡。

这一时期，欧洲仍处于经济、文化发展的低潮。中国的经济、文化在世界上继续处于领先地位。北宋商品经济发达，科技水平高超。出现了世界上最早的纸币，火药兵器广泛应用，罗盘针（指南针）用于航海，发明了活字印刷。这些都极大地推动了世界历史的进步。元朝的疆域比过去的任何朝代都要辽阔，北京是当时闻名世界的大商业都市，意大利人马可·波罗在元世祖当朝时来到中国，居住了十几年，在他所著的《马可·波罗行纪》一书里描述了大都（今北京）的繁华景象。宋朝文学的主要成就是词，元朝戏剧发达，最著名的剧作家是关汉卿等。

The period of the Five Dynasties (the Later Liang, Later Tang, Later Jin, Later Han and Later Zhou) and Ten Kingdoms (Wu, Southern Tang, Southern Ping, Chu, Former Shu, Later Shu, Min, Northern Han, Southern Han and Wu-Yue) started in 907, when the Later Liang Dynasty was established. It ended in 960, when Later Zhou fell and the Northern Song Dynasty was established.

Northern Song was under threat for most of its existence from states set up by minority ethnic groups, such as Liao and Jin in the northeast and Western Xia in the northwest. In 1127, the Jin army captured Kaifeng, the Northern

概述
Introduction

Song capital. Zhao Gou, the emperor, escaped to the south, and set up what is historically known as the Southern Song Dynasty, with Hangzhou as its capital. In 1206, Genghis Khan united the Mongolian tribes. The Mongols went on to build a huge empire. In 1260, Genghis Khan's grandson Kublai founded the Yuan Dynasty, with its capital in today's Beijing. The Yuan army seized Hangzhou in 1276, and in 1279 it crushed the remaining forces of the Southern Song Dynasty and united the whole of China. The Yuan Dynasty endured until 1368, when a rebel army led by Zhu Yuanzhang seized Beijing and established the Ming Dynasty.

Trade flourished in the Northern Song period, as did science and technology. In China there appeared the earliest paper currency in the world, firearms were widely used, the compass assisted navigation, and moveable type was used to print large numbers of books. The territory of the Yuan Dynasty was broader than that of any of the preceding dynasties, and Beijing became a world-renowned commercial metropolis. An Italian merchant named Marco Polo came to China during the reign of Emperor Shizu (1271-1294 AD), and stayed for over 10 years. He described the prosperity of Dadu (today's Beijing) and other parts of China in his book *The Travels of Marco Polo*. The Song and Yuan dynasties were a golden age for literature. In the Yuan Dynasty, especially, great achievements were made in drama, Guan Hanqing being the most outstanding dramatist.

1. 开封龙亭。原为宋代皇宫御苑一部分
Kaifeng Dragon Pavilion used to be part of the Imperial Garden during Song Dynasty.

杯酒释兵权
Relieving the Generals of Their Commands at a Feast

1. 宋太祖请大臣喝酒，言谈间解除他们
   的兵权，史称"杯酒释兵权"
   To prevent revolt against the central authority,
   emperor Taizu took back the military power from
   his ministers at a banquet. This incident is referred
   as "Relieving the Generals of Their Commands
   at a Feast".

唐朝灭亡以后，中国的历史进入五代十国的混乱时期。到了后周（公元951～960年）的时候，周世宗让赵匡胤掌握了军事大权。周世宗死后由他年幼的儿子继位，赵匡胤趁机夺取了皇权，建立了宋朝。他就是宋太祖。

宋太祖赵匡胤做了皇帝以后没多久，就有两个地方节度使反叛宋朝。宋太祖花了很大劲儿，才平定了叛乱。为了这件事，宋太祖心里总不踏实。有一次，他找跟随他多年的赵普说话，问他说："自从唐朝以后，换了许多朝代，不停地打仗，不知道死了多少百姓。这到底是为什么呢？"赵普说："这道理很简单。国家混乱，毛病就出在军事权力不集中，如果把兵权集中到中央，天下就太平了。"宋太祖听了连连点头。他自己就是利用手中的兵权夺取皇位的。为了防止这样的事情再发生，宋太祖决定收回兵权。公元961年秋天的一个晚上，宋太祖在宫中举行宴会，请石守信等几位老将喝酒。他举起一杯酒，先请大家干了杯，说："我要不是有你们的帮助，也不会有今天。但是你们哪里知道，做皇帝日子也不好过呀，还不如做个节度使快乐！"石守信等人听了十分惊奇，连忙问这是什么缘故。宋太祖接着说："这还不明白？皇帝这个位子，哪个不想坐呀？"石守信等人听出话中有话。大家着了慌，跪在地上说："我们决不会对您三心二意。"宋太祖摇摇头说："对你们几位难道我还信不过？只怕你们的部下将士当中，有人贪图富贵，把黄袍披在你们身上。你们想不干，能行吗？"石守信等人吓得满头大汗，连连磕（kē）头，第二天就说自己年老多病请求辞职。宋太祖马上同意了，给他们一大笔财物，收回了他们的兵权。历史上把这件事称为"杯酒释（shì，解除的意思）兵权"。

1. 宋太祖"黄袍加身"处——陈桥驿故址
The site of Chenqiao courier station, where the incident of "Wrapped Around by the Yellow Gown" took place.

After the downfall of the Tang Dynasty, China entered a chaotic period of the Five Dynasties and Ten Kingdoms. In the Latter Zhou Dynasty (951-960 AD), Emperor Shizong let Zhao Kuangyin control the military leadership. After Emperor Shizong died, his young son succeeded to the throne. Taking this chance, Zhao Kuangyin seized the imperial power and established the Song Dynasty. And Zhao Kuangyin was Emperor Taizu.

Not long after Zhao Kuangyin came to the throne, two local military governors revolted against the central authority. It took Zhao Kuangyin a lot of energy to suppress the revolt, which upset him very much. Once he talked with Zhao Pu who had been with him for many years. He said that since the downfall of the Tang Dynasty there had changed many dynasties with endless wars. People had died numerously. What was the reason of all these? Zhao Pu said the reason was very simple. The chaotic situation in a country lay in scattering of the military power. The country would restore to peace as soon as the military power returned to the overall control of the central authority. Emperor Taizu agreed to this opinion, and it was by controlling the military leadership that he had seized the imperial power. In order to prevent the same thing from happening again, Emperor Taizu decided to take back military power from local authorities. In an autumn evening in 961, Emperor Taizu held a banquet in the imperial palace and invited Shi Shouxin and other senior generals. The emperor held up the cup and said, "But for your help, I wouldn't be what I'm like nowadays. But you don't know it's very difficult to be an emperor. In fact it's happier to be a local military governor than to be an emperor." Shi Shouxin and the other generals were very surprised when they heard this and asked why. Emperor Taizu said, "It's quite obvious. Who does not want to be the emperor?" The generals got the underlying meaning of his words and became flustered. They knelt on the ground hurriedly and said, "We won't betray you at any time." Emperor Taizu shook his head and said, "I have confidence in all of you. But I'm afraid your subordinates may be ambitious and hanker after riches and honors. When they wrap the yellow gown (a symbol for emperor) around you and support you to be the emperor, can you refuse them?" The generals were so frightened that their faces were covered with beads of perspiration. The next day they asked to resign and the emperor agreed immediately. He gave them a large amount of money and took back their military power. This was called "relieving the generals of their commands at a feast" in history.

赤胆忠心的杨家将
The Loyal Generals of the Yang Family

杨家将的故事在中国民间家喻户晓。

历史上杨家将的主要人物是杨业。北宋初年，北方的辽国不断进扰宋朝边境。杨业带领部队守卫边境重镇雁门关。公元980年，辽国派10万大军攻打雁门关。那时候，杨业只有几千人马。他就让大部分人马守卫雁门关，自己带领几百名骑兵，悄悄绕到辽军背后，给辽军一个突然袭击。辽军毫无防备，人人心惊胆战，大败而归。

雁门关一仗取得胜利后，杨业又带领宋兵打了几个大胜仗。从此以后，辽军一看到"杨"字旗号，就吓得不敢再战。人们给杨业起了个外号，叫"杨无敌"。

过了两年，宋太宗决定大举攻辽，令宋军分三路进军。杨业担任西路军副帅。开始，三路军进展顺利。后来，东路军轻率冒进，导致溃败，宋军只得撤退。撤退时，由于西路主帅指挥错误，杨业的部队遭到辽国大军伏击。士兵们都战死了，杨业孤军奋战，身受几十处创伤仍坚持战斗，最后被俘。杨业在辽营里宁死不肯投降，绝食了三天三夜，就牺牲了。

杨业死后，杨家子孙继承了他的事业。儿子杨延昭、孙子杨文广都在保卫宋朝边境的战争中立了功。民间传说的杨家将的故事就是根据他们的事迹加工而成的。

There are many stories about the exploits of the generals from the Yang Family and their faithful service to the Northern Song Dynasty.

Yang Ye, his son Yang Yanzhao and his grandson Yang Wenguang fought many glorious battles to repel the incursions by Liao, a kingdom set up in northeast China by the Khitan tribe. Many members of the Yang Family laid down their lives in the war of resistance against Liao, including Yang Ye, who died of a hunger strike after his capture by the Liao troops. The deeds of the Yang Family generals became the stuff of folk legend.

小资料 Data

辽国

公元916年耶律阿保机建契丹国，947年耶律德光改国号为"辽"，定都上京（今内蒙古境内）。国号有时为契丹，有时为辽。

The Kingdom of Liao

In 916, Yelu Abaoji, leader of the Khitan tribe, established a kingdom in the area of modern Manchuria. In 947, the name of the kingdom was changed to Liao, with Shangjing (in today's Inner Mongolia Autonomous Region) as the capital.

1. 杨令公血战西狼山
   General Yang at war

秉公执法的"包青天"
Bao the Upright Judge

中国民间流传着许多有关包公的传说，称他为"包青天"、"青天大老爷"，称赞他执法严明，铁面无私，为老百姓做主。确实，历史上有这样一个清官，他就是宋朝的包拯（zhěng）。

包拯（公元999～1062年）是安徽合肥人，在地方和朝廷都做过官。他在做县官时，据说有一次，他的堂舅犯了法。包拯不讲私情，照样依法办事，派人把他抓到官府，判了死刑。许多亲戚赶来求情，包拯说："不是我没有情义，谁叫他犯法呢？"

后来，包拯又到朝廷做官，他也不怕得罪大官。有一年开封发大水，威胁到老百姓的安全。包拯发现涨水的原因是河道被阻塞了。原来一些大官在河道上修筑了花园亭台。为了保证开封的安全，包拯立刻下命令，要这些人把河道上的建筑全部拆掉。即使是皇亲国戚，违反了法令，包拯也毫不留情，他向皇帝提出自己的意见，直到让这些人受到应有的惩罚，才肯罢休。

对受冤枉（yuānwàng）的老百姓，包拯却充满了同情。每次遇到这样的案情，他总是深入调查，详细分析，替百姓伸冤。人们感激他公正执法，都称他为"包青天"。

包拯做了大官，家里的生活也没什么变化，穿衣吃饭，跟普通老百姓一样。包拯死了以后，留下一份遗嘱说："后代子孙做了官，如果犯了贪污罪，不许回老家；死了以后，也不许葬在包家坟地上。"

包拯一生做官清清白白，受到老百姓的敬仰，民间流传着许多他的故事，大家习惯上都叫他"包公"，包拯的本名倒很少有人提起了。

Many stories have been handed down among the Chinese people about a

2

judge known for his fearless espousal of justice. He is known as "Clear Sky Bao", meaning that no wrongdoing could be hidden from his impartial eye, and was a historical personage during the Song Dynasty.

Bao Zheng (999-1062 AD) was from Hefei, in today's Anhui Province. As a county magistrate, he showed no partiality for friends or relatives, even sentencing one of his uncles to death for a crime.

When Lord Bao, as he came to be known, became a court official, he refused to practice favoritism as regards his fellow officials. One year, there occurred a flood in the capital, Kaifeng, which threatened to engulf the poorer quarters of the city. Bao Zheng found that the flood had been caused by the intrusion of waterside gardens and pavilions built for the pleasure of senior officials. Without any hesitation, he ordered that these constructions be removed.

Bao Zheng had great sympathy for those who were unjustly convicted. He would determinedly carry out detailed investigations and bring justice to the victims. People admired his character so much that they praised him as the "Clear Sky Bao".

Although Bao was a high-ranking official, he lived a simple and frugal life just like commoners. His will declared that if his descendants were to be corrupted officials, they would be forbidden to return home and they would be denied the right to be buried in the family graveyard.

Bao was well respected by people because of his righteousness, and his legend was spread among the regions. Since people were used to call him Lord Bao, his real name was rarely mentioned.

1. 安徽合肥包公祠内的包公铜像
   A bronze statue of Lord Bao in his memorial temple of Hefei, Anhui Province
2. 河南开封包公祠内的狗头铡等
   The guillotines found in Lord Bao's Memorial Temple, Kaifeng, Henan Province
3. 包拯办案绝不徇私，人称"包青天"
   Bao Zheng is known as "Clear Sky Bao" because of his integrity and uprightness.

 **小资料 Data**

包拯小故事

包拯一生清廉，从不贪污受贿。他在端州——今天的广东肇(**zhào**)庆市，当了将近三年官。端州有一种著名的特产——端砚。笔、墨、纸、砚合称为文房四宝，而湖笔、徽墨、宣纸、端砚被称为四宝之最。端砚石质坚实温润，纹理细密，发墨快而不易干，书写流利生辉，从唐代起就很有名，是上贡皇帝的贡品。包拯以前的县官常征收老百姓的端砚，用来贿赂朝中权贵。包拯当县官时不加征端砚，也不贿赂权贵。虽然他十分喜爱书法，但他离开端州时竟然连一块端砚也没带走。

Lord Bao and the Inkstones

Bao Zheng was once the magistrate of Duanzhou (today's Zhaoqing in Guangdong Province). Duanzhou was famous for its manufacture of fine-quality inkstones, used for grinding and mixing ink preparatory to writing. These inkstones were so fine that they were even presented as tribute to emperors. Bao Zheng's predecessors had often extorted inkstones from the people and used them to bribe court officials. But Bao Zheng refused to stoop to such dishonesty; in fact, although he was a keen calligrapher himself, he did not take a single inkstone with him when he left Duanzhou.

忠心报国的岳家军

General Yue Fei,
a Paragon of Loyalty

1. 河南汤阴岳飞庙
   Yu Fei Temple, Tangyin, Henan Province
2. 岳飞塑像
   A statue of Yue Fei
3. 奸臣秦桧（中）像长跪在岳飞坟前
   A statue of the kneeled treacherous minister, Qin Hui (middle), is placed in front of Yue Fei Mausoleum.

岳飞是南宋时期抗击金朝进犯的名将。他从小刻苦读书，特别爱读兵法，20岁时参加了军队，以勇敢出名。

岳飞一心想收复被金朝占领的中原大地，对自己要求十分严格，又关心爱护士兵。他领导的岳家军作战十分勇猛，从没打过败仗。

公元1140年，金大将兀术(wùzhú)带领金朝的军队向南宋进攻。岳飞带领岳家军与金兀术作战。

兀术有一支经过专门训练的骑兵，人马都披上厚厚的铁甲，叫做"拐子马"，向岳家军进攻。岳飞看准了拐子马的弱点，等敌人冲过来，命令士兵弯着身子，专砍马腿。马砍倒了，金兵跌下马来，这样就把拐子马打败了。兀术听到这个消息，伤心得哭了。他说，自从带兵打仗以来，全靠拐子马打胜仗，这下全完了。岳家军乘胜收复了许多中原失地。

但后来，昏庸的宋高宗却与金朝讲和，命令岳飞从前线撤兵，又解除了他的兵权。公元1142年，奸臣秦桧（huì）又以"莫须有"（即当地语言"可能有"的意思）的罪名把岳飞害死了。岳飞死时只有39岁。

Yue Fei was a general of the Southern Song Dynasty, who fought victoriously against the invading forces of Jin, a kingdom established in northern China by the Nuzhen tribe, and drove them out of the Central Plains.

In 1140, the Jin army under General Wu Zhu attacked the Southern Song Dynasty. Their warhorses were clad in thick armor, so Yue Fei instructed his men to hack at the horses' unprotected legs. In this way, the Jin troops lost their advantage, and were crushingly defeated.

However, the fatuous Emperor Gaozong of the Southern Song Dynasty made peace with the Jin. Yue Fei was dismissed, and in 1142 executed on a trumped-up charge.

成吉思汗与忽必烈
Genghis Khan and Kublai Khan

1. 成吉思汗像
   A portrait of Genghis Khan
2. 元世祖忽必烈像
   A portrait of Kublai Khan, Emperor Shizu of the Yuan Dynasty
3. 成吉思汗陵(位于内蒙古伊金霍洛旗，为后人重建。)
   Genghis Khan Mausoleum, located in Ejin Horo Banner in todays' Inner Mongolia Autonomous Region

　　蒙古族是中国北方一个古老的民族。12世纪末，铁木真经过十多年战争统一了蒙古各部，公元1206年被推举为蒙古的大汗，尊称为"成吉思汗(**hán**)"，意思是"坚强的君主"。成吉思汗建立大蒙古国以后，国力强盛，军事行动波及欧洲的多瑙河流域，对世界历史发展进程产生了重大影响。成吉思汗死后，蒙古军队相继灭西夏和金，统一了中国整个北方地区。

　　公元1260年，忽必烈(成吉思汗的孙子)继承了汗位，建都大都(今北京)。到1271年，忽必烈正式称皇帝，建立了元朝(公元1271～1368年)，他就是元世祖。元世祖逐步巩固对北方的统治之后，就集中力量攻打南宋，终于灭了南宋。公元1279年，实现了中国南北大统一。

　　元世祖忽必烈做了皇帝以后，就对中央和地方的行政机构进行改革。他先在中央设立中书省，为最高的行政机构。在全国各地设立了行中书省，简称"行省"，在全国各地共设立十个行中书省，正式作为地方最高的行政机构。另外，吐蕃(今西藏)地区在元朝时也正式成为中国的一个行政区，由中央的宣政院管辖。元朝政府还设置了澎湖巡检司，管辖台湾与澎湖，这是台湾归属中国中央政府管辖的开始。

　　元朝行省制度的建立，加强了中央与行省、行省与行省之间的联系，使元朝中央对边疆少数民族地区的管理比以前任何朝代都有效，有利于多民族统一国家的稳定和发展。这是元世祖忽必烈的一项创举。

　　元朝创设的行省制度一直沿用到今天，但在辖区的数目与大小等方面已有很大的变化。

At the end of the 12th century, Temujin united all the Mongolian tribes after 10 years of warfare. In 1206, he was chosen their khan, with the title of "Genghis Khan", which means "mighty monarch". Under Genghis Khan, the

Mongol Empire grew, until it stretched from the northern borders of China to the Danube River in Europe. Under Genghis Khan's son and successor, the Mongols wiped out the Western Xia kingdom and the Jin Dynasty, and incorporated northern China into their empire.

In 1260, Kublai, the grandson of Genghis Khan, succeeded to the position of khan, and decided on Dadu (today's Beijing) as his capital. In 1271, Kublai Khan formally proclaimed himself emperor, historically known as Emperor Shizu, of the newly established Yuan Dynasty (1271-1368 AD). After consolidating his hold emperor, historically known as over the north, he moved against the Southern Song Dynasty, which fell in 1279, and China was united once more.

Kublai Khan reformed the system of administration, with *Zhongshusheng* (Metropolitan Secretariat) in the central government as the highest administrative institution, and *Xingzhongshusheng* (Branch Secretariat) in local governments as the highest local administrative institutions (called *Xingsheng* for short). There were 10 *Xingsheng* altogether in the whole country. Tubo (today's Tibet) officially became one of China's administrative regions in the Yuan Dynasty, under the direct administration of *Xuanzhengyuan* (Commission for Buddhist and Tibetan Affairs) in the central government. In the Yuan Dynasty, too, the island of Taiwan became part of the administrative region of Penghu. This was the beginning of the Chinese central government's administration over Taiwan.

The setting up of the *Xingsheng* system strengthened the relations between the central and local governments, as well as those between different local governments. It made the central government's administration over border areas more effective than that of any previous dynasty, solidifying the unity of China as a multi-ethnic country. Moreover, it was the basis of the administrative systems of later dynasties, and even of today's China.

小资料 Data

元大都

大都是元代的首都。元灭金后，忽必烈于至元元年（公元1246年），以中都（金的首都）东北风景秀丽的离宫为中心，着手规划建设新都城，至元十三年元大都建成完工。大都城采用外城、皇城和宫城三城相套形制，规模宏伟整齐，功能分区明确。大都是元代最大的商业中心，城市各种市集多达30余处，有综合性的商业中心，也有各行业的街市。明清北京城就是在元大都的基础上改建和扩建而成的，有许多建筑仍保留至今。

Dadu in the Yuan Dynasty

After conquering the Jin Dynasty, in 1246 Kublai Khan embarked on laying out and building a new capital city, on the site of the Jin capital, Zhongdu (present-day Beijing). The construction of Dadu was completed in 1276. The new capital consisted of the Outer City, the Imperial City and the Palace City. With grand buildings and a strictly ordered pattern of streets and quarters, Dadu was the largest commercial center in the Yuan Dynasty. There were over 30 markets of various types, comprehensive commercial centers and downtown streets devoted to different trades. The city of Beijing during the Ming and Qing dynasties was extended on the basis of Dadu, and many of the Yuan Dynasty buildings are still preserved.

历史名臣文天祥
Wen Tianxiang, a Renowned Minister

1. 文天祥像
   A portrait of Wen Tianxiang
2. 江西吉安白鹭洲文天祥纪念馆
   Wen Tianxiang Memorial Hall, Bailuzhou, Ji'an, Jiangxi Province

文天祥是中国历史上的名臣，江西人。他从小爱读历史上忠臣烈士的传记，立志要向他们学习，年轻时就考中了状元。

忽必烈建立元朝以后，开始进攻南宋，一路南下逼近临安(南宋首都，今杭州)。这时南宋朝廷连忙号召各地派兵救援。文天祥在江西响应，组织了几万义兵，准备赶到临安去。有个朋友劝他说，你用这些临时招来的人马去抵抗元军，好比赶着羊群去跟猛虎搏斗，还是不要去吧！文天祥说，国家危急，却没有人为国出力，难道不叫人痛心吗？我明知道自己力量有限，宁愿为国献身。

南宋朝廷在危急中任命文天祥为右丞相，去和元军谈判。文天祥被元军扣留，在押往大都的途中，他趁机逃走。

文天祥逃到福州、广东，重新组织力量抗击元军，后来终因力量悬殊，被元军抓住，随后被押往大都。

文天祥在大都被关了3年多，宁愿死也不肯投降。最后元世祖忽必烈亲自劝他说：你的忠心，我也完全了解。现在你如果能改变主意，做元朝的臣子，我仍旧让你当丞相。文天祥回答说："宋朝已经灭亡，我只求一死，别的没有什么可说了"。1283年，年仅47岁的文天祥去世。

文天祥在监狱中写下的《正气歌》，成为千古传诵的不朽诗篇。

《正气歌》

天地有正气，杂然赋流形。下则为河岳，上则为日星。于人曰浩然，沛乎塞苍冥。
皇路当清夷，含和吐明庭。时穷节乃见，一一垂丹青。在齐太史简，在晋董狐笔。
在秦张良椎，在汉苏武节。为严将军头，为嵇侍中血。为张睢阳齿，为颜常山舌。
或为辽东帽，清操厉冰雪。或为出师表，鬼神泣壮烈。或为渡江楫，慷慨吞胡羯。
或为击贼笏，逆竖头破裂。是气所磅礴，凛烈万古存。当其贯日月，生死安足论。
地维赖以立，天柱赖以尊。三纲实系命，道义为之根。嗟余遘阳九，隶也实不力。
楚囚缨其冠，传车送穷北。鼎镬甘如饴，求之不可得。阴房阗鬼火，春院闭天黑。
牛骥同一皂，鸡栖凤凰食。一朝蒙雾露，分作沟中瘠。如此再寒暑，百沴自辟易。
哀哉沮洳场，为我安乐国。岂有他缪巧，阴阳不能贼。顾此耿耿在，仰视浮云白。
悠悠我心忧，苍天曷有极。哲人日已远，典刑在夙昔。风檐展书读，古道照颜色。

Wen Tianxiang was born in Jiangxi Province. In his youth, he was fond of reading biographies of loyal ministers, and made up his mind to model himself on them. Later, he achieved the first place in the imperial civil examination.

When Kublai Khan's armies approached Lin'an (today's Hangzhou), the capital of the Southern Song Dynasty, Wen Tianxiang raised a volunteer force in his home province. Appointed chief negotiator by Southern Song, Wen was detained by the Yuan side, but managed

to escape. He was captured once more, and spent three years as a prisoner in the Yuan capital, Dadu. It is said that Kublai Khan (Emperor Shizu, founder of the Yuan Dynasty) offered Wen Tainxiang the post of prime minister if he would defect, but Wen remained loyal to the doomed Southern Song. Wen Tianxiang died in 1283, at the age of 47. *The Song of Integrity*, which he wrote behind prison bars, is regarded as a classic of its kind.

Song of Integrity

There is integrity that is embodied in various forms.
On the earth it is mountains and rivers, in the sky it is the sun and stars.
In man it is the noble spirit that fills up the whole world.
The imperial road should be cleared of barbarians and be flooded with light.
In times of great danger man's high moral principle shows itself and leaves its record in history.
This is revealed in the records of Qi, the writings of Dong Hu of Jin.
Zhang Liang's service to Qin and Su Wu's moral courage in the Han Dynasty.
It was General Yan's head, Ji Kang's blood, Zhang Suiyang's teeth and Yan Changshan's tongue.
It was the Liaodong hat that could withstand ice and snow.
It was Zhuge Liang's memorial which was so heroic that it moved the immortals.
It was the river-crossing oar that wiped out the nomad invaders.
It was the mongolian scepter that crushed treacherous vassals' heads.
Integrity is so majestic that it will never die out.
It shoots up to the sun and the moon, and life and death are of no importance before it.
It supports both the earth and the sky.
Our lives hinge on our cardinal guides and our foundation rests on our morality.
But now everything is upside down.
Divested of his headgear this prisoner is kept behind prison bars in the north.
He would be only glad to be burned in the barbarians' crucible.
Ghost flame rages in the room and the courtyard is wrapped in darkness.
Oxen and steeds live in the same fold and chickens and phonixes share the same food.
The earth is shrouded in mist and fog.
If things go on like this, miseries and disasters will spread.
I'm sad that this swamp used to be my paradise-like homeland.
Fallacies can't become truth nor can Yin and Yang be confused.
So I'm worried and look up at the white clouds floating in the sky.
My heart is full of sorrow and I wonder where the sky will end.
The ancient sages are far away, my execution is nearing.
I open a book to read, and there is sunshine on the ancient words.

马可·波罗来华
Marco Polo's Travels in China

元朝同亚、非、欧各国的交往很多，当时来中国的外国人之中，最著名的是意大利威尼斯人马可·波罗。他在元世祖忽必烈时代来到中国。

公元1271年夏天，马可·波罗的父亲和叔父带着他离开故乡，经过4年的艰辛旅程，来到了中国。

马可·波罗聪明好学，来到中国以后，很快学会了蒙古语、骑马和射箭。忽必烈很喜欢他，经常派他出去视察。马可·波罗后来在书中描述中国西北、华北、西南、中南和华东的许多地方，其中多数是他游历过的，但也有一些可能来自传闻。除此之外他还到过南洋很多国家。据说，他在扬州呆过，还当了3年总管呢。

在中国时间久了，3个欧洲人非常怀念故乡，一再要求回国。获得批准后，他们再次踏上了充满艰险的归途。路上花了4年多时间，终于在1295年回到了威尼斯。

这时他们已经远离故土24年，当地人以为他们已经死在国外了。现在他们却穿着东方的服装回来了。人们认为他们带回了无数黄金珠宝，给马可起了个外号，叫"百万"。

没有多久，威尼斯和另外一个城邦热那亚打起了仗。马可·波罗自己花钱买了一条船，亲自驾驶参加威尼斯的舰队。结果威尼斯打了败仗，他做了俘房，被热那亚人关进了监狱。热那亚人听说他到过东方，常常到监狱里听他讲东方和中国的见闻。牢里关着一个作家，把马可讲的事都记了下来，编成了一本书，叫《马可·波罗行纪》。

在这本游记里，马可·波罗描绘了一个新奇的东方世界，详细介绍了中国的著名城市，如大都、苏州、扬州、杭州等。这本书一出版，就受到了欧洲人的欢迎，激起了他们对东方文明的向往。

15世纪以后，欧洲的航海家、探险家，普遍受到了马可·波罗的影响，去东方寻找一个遍地黄金的国家。

The Yuan Dynasty had worldwide contacts. Among the many foreigners who came to China at that time, Marco Polo — an Italian from Venice — was the most famous. He wrote a book about the 17 years he spent in China, which is still a popular travelogue.

In the summer of 1271, Marco Polo arrived in China with his father and uncle after a journey which had taken four years.

He became a favorite of Kublai Khan, who often sent him on inspection tours. It is said that he served as the magistrate of Yangzhou for three years. He also traveled to Southeast Asia during this time.

The three Europeans returned to their homeland in 1295.

Marco Polo wrote his account of his journey to China in his *The Travels of Marco Polo* while in jail, having been captured by enemy forces during a war between Venice and Genoa.

Marco Polo's description of the fabulous wealth of China under the Yuan Dynasty, and the prosperous cities of Dadu, Suzhou, Yangzhou and Hangzhou, roused the interest of merchants and explorers. The result was expanded contacts and trade between China and Europe.

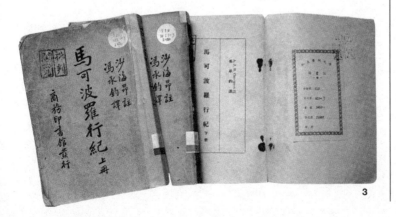

小资料 Data

马可·波罗来华背景

公元1260年，马可·波罗的父亲和叔父经商时，第一次来到中国，受到了忽必烈的接见。忽必烈向他们了解西方各国和罗马的情况，并让他们作为去罗马的使者。他们完成了任务后，就带上马可·波罗一起到了中国。

How Marco Polo Came to China

In 1260, Marco Polo's father and uncle came to China for the first time for trade, and were received by Kublai Khan. The emperor questioned them about Europe, and appointed them envoys to Rome. After completing their mission to Rome, they returned to China, taking young Marco Polo with them.

1. 马可·波罗像
   A portrait of Marco Polo
2. 《马可·波罗行纪》德文译本封面。封面人物是马可·波罗本人
   The German edition of *The Travels of Marco Polo*. The cover of the book is Marco Polo himself.
3. 《马可·波罗行纪》曾经在欧洲引起轰动，各种文字的译本有几十种
   The Travels of Marco Polo (The book has been translated into dozens of languages. This is the Chinese version, translated in 1935.)

四大发明
The Four Great Inventions

1

2

造纸术

西汉时期已经出现早期的植物纤维纸，但比较粗糙，书写不方便。东汉时的宦官蔡伦，改进了造纸方法，用树皮、麻头、破布和旧鱼网作原料，制造出既美观又便宜，并且书写方便的纸张，并使这种以麻为主要原料的纸得到推广，对书写起到了重要的推动作用。造纸术逐步推广开来，到了公元三、四世纪，纸取代竹简和丝帛成为中国的主要书写材料。

指南针

战国时，人们用天然磁石磨成"司南"，这是世界上最早的指南针，到今天已经有两千多年了。司南磁性较弱，指南效果比较差。

到了宋朝，发明了人造磁铁，磁性比天然磁铁稳定。指南针的装置也有很大改进，人们发明了指南鱼、指南龟、水浮指南针等指南工具。

在宋代，海外贸易非常发达。为了克服在海洋中航行的困难，到北宋末年，在航海上已经应用了指南针。南宋时还出现了将指南针安装在刻着度数和方位的圆盘上的罗盘针，使海上航行的人，在没有太阳的白天，没有月亮的夜晚，也能辨别方向。

印刷术

在人类文明发展史上，印刷术的地位非常重要。大约在隋朝的时候，雕版印刷术被发明了出来。但雕版印刷费时长，花钱多。

3

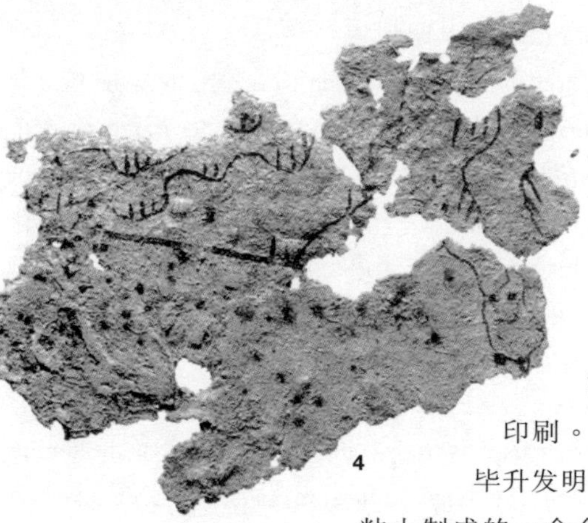

毕升是北宋时一个聪明能干的印刷工人，熟悉雕版印书的情况，他想发明一种既省时省力又经济的印刷方法，创造了活字印刷。

毕升发明的是泥活字。先在粘土制成的一个个小方块上刻出反字。制成一批后，就放在窑中烧硬成为陶字。排版时，在一块铁板上铺上一层用松香、蜡和纸灰混合的粉末，把一个个陶字排在有框的铁板上，然后把铁板放到火上加温，等粉末熔化后，用一块平板把字压平。铁板温度降低后，活字固定，就可以印刷了。印板中如果有错别字，可以随时更换，印完一板，活字拆了，铁板可以再用。

毕升为印刷术的改进打下了基础，西夏有了木活字，明代改成铜活字，直到后来使用的铅活字。

火药与火器

中国古代有专门炼丹的人，他们中有人把硫磺、硝石、木炭放在一起烧炼，引起了燃烧和爆炸，人们把这三种物质的混合叫做"火药"。唐朝中期的书籍里记载了制成火药的方法。唐朝末年，火药开始用于军事。

在宋代，火药得到了广泛使用，火药不仅被用在生活中，狩猎、开石、采石、制造爆竹和焰火，更多地被用在军事上。火器的制造技术也提高到了一个新的阶段。北宋制造的火药武器主要是燃烧性的、爆炸性的，如火箭、霹雳 (pīlì) 火球、蒺藜 (jílí) 火球等。到了南宋，发明了管状火器，把火药装在竹筒里点火喷射。有一次，宋朝军队和蒙古军队打仗，宋军发明了管状"突火枪"，即把火药装在竹筒里，然后装上"子窠 (kē)"。"子窠"和子弹的性质差不多，是用石子和铁块做的。这是世界上最早使用原始步枪。它的出现是火器制造历史上划时代的进步。

4

1. 北宋出现了世界上最早印刷的"纸币"，即交子
   Jiaozi — the earliest paper currency of the world — was printed in Northern Song Dynasty.
2. 江苏苏州曲园木刻原版
   The original wood tablet for printing is found in Quyuan, Suzhou, Jiangsu Province.
3. 古代造纸流程图
   The ancient paper-making procedure
4. 甘肃汉墓出土的西汉早期麻纸地图，是目前世界上发现的最早的纸绘地图
   The earliest paper map of the world — plant-fibre map of early Wester Han — was unearthed from the Han Mausoleum, Gansu Province.

小资料 Data

印刷术和指南针对世界的影响

印刷术首先传入朝鲜和日本，后经中亚传到埃及，直到欧洲。印刷术被称为"文明之母"。它的广泛传播，为全世界大量出版书籍打下了基础。

指南针应用于海上交通，成为航海罗盘。后来罗盘经阿拉伯人传至欧洲，促进了航海事业的发展，对欧洲人成功发现新航路与新大陆，作出了贡献。

The Impact of Printing and the Compass

The art of printing first spread from China to Korea and Japan. Then it reached Egypt by way of Central Asia, and then Europe. The new technique of printing gave a great boost to literacy all over the world.

The compass was introduced to Europe by Arab merchants who had acquired the invention from China. It spurred the development of navigation and made a major contribution to the Europeans' successful discovery of new maritime routes and new continents.

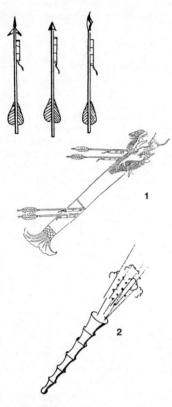

The Technique of Making Paper

A crude type of paper was used for writing on as early as in the Western Han Dynasty. It was made from plant fiber, and was rather rough. Cai Lun, a eunuch of the Eastern Han Dynasty, used tree bark, rags and old fishing nets as raw materials, and produced a smoother and more convenient type of paper. By the fourth century, paper had replaced bamboo slips and silk as the main material for writing on.

The Invention of the Compass

Natural magnets were used as crude compasses as early as in the Warring States Period. By the Song Dynasty, artificial magnets had been invented, whose magnetism was more stable than that of natural magnets. With such artificial magnets, compasses were developed and used for navigation, together with degree markings. This greatly stimulated maritime trade.

The Technique of Printing

Printing has played a very important role in the history of civilization. Woodblock printing was in use at the time of the Sui Dynasty. But it involved laborious and expensive processes.

Bi Sheng of the Northern Song Dynasty determined to improve the printing technique, and he invented moveable type. He carved characters in reverse on blocks of clay, and baked the blocks in a kiln. The slugs of type were pressed onto a coating of rosin, wax and paper ash spread on an iron tray, which was then heated and cooled to fix the slugs. If there was a wrong character, it could easily be replaced, and the tray, slugs and coating could be used over and over again.

In the Ming Dynasty, bronze type was invented, and later lead type was used.

Gunpowder and Firearms

Alchemists were the first people in ancient China to dabble in chemistry. In the search for "pills of immortality", it was found that a mixture of sulfur, saltpeter and charcoal could cause an explosion. This mixture was mainly used for making fireworks, until the Song Dynasty, when it began to be applied for military use. Fire arrows and bombs were made using gunpowder, and crude muskets were used with devastating effect against Mongolian invaders.

1. 北宋火箭
   The fire arrows of the Northern Song Dynasty
2. 南宋突火枪
   The flamethrower of the Southern Song Dynasty

小资料 Data

火药

制造火药的主要原料硫磺和硝石，在中国古代是贵重药材，而硫磺、硝石和木炭磨成细末，放在罐中烧炼，会引起大火，因此人们把这种容易着火的药叫火药。

Gunpowder

The main materials of gunpowder are sulfur and saltpeter, which were regarded as precious medicinal materials in ancient China. The explosive mixture of sulfur, saltpeter and charcoal has been used in fireworks for thousands of years in China.

清明上河图
The Social Genre Painting
Riverside Scene on the Pure Brightness Festival

1. 《清明上河图》局部
   The Rainbow Bridge, from *Riverside Scene on the Pure Brightness Festival*

宋朝绘画，除了人物画、山水画、花鸟画之外，还出现了描写城乡生活的社会风俗画。生活在北宋末年南宋初年的张择端所画的《清明上河图》是其中最优秀、最有名的。《清明上河图》描绘了北宋首都东京（今河南开封）汴（biàn）河两岸清明节前后的风貌。

《清明上河图》现收藏在北京故宫博物院。长卷共分三部分：第一部分画晨光下，郊外河岸上慢慢行进着的一支驮着重物的驴队；第二部分描写汴河交通繁忙的景象，尤其引人注目的是像彩虹般横跨汴河两岸的"虹桥"，桥上熙熙攘攘，车水马龙，非常热闹；第三部分画市区街景，各行各业，应有尽有，街上行人，来来往往。整幅画宽25.5厘米，长525厘米，共画了各类人物800多个，牲畜94头，树木170多棵。它把汴京郊外的菜园风光、汴河上的交通运

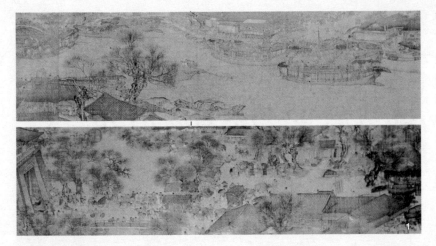

输、街头的买卖状况、沿街房屋的建筑特征、船夫们的紧张劳动、士大夫们的悠闲自得、雄伟的虹桥、巍峨的城楼以及车子、轿子、骆驼，一一描绘得十分逼真。这幅画感染力强，欣赏价值高，受到人们的普遍喜爱，并被很多画家摹仿。

1. 《清明上河图》局部
   Street scene, from *Riverside Scene on the Pure Brightness Festival*

《清明上河图》直观地反映了北宋时代东京的城市面貌。它不仅欣赏价值高，而且是研究北宋时期东京的重要材料。

The Song Dynasty produced masterpieces of figure painting, landscape, flower-and-bird painting, and social genre painting describing both urban and rural life. The most famous of the latter works is one known as *Riverside Scene on the Pure Brightness Festival*. It was painted by Zhang Zeduan, who lived in the late Northern Song Dynasty and early Southern Song Dynasty. It depicts scenes along the Bianhe River at Dongjing (today's Kaifeng in Henan Province), the capital of the Northern Song Dynasty, at the time of the Pure Brightness Festival. This traditional festival is held in early April, and is the time when people visit their ancestral tombs.

Now in the collection of the Palace Museum in Beijing, the painting is divided into three parts: The first part shows a team of pack mules plodding along the river bank in the suburbs in the morning light; the second part shows the bustling scene around the Rainbow Bridge spanning the river; the third part depicts the downtown streets, thronged with people plying all sorts of trades, and their customers. The whole scroll is 25.5 cm wide and 525 cm long, and has over 800 human and 94 animal figures, and 170 trees. This fascinating painting shows a wealth of detail of life in those days, covering customs, transportation, business, architecture and the activities of boatmen, sedan-chair carriers, scholars, etc. It provides valuable material for the study of life in the Northern Song capital.

司马光和《资治通鉴》
Sima Guang and His History Book

司马光（公元1019～1086年），北宋政治家、史学家，陕州夏县人（今属山西省），出生在一个官僚的家庭，曾经做过宰相。

司马光平生最大的成就之一就是主持编写了《资治通鉴》。司马光认为治理国家的人一定要了解历史，他用了两年的时间，写成了一部从战国到秦末的史书，名叫《通志》。后来他把《通志》拿给宋英宗看，宋英宗很满意，让他把这本书编下去。宋英宗允许司马光自己挑选编写人员，阅读官府藏书。司马光非常高兴，马上成立书局，邀请当时许多著名史学家做助手，共同编写通史。他们收集了大量材料，其中有很多在以前的历史书中都没有见到过的历史资料，非常珍贵。

1. 司马光因编《资治通鉴》被后人公认为司马迁之后又一史学大家
   A portrait of Sima Guang (His book, *Comprehensive Mirror for Aid in Government*, is an outstanding masterpiece that made him the greatest historian after Sima Qian.)
2. 《资治通鉴》是一部编年体通史，这是有关唐朝军队攻打突厥的记载
   The *Comprehensive Mirror for Aid in Government* is a magnum opus History of China. The text here is about the war on Tujue during the Tang Dynasty.

为了编写这本书，司马光花费了大量心血。为了防止自己睡觉过多，耽误编书，他还特意请人用圆木做了一个枕头。睡觉时，只要一翻身，枕头就会滚掉，人也就醒了。这个枕头被称为"警枕"。

司马光用了19年完成了这部历史巨著。继位的宋神宗觉得很好，定名为《资治通鉴》。《资治通鉴》是一部编年体通史，记载了从公元前403到公元959年间1,362年的历史，共294卷，300多万字，材料详细真实，文字优美通畅，是后人编写编年体史书的典范，也是中国古代宝贵的文化遗产。

司马光砸缸

传说司马光7岁那年，跟小伙伴在院子里玩。院子里有一口大水缸，有个小孩爬到缸沿上，不小心掉进了水缸。缸很大，水很深，眼看孩子快被淹死了，别的孩子都哭喊着往外跑。司马光没有慌，想出了一个主意，拿起一块大石头，用尽力气砸向水缸，缸破了，水流了出来，小孩得救了。

Smashing the Vat

It is said that one day at the age of seven when Sima Guang was playing with other children in the courtyard of his house, one child fell into a big vat of water. While the other children were running around howling in a panic, Sima Guang coolly picked up a large stone, and smashed the side of the vat with it. The water flowed out through the hole, and the drowning child was saved.

1. 《资治通鉴》之草稿
   The preliminary draft of the *Comprehensive Mirror for Aid in Government*
2. 线装版本《资治通鉴》
   The thread bound *Comprehensive Mirror for Aid in Government*

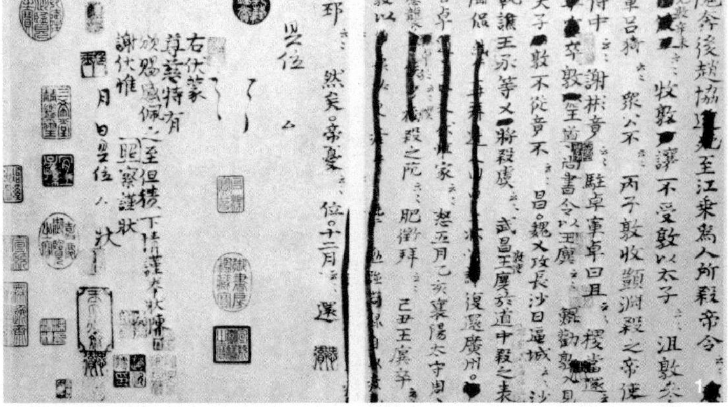

Sima Guang (1019-1086) was a statesman and historian of the Northern Song Dynasty. He was born in today's Shanxi Province into an official's family. He served as a prime minister for the Song court at one time.

Sima Guang was convinced that those governing the country should be well versed in history. He spent a total of 19 years writing a history of China covering 1,362 years — from 403 BC to 959 AD. This magnum opus work comprises 294 volumes containing more than 3,000,000 words. Sima Guang had the encouragement of first Emperor Yingzong and then his successor Emperor Shenzong. He also had the assistance of many famous scholars.

Sima Guang was so absorbed in his work that he even invented an "alarm pillow" which prevented him from sleeping too long. The wooden pillow was designed to slip from under his head whenever he turned over.

It was Emperor Shenzong who gave Sima Guang's history its title of *Zi Zhi Tong Jian* (*Comprehensive Mirror for Aid in Government*).

宋词与元曲
Song *Ci* Poetry and Yuan Drama

宋朝文学的主要成就是词。词是一种新体诗歌，唐朝时已经出现，最初在民间流行。句子有长有短，便于演唱。经过五代到两宋，词得到极大的发展。两宋时期，优秀词人不断出现。苏轼、李清照、辛弃疾、柳永、周邦彦、姜夔 (kuí) 等的词代表了宋词的最高成就。

苏轼 (公元1037～1101年)，号东坡居士，四川人，中国古代著名文学家，具有多方面的艺术才能和造诣。他的词豪迈奔放，描绘壮观的景物，给词注入了生命力，对词的发展作出了突出的贡献。他的"大江东去，浪淘尽，千古风流人物"(《念奴娇·赤壁怀古》)，"但愿人长久，千里共婵娟 (指月亮)"(《水调歌头·明月几时有》) 被世世代代的中国人千古传诵。

李清照，生活在北宋末年南宋初年，济南人，中国文学史上杰出的女词人。她前半生，婚姻生活美满，词写得精巧、优美，如"帘卷西风，人比黄花瘦"(《醉花阴·薄雾浓云愁永昼》)，"才下眉头，却上心头"(《一剪梅·无言独上西楼》) 等词，写出了一个生活悠闲自在的妇女对出门在外的丈夫的深情思念，前一句因思念而消瘦，后一句因思念而烦恼。后期，由于丈夫病死，国家破碎，她的词变为哀怨、悲愤，一直没能摆脱"寻寻觅觅，冷冷清清，凄凄惨惨戚戚"(《声声慢》) 的悲凉、忧伤情绪。

元朝文学的主要成就是元曲。元曲由散曲和杂剧组成。散曲是在民间歌词的基础上，吸收少数民族音乐，形成的长短不齐的新的诗歌形式。马致远、关汉卿 (qīng)、白朴、张可久、贯云石 (维吾尔族)、张养浩等人的作品代表了元曲的成就。描写出门在外凄凉的"枯藤老树昏鸦，小桥流水人家"(马致远《天净沙·秋思》)；概括了作为一个普通老百姓生活艰辛的"兴，百姓苦！亡，百姓苦！"(张养浩《山坡羊·潼关怀古》) 等都是人们非常喜欢的精彩语句。

1. 《西厢记》插图
An illustration for Romance of the Western Chamber

元朝戏剧空前发达，出现了元杂剧。元杂剧是一种把音乐、歌舞、动作、念白（对话、独白）相结合的综合艺术。现有剧目二百多种。关汉卿的《窦娥冤》、马致远的《汉宫秋》、郑光祖的《倩女离魂》、白朴的《梧桐雨》及王实甫的《西厢记》等都是经典的元杂剧。

关汉卿，大都人，是元杂剧作家中最杰出的一位。他一生从事戏剧创作活动，长期生活在演员中间，有时亲自登台演出。他是一位高产作家，写了60多种杂剧，流传至今的有18种。关汉卿因为经常在作品中揭露社会的黑暗，常常受到威胁，但他毫不动摇，在一首曲子中自称是"蒸不烂、煮不熟、捶不扁、炒不爆、响当当一粒铜豌豆"。

The main literary achievement in the Song Dynasty was *Ci* (poetry written to certain tunes with strict tonal patterns and rhyme schemes, in fixed numbers of lines and words, originating in the Tang Dynasty and fully developed in the Song Dynasty). *Ci* have sentences of different lengths, which are convenient for singing. Many outstanding writers of *Ci* appeared in the two Song dynasties, such as Su Shi, Li Qingzhao, Xin Qiji, Liu Yong, Zhou Bangyan and Jiang Kui.

Su Shi (1037-1101 AD) is also known by his literary name Dongpo (Eastern Slope). He was from Sichuan Province, and contributed greatly to the development of *Ci*. Famous lines of his, which are still quoted today include "The endless river eastward flows/ With its huge waves are gone all those gallant heroes of bygone days" and "May we live a long life/ And together share the beauty of the moonlight".

Li Qingzhao lived in the period of the late Northern Song Dynasty and early Southern Song Dynasty. She was born in Jinan, Shandong Province. Her early life was pleasant and comfortable, with a happy marriage. Her delicate and cheerful poetry written in this period reflects this. However, following the death of her husband and the rise of turmoil in the country, her works started to betray melancholy and pessimism.

The main literary achievement in the Yuan Dynasty was Yuan drama. Leading exponents of this genre, which used a new type of lyrical poetry for the dialogue, were Ma Zhiyuan, Guan Hanqing, Bai Pu, Zhang Kejiu, Guan

 **小资料 Data**

元曲四大家

著名剧作家关汉卿、马致远、郑光祖、白朴被称为"元曲四大家"。

Four Masters of Yuan Drama

The four masters of Yuan drama were Guan Hanqing, Ma Zhiyuan, Zheng Guangzu and Bai Pu.

Yunshi (ethnic Uygur) and Zhang Yanghao. "Withered branch, old tree and a crow in the dusk; a little bridge, flowing water and a cottage" describes the loneliness of a traveler far from home. "The rise of the nation brings misery to the people, and its fall also brings misery to the people!" is a biting social commentary. Both these verses are typical of the Yuan style of lyrics.

Drama reached its heyday during the Yuan Dynasty. Yuan drama combined music, dancing, acting and speaking (dialogue and monologue) all together. Classical Yuan plays include *The Injustice Suffered by Dou E* by Guan Hanqing, *Autumn in the Palace of Han* by Ma Zhiyuan, *A Beautiful Girl Loses Her Soul* by Zheng Guangzu, *The Parasol Tree and the Rain* by Bai Pu, and *Romance of the Western Chamber* by Wang Shifu.

Guan Hanqing was born in Dadu. He was the most prominent dramatist of the Yuan Dynasty. He devoted his life to the stage. He lived among actors, and went on the stage to act sometimes. He was a prolific writer, producing over 60 plays, 18 of which are extant. Guan Hanqing often discloses the dark side of society in his works, and thus came under official suspicion from time to time. But he never wavered in his commitment to portraying real life problems. He once called himself "a bronze pea which cannot be destroyed by steaming, cooking, smashing or frying".

1. 《窦娥冤》插图
   A portrait of *The Injustice Suffered by Dou E*
2. 杂剧图壁画
   A mural of the drama team

小资料 Data

《窦娥冤》内容提要

窦娥是一个寡妇，跟着丈夫的母亲蔡婆一起生活。恶棍张驴儿看中了窦娥，就想用药毒死蔡婆，没想到却毒死了自己的父亲。审案的官员因为受了张驴儿的贿赂，诬陷窦娥杀人，判了她死刑。在刑场上窦娥强烈地控诉了那个不合理的社会，发了三个誓愿，如果她被杀了，那么六月里就会下雪，杀她时的血渍就会溅到刑场上的白布上，在她死去的地方就会三年干旱。窦娥被杀了，果然前两个誓愿当时就实现了，而第三个誓愿也在三年中被证实了。三年后，她的父亲做了官，她的鬼魂向父亲哭诉了冤情，最终逮捕了凶手。窦娥的反抗性在当时的社会是少见的。

The Injustice Suffered by Dou E

Dou E was a widow who lived with her mother-in-law, Granny Cai. In an attempt to remove Granny Cai and marry Dou E, the villainous Donkey Zhang poisons his own father by mistake. Zhang bribes the local magistrate, and gets Dou E accused of the crime. On the execution ground Dou E protests against the injustice being done to her, and calls on Heaven to prove that she was innocent in three ways after her death: by sending snow in the sixth lunar month; by making her blood splash upward onto a white cloth; and by inflicting three years of drought on her hometown. These three phenomena are in fact manifested, Donkey Zhang is executed, and the soul of Dou E is appeased.

概述
Introduction

　　14至19世纪，是中国封建社会衰落的明清时期。明朝从朱元璋(公元1368年)在南京建立，到1644年崇祯皇帝吊死北京煤山，历时280多年。从1644年清朝顺治皇帝入主北京，到1840年鸦片战争爆发，清朝前期的统治长达190多年。明朝时，统一的多民族国家进一步发展。明朝前期经济发展，社会繁荣，郑和多次出使西洋各国，促进了中外友好交往。清朝的康熙、雍正和乾隆时期，出现了繁荣的"盛世"。明清时期，中国人民创造了丰富的物质财富和精神财富，涌现出许多政治家、思想家、军事家、探险家、科学家，他们在中华民族的史册上谱写了光辉的篇章。

　　这一时期，世界历史进展迅猛，东西方经济文化接触日益频繁，新航路的开辟使世界密切联系起来。14、15世纪，欧洲地中海沿岸一些城市出现了资本主义萌芽。17～18世纪，英、美、法三国先后发生资产阶级革命，世界历史进入新的时期。西方先进国家已经进入工业革命的成熟阶段，资本主义发展迅速。相比之下，中国却未能同步发展。虽然中国从明朝中后期产生资本主义萌芽，但由于封建制度的束缚，生产力发展受到严重阻碍，商品经济发展艰难，封建社会由盛而衰。随着中国社会发展的逐步落伍和西方殖民主义侵略势力的到来，中国封建统治者对外部世界的态度，逐渐由交往转向闭关锁国，同西方国家的差距迅速拉大。

统一的多民族国家进一步发展和
封建社会由盛而衰时期——

明、清 (鸦片战争以前)

Further Development of the Unitary Multi-ethnic Country and Decline of Feudal Society – The Ming and Qing Dynasties (Before the Opium War of 1840)

The final phase of Chinese feudal society is represented by the period of the Ming and Qing dynasties, from the 14th to the 19th centuries. The Ming Dynasty lasted over 280 years from its establishment by Zhu Yuanzhang in Nanjing in 1368 AD to Emperor Chongzhen's suicide in 1644. The early reign of the Qing Dynasty lasted over 190 years from Emperor Shunzhi's entry into Beijing in 1644 to the outbreak of the Opium War in 1840. In the Ming Dynasty, there was a closer integration of the many ethnic groups that composed China. In the first half of the dynasty, the economy developed rapidly, and society was prosperous. Admiral Zheng He made seven long-distance voyages with huge merchant fleets, and promoted China's friendly relations with foreign countries. The reigns of emperors Kangxi, Yongzheng and Qianlong of the Qing Dynasty are regarded as a golden age both materially and culturally, and there emerged great numbers of statesmen, thinkers, strategists, explorers and scientists in those days.

During this period also, economic and cultural contacts between the East and the West became more and more frequent. The opening of new navigation routes linked almost all corners of the globe. With the Industrial Revolution in the West, capitalism progressed rapidly. However, China was left behind during this phase of history, due to the restrictions imposed by the feudal political and economic structure, which hampered the development of commerce. But aggression by Western colonialists forced the Chinese feudal rulers to change their attitude to the outside world.

明朝开国皇帝朱元璋
Zhu Yuanzhang, the First Emperor of the Ming Dynasty

小资料 Data

明孝陵

位于南京东郊风景区，是朱元璋和马皇后的墓。公元1381年修建，1383年完成。1382年马皇后死，葬在这里。马皇后死后封为"孝慈"，所以称为"明孝陵"。公元1389年朱元璋死后，也葬在这里。明孝陵由下马坊、大金门、碑亭、方城、宝城等组成，是中国现存的最大的皇帝陵墓之一。

The Tomb of Zhu Yuanzhang

Located in the eastern suburbs of Nanjing, the tomb of Zhu Yuanzhang and Empress Ma was constructed in 1381-1383 AD. Empress Ma died in 1382 and was buried there. After she died, she was given the title "Xiaoci" (filial and kind), so the tomb was called the"Ming Xiao Tomb." After Zhu Yuanzhang died, he was also buried in this tomb. The Ming Xiao Tomb is composed of the Xiama (Dismount) Archway, Dajin (Great Gold) Gate, Tablet Pavilion, Square City and Bao (Treasure) City. It is one of the largest imperial tombs existent in China.

元朝末年，统治者昏庸无能，社会经济发展迟缓，甚至倒退，黄河又多次决口。连年的天灾人祸，农民几乎没有办法生活下去，于是在14世纪中叶爆发了大规模的农民起义。

朱元璋(公元1328～1398年)，是元末农民领袖之一，他出生于濠(háo)州(今安徽凤阳)一个贫苦农民家庭。1352年，郭子兴率领农民在濠州起义，朱元璋参加到这支队伍中来，作战勇敢又足智多谋，很快就得到郭子兴的重用。郭子兴死后，朱元璋成了这支队伍的首领。1356年3月，朱元璋亲自带领大军，攻占了集庆(今南京)，并改名为"应天府"。他接受谋士的建议，在应天召集了许多有才能的人。同时朱元璋以应天为中心，采取先易后难的战斗策略，一个一个地消灭附近的元军。这时候，原来的其他起义队伍也都各霸一方，割地称王。1364年，朱元璋消灭了他最强大的敌人——陈友谅的起义队伍，此后，其他农民起义队伍都被他一个个打败。

1368年，朱元璋在应天称帝，定国号为明，史称明朝，朱元璋就是明太祖。同年秋天，攻克元大都，结束了元朝在全国的统治。此后，他又用近20年的时间，完成了统一大业。

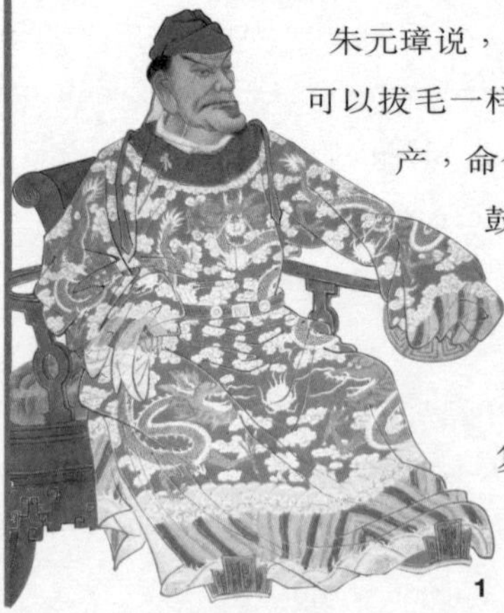

1. 朱元璋像
A portrait of Zhu Yuanzhang

朱元璋说，国家刚刚稳定，就像小鸟刚出窝不可以拔毛一样，需要好好管理。他重视农业生产，命令在战争中流亡的农民回家种田，鼓励他们开垦新的农田；提倡种植棉、桑、麻等经济作物，免除他们三年的赋税。到1393年，全国可耕种的土地是元末的四倍。他恢复了手工艺人的自由身份。他还重视水利，建国后，修建了许多水利工程。这些措施对全国社会经

济文化的进一步发展提供了有利的条件。明太祖废除丞相，在中央设立六部，六部直接对皇帝负责，加强了中央集权。他还严厉处罚贪官污吏，制定法律。为明朝的统治打下了良好的基础。

A combination of incompetent rulers and natural disasters led to peasant uprisings which overthrew the Yuan Dynasty.

Zhu Yuanzhang (1328-1398 AD) was a leader of one of these peasant uprisings. He was born into a poor peasant's family in Haozhou (today's Fengyang, Anhui Province). In March 1356, Zhu Yuanzhang captured Jiqing (today's Nanjing) and changed its name to Yingtian. With this major city as his base, he defeated not only the Yuan armies sent against him but also rival peasant rebel forces.

In 1368, Zhu Yuanzhang proclaimed himself emperor, historically known as Emperor Taizu, of the Ming Dynasty in Nanjing. In the autumn of the same year, the Ming army took Dadu, the capital of the Yuan Empire, putting an end to the rule of the Mongols. However, it took Zhu Yuanzhang nearly 20 more years to consolidate his hold over the whole country.

Emperor Taizu's first concern was to restore agricultural production, which had been severely disrupted during the wars. He encouraged peasants who had fled from their homes during the fighting to return to their fields and to open up new land. He advocated the planting of cash crops such as cotton, mulberries and hemp, offering tax exemptions as an incentive. By 1393, the area of agricultural land had grown to four times as big as that at the end of the Yuan Dynasty, and irrigation works had been expanded greatly. Emperor Taizu also extended preferential treatment to craftsmen. All these measures provided advantageous conditions for the further overall development of society, economy and culture nationwide. Emperor Taizu abolished the position of prime minister, and set up six offices known as "boards" in the central government, which were directly responsible to the emperor. This method strengthened the centralization of authority. At the same time, the emperor made a thorough overhaul of the existing laws, increasing the penalties for offenders.

明统一经过略图
Sketch Map of the Ming Campaigns to Unite China

 小资料 Data

明成祖迁都

明成祖朱棣（dì）是明朝的第三个皇帝。明太祖朱元璋60多岁的时候，太子朱标死了，于是立朱标的长子朱允炆（wén）为皇太孙。朱元璋死后，朱允炆即位。朱元璋的四子燕王朱棣看到皇位落到了侄子的身上，心中不服。公元1399年朱棣以帮助皇帝除掉奸臣为理由，从北平起兵南下，1402年攻入了都城南京，夺得了帝位。朱允炆在兵乱中下落不明。朱棣当上了皇帝之后，决定把都城迁到北平，改北平为北京。

Emperor Chengzu Moves the Capital

Zhu Di, Emperor Chengzu, was the third emperor of the Ming Dynasty. Zhu Biao, Emperor Taizu's crown prince, died before his father, and his place was taken by Zhu Biao's eldest son, Zhu Yunwen. After the new emperor came to the throne, Zhu Yunwen's uncle, Zhu Di, the fourth son of Zhu Yuanzhang, dispatched an army from his power base of Yan (the present-day Beijing area) in 1399, on the pretext of helping to restore order. In 1402, this army captured Nanjing. Zhu Yunwen disappeared in the turmoil, and Zhu Di declared himself Emperor Chengzu. Feeling insecure in Nanjing, Emperor Chengzu removed the capital to Beiping, and changed its name to Beijing.

郑和下西洋
Zheng He's Voyages

1. 郑和下西洋宝船模型
   A model of one of Zheng He's ships
2. 郑和像
   A statue of Zheng He
3. 福建南山塔下的"天妃灵应碑"详细记载了郑和七次下西洋的事迹
   The story of Zheng He's seven voyages to the western ocean is inscribed on the Tianfei Memorial Tablet at Nanshan Pagoda, Fujian.

郑和航海图
Sketch Map of Zheng He's Voyages

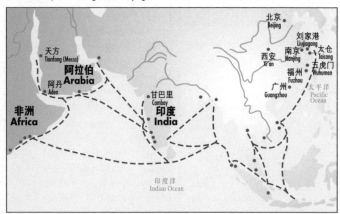

明朝前期，中国是世界上最先进、最发达的国家之一。为了弘扬国威和加强与世界各国的联系，明成祖朱棣派郑和多次出使西洋（西洋指文莱以西的东南亚和印度洋一带）。

郑和（公元1371～1435年），云南回族人，小名三保，又称三宝太监。他聪明好学，立过战功，明成祖非常信任他，派他出使西洋。公元1405年6月，郑和奉命第一次出使西洋。他率领两万多人，包括水手和士兵，还有技术人员、翻译等，携带大量的金、帛等货物乘坐200多艘海船，从江苏太仓刘家港出发，先到占城（今越南中南部），一路经过爪哇、孟加拉等地，到达红海沿岸，后从锡兰、古里（今印度卡里卡特）回国，历经两年，于公元1407年秋，返回南京。郑和的船队满载着金银珠宝、丝绸、瓷器等中

国特产，每到一个国家或地区，郑和都把明朝的礼物送给他们，表达了和他们友好交往的愿望。西洋各国非常友好地接待了他和他的船队，有些国家还派遣使者跟随郑和前来朝见中国皇帝，同时也从各国换回了珠宝、香料等特产。明成祖对郑和的成绩非常满意。郑和前后7次出使西洋，最远到达非洲东海岸和红海沿岸。

这一时期南洋、西洋许多国家的国王、使臣和商队纷纷来到中国。郑和的出航也为人类航海史作出了巨大的贡献，郑和下西洋比哥伦布发现美洲大陆早半个多世纪。郑和下西洋是世界航海史上的壮举，现在东南亚一带还有许多纪念郑和的建筑物，表达了人们对他的崇敬。

In the early Ming Dynasty, China was one of the most advanced and developed countries in the world. In order to transmit the national power and strengthen contacts with other countries, Empeor Chengzu sent Zheng He, a senior general and eunuch, on six voyages to the Western Ocean (Southeast Asia west of Brunei and the Indian Ocean) on diplomatic missions. Zheng He's seventh and last voyage was authorized by Emperor Chengzu's successor, Emperor Renzong.

Zheng He (1371-1435 AD), ethnic Hui (Moslem), was born in Yunnan Province. In 1405, Zheng He embarked on his first voyage. His fleet of more than 200 ships carried well over 20,000 men, including sailors, soldiers, technical personnel, interpreters, etc., and large amounts of gold, precious stones, porcelain and silk to be used for trade and as gifts. The fleet set out from Liujiagang in Jiangsu Province, and sailed westward as far as the Red Sea. The round trip took two years. Some of the countries Zheng He visited dispatched envoys bearing tribute to the Ming court on his ships. Subsequent voyages took Zheng He to the eastern coast of Africa. Zheng He's voyages were a great feat in the world's navigation history. There are still many buildings in present Southeast Asia dedicated to his memory.

小资料 Data

郑和七次下西洋
第一次	公元1405～1407年到锡兰山、古里等地。
第二次	1407～1409年到古里、小葛兰等地。
第三次	1409～1411年到忽鲁莫斯（波斯湾）、阿拉伯等地。
第四次	1413～1415年到非洲东海岸。
第五次	1417～1419年到东非。
第六次	1421～1422年到忽鲁莫斯（波斯湾）、阿拉伯等地。
第七次	1431～1433年到红海、麦加等地。

Zheng He's Seven Voyages to the Western Ocean

First: 1405-1407 AD reached Sri Lanka

Second: 1407-1409 AD called at Calcutta and Sri Lanka

Third: 1409-1411 AD reached Hormuz on the Persian Gulf and Arabia

Fourth: 1413-1415 AD reached the east coast of Africa

Fifth: 1417-1419 AD revisited East Africa

Sixth: 1421-1422 AD revisited Hormuz (Persian Gulf) and Arabia

Seventh: 1431-1433 AD reached the Red Sea and Mecca

戚继光抗倭
Qi Jiguang Repels Japanese Pirates

元末明初，一些日本海盗时常骚扰中国沿海地区，威胁沿海人民的生命安全。当时的人们把这些人叫做"倭寇"（wōkòu）。到了明朝中期，倭寇与中国海盗勾结在一起走私抢掠，杀人放火，无恶不作，对沿海人民的危害越来越大。朝廷下决心整治海防，命令戚（qī）继光平定倭寇。

戚继光（公元 1528～1587年），山东蓬莱人，是中国历史上著名的民族英雄。公元1556年，年轻的将领戚继光被派到浙江东部沿海地区抗击倭寇。他到了浙江以后，发现明朝军队纪律不严，战斗力不强，于是决定重新招募军队，训练精兵，他很快就召集了一支4千人左右的队伍。戚继光根据沿海地区的特点，精心训练士兵。经过两个月的严格训练，队伍纪律严明，战斗力很强，与敌人作战屡战屡胜，当地的人们亲切地称他们为"戚家军"。1561年倭寇假装侵犯奉化、宁海，实际想进攻台州。戚继光识破了倭寇的诡计，在台州打败了倭寇。戚继光在台州先后九战九捷，消灭了浙东的倭寇。以后，倭寇到哪里，戚继光就打到哪里，打得倭寇落花流水。经过近10年的艰苦作战，到1565年，倭寇基本上被赶出了东南沿海。

3

1.　戚继光塑像
    A statue of Qi Jiguang
2.　大福船（模型，明军的主要战船。）
    A model of a Ming Dynasty battleship
3.　倭寇刀
    The swords used by Japanese pirates
4.　为抗倭寇而建的福建惠安崇武古城。
    戚继光曾在此操练兵马
    Chongwu Stone Fortress (Huian, Fujian Province)
    was built to defend itself against the Japanese
    Pirates. Qi Jiguang was here to raise and train
    his own army.

At the end of the Yuan Dynasty and in the early years of the Ming Dynasty, Japanese pirates often harassed China's coastal areas, sometimes in collaboration with Chinese pirates. Finally, the Ming court resolved to bolster the coastal defenses, and ordered Qi Jiguang to put an end to the pirate menace.

Qi Jiguang (1528-1587 AD) was born in Penglai, Shandong Province. In 1556, he was assigned to deal with the problem of Japanese pirates in the coastal areas of Zhejiang Province. Dismayed at the low morale and lack of training of the soldiers he found there, Qi decided to raise and train his own army. Soon, he had a force of about 4,000 crack troops. They were known locally as "Qi's army", and soon distinguished themselves. In 1561, the Japanese pirates pretended to invade Fenghua and Ninghai with the real aim of attacking Taizhou. Qi Jiguang saw through the enemy's trick, and defeated the invaders at Taizhou. After ridding Zhejiang of the pirate scourge, Qi Jiguang fought Japanese pirates wherever they appeared along Chinese coastal areas. After nearly 10 years of hard fighting, he succeeded in driving the Japanese pirates from the coastal areas of southeast China by 1565.

4

清官海瑞
Hai Rui, an Upright and Incorruptible Official

1. 海瑞墓墓道旁的石马
   The stone horse by the hallway of Hai Rui Mausoleum
2. 海瑞一生清廉，名垂青史
   Hai Rui is known as an upright and incorruptible official.
3. 一代清官长埋于海南家乡
   The incorruptible official is buried at his hometown of Hainan Province.

　　海瑞 (公元1514～1587年)，海南琼州人。1558年，他被任命为浙江淳安县知县。在他来之前，县里的官吏贪赃枉法，处理案件都是胡乱结案。海瑞到任后，认真处理案件，纠正了许多冤案错案，老百姓非常敬重他。

　　1564年，海瑞被调到京城做官。当时的皇帝明世宗相信长生不老，整天跟道士在皇宫里修炼，有20多年没上朝处理国家大事了。当时的大臣都不敢劝皇帝。海瑞官虽不大，胆子却不小，他在1565年写了一道奏章批评明世宗，海瑞估计明世宗看了这一道奏章以后，可能杀自己的头，于是自己买了一口棺材，告别妻子，并且把他死后的事交代好。明世宗看到他的奏章后，果然大怒，把海瑞逮捕入狱。明世宗死后，海瑞获释。

　　1569年，海瑞又被任命为江南巡抚，巡视应天十府 (包括苏州、应天、松江、常州、镇江、徽州等地)。应天府是明朝经济、文化最发达的地区，但也是大官僚大地主最集中，国家最难管理的地方。大官僚大地主霸占了大量的良田。海瑞坚决要求他们把霸占的土地无偿退还给农民，大官僚大地主因此非常仇恨海瑞，于是和朝廷内的一些官员相勾结，在皇帝面前说海瑞的坏话，皇帝被这些人欺骗了，罢免了海瑞的官职，海瑞从此闲居10多年。

　　明神宗时，年迈的海瑞又被起用，1587年，海瑞死于南京任上。海瑞做官几十年，为人民做了许多好事，人们都叫他"海青天"。

Hai Rui (1514-1587 AD) was born in Qiongzhou, Hainan Province. In 1558 AD, he was appointed county magistrate of Chun'an County in Zhejiang Province. He cleaned up this notoriously corrupt county, setting an example of honest government.

In 1564, Hai Rui was transferred to an official post in the capital. The emperor, Shizong, was obsessed with Taoism and the "search for immortality" and completely neglected state affairs. Though only a very junior official, Hai Rui had the courage to send a memorial to the throne, censuring the emperor. Fully convinced that the emperor would have him executed, Hai Rui bought a coffin, bade farewell to his wife, and settled his affairs. He was not, in fact, executed, but thrown into prison and not released until after Emperor Shizong's death.

In 1569, Hai Rui was appointed imperial inspector of the 10 areas under the administration of Yingtian (including Suzhou, Yingtian, Songjiang, Changzhou, Zhenjiang, Huizhou, and others). Yingtian was the most advanced region in both economy and culture in the Ming Dynasty. Senior officials had carved out large estates for themselves there, depriving the state of large amounts of fertile land. Hai Rui insisted on the breaking up of these estates, and the return of the land to the peasants unconditionally. His enemies thereupon banded together to slander him to the emperor, Muzong, and Hai Rui was stripped of his official rank. After 10 years living in retirement, the new emperor Shenzong made Hai Rui magistrate of Nanjing. He held this post until his death in 1587. He was renowned far and wide as a model of an upright and incorruptible official.

小资料 Data

海瑞墓

位于海南省海口市西滘村。海瑞一生为官清廉，公元1589年死于南京任上，朝廷命钦差送到海南安葬。海瑞墓始建于1589年，全部用石头建成，陵园是长方形，基是圆锥形，墓前有明刻石碑。墓道两边有石马、石狮、石羊等。陵园里还种着松树、椰树等。

Hai Rui's Tomb

Hai Rui's last resting place is located near Haikou City, Hainan Province. When he died, the court dispatched imperial envoys to escort his coffin all the way from Nanjing to Haikou. Construction of the stone tomb began in 1589. Before the tomb stands an official stone tablet. Stone horses, lions and sheep line the avenue leading to the tomb, which is shaded by pine and coconut trees.

闯王李自成
Li Zicheng and the Fall of the Ming Dynasty

明朝后期，由于皇帝腐朽无能，宦官专权，政治黑暗腐败。官僚地主霸占了全国绝大部分的良田沃土，很多农民失去了土地，政府还不断地向农民征收赋税，困苦不堪的农民又遭到蝗灾、旱灾等自然灾害。在这种情况下，农民起义迅速地在全国酝酿 (yùnniàng)，公元1627年，农民起义首先在灾情严重的陕北爆发。农民战争发展迅猛，短短几年内，就涌现出几十支起义军，其中以高迎祥领导的起义军规模最大。高迎祥死后，起义军主要有两支：一支由张献忠率领，另一支由李自成率领。

李自成(公元1606～1645年)，陕西米脂人。1630年在家乡米脂起义，不久投奔高迎祥，成为高迎祥手下的一名闯将，高迎祥死后，被拥为"闯王"，率领一支起义军转战于河南一带。当时，河南是灾情比较严重的地区，李自成在谋士的帮助下，提出"均田免粮"的口号，赢得了广大农民的支持，人们互相流传"杀牛羊，备酒浆，开了城门迎闯王"。起义军迅速壮大，发展到百万人。1641年，李自成起义军攻占了洛阳，活捉并杀死了福王朱常洵，没收王府中的财物，分给老百姓。1644年，李自成在西安建立了大顺政权，同年，乘胜进攻北京，明朝最后一个皇帝崇祯在煤山(今北京景山)上吊自杀，三月，李自成大军占领了北京。

农民军进了北京之后，严整军纪。大顺政权命令明朝的贵族、官僚、富户交出大量钱财，还镇压了一批罪大恶极的达官贵人，大顺政权控制了长城以南、淮河以北的广大地区。

李自成进北京的消息传到关外，满清摄政王多尔衮 (gǔn) 急忙率兵南下，降服了驻守山海关的明将吴三桂。不久，李自成亲自率农民军同吴三桂的军队和清军在山海关展开大战，农民军战败。李自成被迫率军撤出北京，转战于河南、陕西等地。1645年，李自成战死于湖北九宫山。

The emperors in the late years of the Ming Dynasty were fatuous and incompetent, and power gradually slipped into the hands of eunuchs. Bureaucrats and landlords forcibly occupied large tracts of the fertile lands, leaving many peasants landless. Taxes and natural disasters, which officials did little to relieve, added to the burdens on the peasants, and eventually, in 1627 AD, a large-scale uprising broke out in the area of what is now northern Shaanxi Province. The unrest spread throughout the country. The strongest of the rebel peasant armies was led by Gao Yingxiang. After Gao's death, his army divided into two main parts: one was led by Zhang Xianzhong, and the other by Li Zicheng.

Li Zicheng (1606-1645 AD) was born in Mizhi, Shaanxi Province. In 1630, he joined the uprising, rising rapidly to become a general under Gao Yingxiang. With the death of Gao, he took command of the rebel forces in present-day Henan Province. Li Zicheng won the support of the people in this disaster-stricken area by a policy of land reform and abolition of agricultural taxes. Li's army grew rapidly to become a million-strong force. Wherever Li Zicheng's army went, it distributed the property of the landlords among the people. In 1644, Li Zicheng established the Dashun Dynasty in Xi'an. In the same year, he marched on to Beijing. As the rebels entered the capital, Emperor Chongzhen, the last Ming emperor, committed suicide by hanging himself on Coal Hill (Jingshan), just behind the Forbidden City.

Li Zicheng enforced strict military discipline, punished officials guilty of crimes and corruption, and paid much attention to the people's welfare. The regime controlled a vast area from south of the Great Wall to north of the Huaihe River.

Meanwhile, Dorgon, the prince regent of the Qing Dynasty, which had been set up in 1636 by the united Manchu tribes of northeast China, hurriedly led an army southward. Breaking through the strategic Shanhai Pass, Dorgon drove Li Zicheng from Beijing. In 1645, Li Zicheng was killed in battle at Mount Jiugong, in present-day Hubei Province.

小资料 Data

清军入关

公元1616年，女真首领努尔哈赤建立金，史称"后金"。1626年，皇太极继承皇位。1635年他改族名"女真"为"满洲"；次年，改国号为"清"，称皇帝。1644年，清军进攻山海关，山海关守将吴三桂投降。10月，清顺治皇帝从盛京(今沈阳)迁都北京，开始了对全中国的统治。

The Qing Army Pours Through Shanhai Pass

In 1616, Nurhachi, leader of the Jurchen (Nuzhen) tribes, established the Jin regime, called "Later Jin" in history. In 1626, Huangtaiji succeeded to the throne. In 1635, he changed the name of Jurchen to Manchu; the next year, he changed the title of the regime to Qing, and proclaimed himself emperor. In 1644, the Qing army attacked Shanhai Pass. Wu Sangui, the general garrisoning the pass, submitted to the Qing army. In October, Emperor Shunzhi of the Qing Dynasty moved the capital from Shengjing (today's Shenyang) to Beijing, and commenced to reign over the whole of China.

1. 李自成进北京插图
   A portrait of Li Zicheng entering Beijing
2. 湖北通山县李自成墓
   The mausoleum of Li Zicheng, Tongshan County, Hubei Province

郑成功收复台湾
Zheng Chenggong Recovers Taiwan

宝岛台湾自古以来就是中国不可分割的领土，它风景秀丽，物产丰富。

从公元1624年开始，荷兰殖民统治者采用欺骗的手段逐步侵占了台湾，欺负台湾人民。台湾人民忍受不了他们的压迫和掠夺，不断地反抗，可是因为他们力量弱小，都没有成功，在东南沿海抗清的将领郑成功决心赶走荷兰殖民者。

1661年3月，郑成功亲自率领大军，从金门出发，在台湾当地人的带领下登上了台湾岛。台湾人民听说郑成功来了，成群结队，去迎接自己的亲人。等到荷兰人知道时，中国军队已经像神兵天将一样遍布岛上、海上。郑成功的军队与荷兰殖民者展开了激烈的战

1

2

斗，把敌军包围在赤嵌（qiàn）城（今台南市），断绝了他们的水源，守城的荷兰军队如果不投降就只能渴死、饿死。荷兰殖民头领提出给郑成功10万两白银，请求他退兵。郑成功断然拒绝，他说台湾历来是中国的领土，荷兰殖民者必须退出。荷兰人不甘心，又派了援兵，企图打败郑成

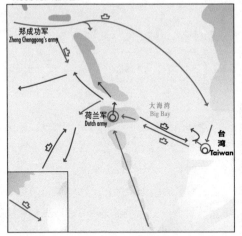

郑成功收复台湾略图
Sketch Map of Zheng Chenggong's Campaign to Recover Taiwan

郑成功军
Zheng Chenggong's army

荷兰军
Dutch army

大海湾
Big Bay

台湾
Taiwan

功，可是早有防备的郑成功给敌人援军一个迎头痛击，彻底打碎了他们的梦想，殖民者最终向郑成功投降。1662年，中国收回了台湾。

收复台湾是中国军民抗击外来侵略的一次大胜利，郑成功也因此成为中国历史上的民族英雄。

Taiwan has been an inseparable part of China since ancient times. It has beautiful scenery and is rich in agricultural products.

In 1624 AD, Dutch colonialists started to build forts and seize territory on Taiwan. In 1661, Zheng Chenggong, a Ming general who was resisting the Qing Dynasty in the coastal area of southeast China, set out with an army from Jinmen, resolved to drive the Dutch from Taiwan.

Zheng Chenggong's forces besieged the Dutch in Chiqian (today's Tainan City) and cut off their water supply. Refusing a huge bribe from the Dutch commander, Zheng forced the enemy to surrender, and expelled the Dutch from Taiwan once and for all in 1662.

The recovery of Taiwan was a great victory for the Chinese people in their resistance to colonial invaders. For this, Zheng Chenggong became a national hero.

1. 郑成功像
   A statue of Zheng Chenggong
2. 郑成功率领大军，跨过台湾海峡，赶走荷兰殖民统治者，收复台湾
   Leading his armies across the Taiwan Straits, Zheng Chenggong recovered Taiwan from the Dutch colonialists.

 小资料 Data

中国对台湾的管辖简史
公元230年，吴主孙权派卫温到台湾。
607年，隋炀帝派朱宽到台湾安抚当地人。
1292年，元世祖忽必烈派大臣到台湾安抚当地人。
1335年，元朝设"澎湖巡检司"正式管辖台湾。
1684年，清朝设立台湾府。

A Brief History of China's Administration of Taiwan

In 230 AD, Sun Quan, ruler of the State of Wu in the Three Kingdoms Period, sent his envoy Wei Wen to Taiwan.

In 607 AD, Emperor Yangdi of the Sui Dynasty sent Zhu Kuan to Taiwan to reassure the local people.

In 1292 AD, Kublai Khan, Emperor Shizu of the Yuan Dynasty, sent ministers to Taiwan to reassure the local people.

In 1335 AD, the Yuan Dynasty set up the Penghu Inspectorate as the official administration of Taiwan.

In 1684 AD, the Qing Dynasty set up the Taiwan Prefecture.

康乾盛世
The Golden Age of Three Emperors

清朝康熙（公元1661～1722年在位）、雍正（1722～1735年在位）和乾隆（1735～1796年在位）三位皇帝治理国家时，政治经济等出现的繁荣时期，史称"康乾盛世"。

康熙是中国历史上在位时间最长的皇帝。1661年康熙即位时，还是一个小孩子，那时明朝的旧臣想推翻清朝，恢复明朝的统治，形势十分危急。为了缓和矛盾，稳定政治局面，康熙把儒家学说定为官方思想，任用汉人做官，提倡汉文化。康熙还非常注重农业生产，并采取减轻农民负担等一系列措施，让被战争破坏的经济迅速恢复。他还经常巡视各地，了解民情，关心人民的疾苦。康熙平定了西南吴三桂叛乱、蒙古准噶尔部的分裂活动和西藏叛乱，从郑成功后代手中收回了台湾，两次与沙俄在雅克萨作战，维护了清朝领土的完整，康熙对国家统一作出了很大贡献。康熙在位期间，社会经济发展，人民生活安定。

雍正在位时间较短，保持了清朝的持续发展。乾隆皇帝是雍正的儿子，1735年即位后，他鼓励农民开垦荒地，组织移民，并行农业生产。多次减免农民的赋税。他调整了雍正时中央与地方地主官僚的紧张关系。惩罚官吏结党营私，改善了官吏队伍。平定了回部贵族叛乱，并对西藏进行了政治和宗教改革，加强了对西藏的管理。消灭了西南少数民族地区的割据政权，这些措施奠定了近代中国的版图。与康熙、雍正时相比，乾隆时的清朝更加强大富有，达到了清朝的最强盛时期。

The reigns of the Qing emperors Kangxi (1661-1722 AD), Yongzheng (1722-1735 AD) and Qianlong (1735-1796 AD) marked a

1. 康熙皇帝
   A portrait of Emperor Kangxi
2. 乾清宫（清朝皇帝处理国家大事的地方）
   The throne room of the Qianqing Palace, where Qing emperors handled state affairs
3. 雍正皇帝
   A portrait of Emperor Yongzheng

清代强盛时期疆域略图
Sketch Map of the Qing Dynasty's Territory in its Heyday

俄罗斯 Russia
库页岛 Sakhalin Is.
哈萨克 Kazakhstan
咸海 Aral Sea
唐努乌梁海 Tangnuwulianghai
乌里雅苏台 Wuliyasutai
外蒙古 Outer Mongolia
蒙 古
满洲 Manzhou
奉天 Fengtian
日本 Japan
准噶尔 Junggar
伊犁 Ili
内蒙古 Inner Mongolia
北京 Beijing
天津 Tianjin
朝鲜 Korea
波 斯 Persia
新疆 Xinjiang
甘肃 Gansu
山西 Shanxi
直隶
山东 Shandong
青海 Qinghai
陕西 Shaanxi
河南 Henan
安徽 Anhui
江苏 Jiangsu
上海 Shanghai
西藏 Tibet
四川 Sichuan
湖北 Hubei
武汉 Wuhan
南京 Nanjing
浙江 Zhejiang
喜马拉雅山 The Himalayas
拉萨 Lhasa
尼泊尔 Nepal
湖南 Hunan
江西 Jiangxi
福建 Fujian
印度 India
不丹 Bhutan
哲孟雄(锡金) Sikkim
贵州 Guizhou
广西 Guangxi
广州 Guangzhou
台湾 Taiwan
香港 Hong Kong
东 Guangdong
云南 Yunnan
缅甸 Myanmar
越 南 Vietnam
暹罗 Siam
海南岛 Hainan Is.
菲律宾 The Philippines
印度洋 Indian Ocean
南海 South China Sea
太平洋 Pacific Ocean
贝加尔湖 Lake Baikal

1775年清势力范围
Qing's sphere of influence in 1775
1911年清疆界
Borders of the Qing Dynasty in 1911
朝贡国
Tributary states

3

period of unprecedented prosperity both politically and economically.

Kangxi enjoyed the longest reign in Chinese history. When he ascended the throne in 1661, he was still a child. He quickly became versed in statecraft, however, and to appease officials of the old regime, he promoted a program of Sinicization of his government. He appointed Han officials, instituted Confucianism as the state ideology and enthusiastically promoted Han culture among the ruling Manchu class. Kangxi also attached importance to the restoration of agricultural production, which had been devastated by years of war and official neglect. He adopted a series of measures to lighten the burden on the peasants, and prosperity rapidly returned to the countryside. During his reign, the last of the armed Ming loyalists were put down, separatist activities in Mongolia and Tibet were quashed, and control of Taiwan was wrested from Zheng Chenggong's descendants. In addition, encroachment from tsarist Russia was halted. Kangxi thus made great contributions to the territorial integrity of the country, as well as to its security and prosperity.

Emperor Yongzheng proved a worthy successor to Kangxi's policies. Emperor Qianlong succeeded to the throne in 1735. He encouraged peasants to cultivate waste land, and lightened their tax burden. He also strengthened the central government's control over the ethnic-minority areas, particularly in Tibet.

小资料 Data

达赖与班禅

公元1653年，清政府册封达赖五世为"西天大善自在佛所领天下释教普通瓦赤喇怛喇达赖喇嘛"。正式确定达赖喇嘛为西藏佛教最高领袖。1713年又封班禅五世为"班禅额尔德尼"，颁发金印金册。正式确立其地位。以后历世达赖、班禅必经中央政权册封成为定制。

The Dalai and Panchen Lamas

In 1653, the Qing government officially recognized the fifth Dalai Lama as the supreme head of Tibetan Buddhism, and in 1713, it recognized the fifth Panchen Lama as the head of the Tashilhunpo Monastery, the headquarters of a powerful sect of Tibetan Buddhism. From that time on, both the Dalai and Panchen lamas had to be confirmed by the central authority.

科学巨匠与巨著
Great Scientists and Their Contributions

明代经济发展的同时，科学、医学也取得很大的成就，涌现了许多优秀的科学家和科学著作。

李时珍和《本草纲目》 李时珍（公元1518～1593年）是明代著名的医学家和药物学家，出生于湖广蕲（qí）州（今湖北蕲春）一个世代行医的家庭。他受到家庭的影响，从小就对医学有着浓厚的兴趣，并决心做一个给人们解除病痛的好医生。李时珍24岁就开始正式给人治病，由于他刻苦钻研，医术高超，治好了许多疑难病症。

可是，李时珍在行医的过程中，发现前人编著的医药书中有许多遗漏，甚至还有许多错误。他决心重编一本比较完善的药物著作。为了实现这一理想，李时珍阅读了大量的医学著作，还注重实地考察和采集草药。经过差不多30年的努力，他终于在60岁的时候写成了《本草纲目》一书。这本书内容十分丰富，收入药物1,800多种，新增药物370多种，医方一万多个，配有插图1,000多幅。书中关于植物的分类方法，也是当时世界最先进的。《本草纲目》是中国药物学研究的总结，已被译成多种文字，被誉为"东方医学巨典"。

徐光启和《农政全书》 徐光启（公元1562～1633年）上海人，明朝科学家，曾跟随意大利传教士利玛窦（dòu）学习西方的天文、历算、火器等知识。他钻研科学文化知识，在介绍西方自然科学和发展中国的农业、天文、数学等方面作出了重大贡献。他的《农政全书》是关于农业科学的著作，用科学的方法总结了中国传统的农业知识和技术，并介绍了欧洲的水利技术，书中有图，有注解，有说明，内容丰富，是一部农业百科全书。

宋应星和《天工开物》 宋应星（公元1587～约1666年），江西人，明朝末年科学家。他一生写了许多著作，《天工开物》是其中影响最大的一部书。这本书是明朝农业和手工业生产技术的总结，内容十分广泛，几乎包括了当时社会生活的各个方面，反映了当时的社会发展水平，被誉为"中国17世纪的工艺百科全书"。

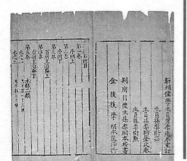

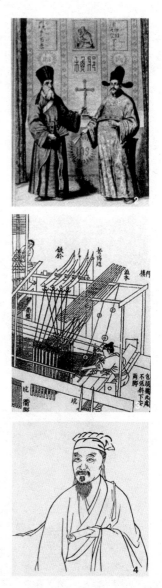

徐霞客和《徐霞客游记》 徐霞客（公元1586～1641年），江苏人，中国17世纪杰出的旅行家和地理学家。徐霞客读了很多书，对地理、历史、游记类的书特别感兴趣。他发现，有些地理书籍的记载是错误的，因而决心考察祖国的山河。22岁那年，徐霞客开始了他的野外考察生活，直到他逝世的那一年。在30多年的考察生活中，徐霞客几乎跑遍了全中国。《徐霞客游记》以日记的形式记录了作者旅行考察中的见闻和内心感受。徐霞客以实地考察的第一手资料，记录了中国的山川河流、地形地貌、矿产分布等。《徐霞客游记》是研究中国地貌、水文、动植物分布等的重要参考资料。

At the same time as the economy was developing rapidly during the Ming Dynasty, great strides were also made in science and medicine.

Li Shizhen (1518-1593 AD) came from a long line of doctors in present-day Hubei Province, and devoted himself to the art of healing. Noticing that the classical works on medicine contained many mistakes and obscurities, he determined to write a definitive materia medica. He spent 30 years on his life's work, which he completed at the age of 60. His book, titled *Bencao Gangmu (Compendium of Materia Medica)*, contains details of over 1,800 kinds of herbs and other medicinal materials, 10,000 prescriptions and over 1,000 illustrations. It was the most scientific description of traditional Chinese medicine of its time, and is still used today, having been translated into several major languages.

Xu Guangqi (1562-1633 AD), born in Shanghai, studied astronomy, mathematics and the art of making firearms under Matteo Ricci, an Italian missionary. He made great contributions to the introduction of Western natural science to China and to developing science in China, including scientific agriculture, as embodied in his *Encyclopedia of Agriculture*.

Song Yingxing (1587-c.1666 AD), born in Jiangxi, contributed much to the devclopment of agriculture and handicrafts. Among the many books he wrote, his *Exploitation of the Works of Nature* was the most influential. Its contents cover almost every aspect of social and economic life in 17th century China.

Xu Xiake (1586-1641 AD), born in Jiangsu, was an eminent traveler and geographer of the 17th century. Puzzled by conflicting references in books of geography, history and travels, he decided to investigate for himself. From the age of 22, Xu Xiake spent 30 years traveling all over China. He recorded his observations in diary form in his *Xu Xiake's Travels*. This book is still of great importance for the study of China's landforms, hydrology, distribution of animals and plants, mineral resources, etc.

1. 《本草纲目》书影
   A copy of Li Shizhen's *Compendium of Materia Medica*
2. 徐光启与利玛窦画像
   A portrait of Xu Guanqi (right) and Matteo Ricci
3. 《天工开物》织机图
   An illustration of a loom in the *Exploitation of the Works of Nature*
4. 徐霞客像
   A portrait of Xu Xiake

四大名著
The Four Great Classical Novels

明清时代，古典小说蓬勃发展。出现了中国文学史上的"四大名著"，它们是《三国演义》、《水浒传》、《西游记》和《红楼梦》。

《三国演义》原名《三国志通俗演义》，是著名的历史小说，作者罗贯中依据民间流传的三国故事和历史著作《三国志》创作而成。罗贯中，元末明初人。小说主要描写的是曹操、孙权、刘备割据一方，形成三国鼎立局面的故事，是中国第一部章回体长篇历史小说。

《水浒传》又叫《忠义水浒传》，与《三国演义》差不多同时出现，是施耐庵根据北宋末年宋江起义的故事加工而成的长篇小说。小说以"官逼民反"为主题，描写了水泊梁山108名英雄好汉起义的故事，揭露了封建统治者的残忍与腐朽，歌颂了好汉们除暴安良的英雄行为。

《西游记》是明朝人吴承恩把唐僧取经的故事和民间传说相结合写成的。小说描写了曾经大闹天宫的神猴孙悟空护送师父唐僧去西天取经，在途中经历了九九八十一难，最终取得真经的故事。《西游记》想像丰富，故事精彩，语言生动，是中国著名的长篇神话小说。

1

2

3

4

《红楼梦》又叫《石头记》，全书120回，清朝人曹雪芹写了前80回，高鹗（è）续写了后40回。这部小说以贾宝玉和林黛玉的爱情悲剧为线索，描写了封建官僚贾、王、史、薛四大家族特别是贾家的衰落过程，揭露了封建统治者的罪恶，说明了封建王朝必将衰落的历史命运。《红楼梦》是中国古典文学中艺术性和思想性结合得最好的一部长篇小说，是中国文学中伟大的现实主义杰作。

　　这个时期出现的"四大名著"和其他一些优秀小说都反映了当时的生活，具有一定的现实意义。

1. 齐天大圣孙悟空（《西游记》）
   The "Monkey King", Sun Wukong, is a figure from *Journey to the West.*

2. 《西游记》作者吴承恩在江苏淮安的故居
   The residence of Wu Cheng'en, author of *Journey to the West*, in Huaian, Jiangsu Province

3. 大观园全图（《红楼梦》）
   The Grand View Garden in *A Dream of Red Mansions*

4. 武松打虎（《水浒传》）
   An illustration from *Outlaws of the Marsh*

5. 《红楼梦》作者曹雪芹的纪念馆
   The memorial hall of the author of *A Dream of Red Mansions*, Cao Xueqin

5

During the Ming and Qing dynasties literary creation flourished. It was in this period that the four great Chinese classical novels were written, namely, *Romance of the Three Kingdoms, Outlaws of the Marsh, Journey to the West* and *A Dream of Red Mansions.*

Luo Guanzhong, the author of *Romance of the Three Kingdoms*, based his novel on both folk tales and historical records of the conflicts between the kingdoms of Wei, Shu and Wu (220-265 AD), established by Cao Cao, Liu Bei and Sun Quan, respectively. Written in the early Ming Dynasty, it

《聊斋志异》

是清朝康熙年间山东淄川（今山东淄博）人蒲松龄写的一部著名的短篇小说集。其中的故事多是借讲狐仙鬼怪来反映当时社会的现实生活，有的讽刺贪官污吏，有的揭露科举制度，有的歌颂青年男女真挚的爱情，还有的赞扬了劳动人民的反抗精神。

Strange Stories from a Chinese Studio

This work is a collection of fantastic stories collected and edited by Pu Songling, who was born in today's Zibo, Shandong Province, during the reign of Emperor Kangxi. Through these weird tales, Pu Songling satirized the corruption of officialdom, uncovered the dark side of the imperial civil examination system, praised true love between young men and women, and eulogized the rebellious spirit of the laboring people.

1. 《红楼梦》详细地描述了古代上流贵族的生活
   A Dream of Red Mansions depicts the life of the feudal noble families in details.
2. 桃园结义图（《三国演义》）
   An illustration from *Romance of the Three Kingdoms*: Emperor Liu Bei, Guan Yu and Zhang Fei forming a pact of friendship to death

was the first historical novel to appear in China.

Outlaws of the Marsh, which was written at almost the same time as *Three Kingdoms*, was written by Shi Nai'an. It is based on folk tales about a band of rebels led by Song Jiang at the close of the Northern Song Dynasty. There are 108 heroes and heroines in the novel, which is a savage satire on official corruption and feudal oppression.

Journey to the West was written by Wu Cheng'en of the Ming Dynasty. It is based on the true story of a Tang Dynasty monk who made a perilous overland trip to India to fetch back the Buddhist scriptures. In the novel, the monk is led and protected by Sun Wukong, the "Monkey King," a figure from folk legend.

A Dream of Red Mansions, also named *Tale of the Rock*, has 120 chapters, of which the first 80 were written by Cao Xueqin, and the remaining 40 by Gao E. With the tragic love story of Jia Baoyu and Lin Daiyu as the main theme, the novel describes the decline of four feudal noble families. The novel is a treasure house of information about the way aristocratic families lived in the Qing Dynasty.

概述
Introduction

　　英国于公元1840年前后在世界上率先完成工业革命，成为当时最强大的资本主义国家。英国为了扩大工业品的销售市场，占领更广阔的工业原料产地，发动了侵略中国的鸦片战争，中国在鸦片战争中战败，被迫与英国签订了《中英南京条约》等不平等条约。从此，中国的主权与领土完整遭到破坏，开始沦为半殖民地半封建的国家。所以，史学界以1840年作为中国近代史的开端，此后110年的历史，是中国的近代史。鸦片战争后的100多年中，列强又多次发动对中国的侵略战争，使中国的主权与领土完整继续遭到破坏，使中国人民遭受殖民主义者的欺辱；同时，中国也涌现出许许多多的抵抗侵略，挽救国家危亡的可歌可泣的事迹。如太平天国运动、戊戌变法运动、义和团运动等，特别是1911年孙中山领导的辛亥革命，推翻了中国2,000多年的封建君主专制制度，建立了中华民国；1919年的五四运动，为中国共产党的诞生奠定了基础；1921年，中国共产党的诞生，使中国革命出现了新局面。

　　1949年，在中国共产党的领导下，中国人民赶走了帝国主义势力，推翻了国民党在大陆的统治，结束了半殖民地半封建社会的历史，取得了革命的胜利。

Britain was the first country in the world to complete the Industrial Revolution, in the early 19th century, and became the most powerful capitalist country at that time. As part of its efforts to expand the markets for its industrial products and to secure more sources of industrial raw materials, Britain launched a war against China — the Opium War — in which China was defeated and was forced to sign unequal treaties, including the *Treaty of Nanking*. From that time on, China's sovereignty and territorial integrity were threatened continually, and China began to sink to the level of a semi-colonial and semi-feudal country. So historians regard 1840 as the beginning of China's modern history, and the following 110 years as the history of modern China. During the 100 years following the Opium War, the imperialist powers launched wars of aggression against China many times. At the same time, resistance movements emerged, such as that of the Taiping Heavenly Kingdom, the Reform Movement of 1898 and the Yihetuan Movement. Among all these movements that which had the greatest significance was the Revolution of 1911 led by Dr. Sun Yat-sen, which overthrew the 2,000-year-old autocratic feudal monarchy, and established the Republic of China. The May 4 Movement of 1919 laid the groundwork for the foundation of the Chinese Communist Party, which finally liberated China from imperialist oppression in 1949.

林则徐与虎门销烟
Lin Zexu Destroys the Opium

公元1839年6月3日，在广东虎门的海边，许多箱子堆得像小山一样高，周围有成千上万的群众，他们都在激动而兴奋地等待着……这是怎么一回事呢？

原来，箱内装的都是大烟。大烟正式的名字叫鸦片，是一种毒品，人吸了就会上瘾（yǐn）。常吸大烟的人身体虚弱，精神萎靡（wěimǐ），被叫做"大烟鬼"。从19世纪初开始，英国等西方国家大量向中国偷运走私鸦片，在不到40年里，就使中国吸鸦片的人数达到两百多万。鸦片给英国商人带来巨额的利润，却给中国社会带来了巨大的危害：它不但损害人民的健康，而且使中国的白银大量外流，社会经济受到很大影响。另外，由于军队中的"大烟鬼"增多，军队的士气和战斗力也大大下降。

面对这种严重的形势，以湖广总督林则徐为代表的大臣们多次向道光皇帝上书，主张严厉禁止鸦片。1839年，皇帝终于下决心派林则徐去广州禁烟。

林则徐（公元1785～1850年）在1838年任湖广总督时，禁止鸦片，效果显著。林则徐到广州后，与外国毒贩展开了坚决的斗争。他先进行调查，摸清情况，然后命令毒贩们交出全部鸦片，并且保证永远不再走私。外国毒贩们不相信林则徐真能禁绝鸦片。他们不交鸦片，有的还准备逃跑。林则徐派兵抓回了逃犯，包围了英国商馆，撤出了商馆里的中国雇工，断绝了商馆的饮食供应，给外国毒贩及其支持者的生活造成极大的不便，并且说："若鸦片一日未绝，本大臣一日不回！誓与此事相始终！"毒贩们这下儿可害怕了，知道没有希望了，只好交出鸦片，一共有2万多箱，110多万公斤！

林则徐命令将这2万多箱大烟全部销毁，于是就发生了开篇的那一幕。由于大烟数量太多，销烟工作整整进行了23天。虎门销烟是一件震撼（zhènhàn）世界的壮举，林则徐也因此成为中国近代史上的民族英雄。

From the early 19th century, Britain and other Western countries began to smuggle opium into China. In no more than 40 years, the number of China's opium addicts had reached over two million. Opium brought huge profits to British merchants, but posed a great danger to China. It not only harmed people's health, but also drained the country of silver. What was more, the morale and strength of the army were also harmed with the increase of opium addiction in the ranks.

2

Emperor Daoguang was repeatedly urged by his ministers to stop the scourge of opium spreading, and in 1839 he dispatched Lin Zexu to Guangzhou to implement the banning of opium smoking and the opium trade.

Lin (1785-1850 AD) had been successful in banning opium smoking and the opium trade when he was viceroy of Hubei and Hunan. After arriving in Guangzhou, he forced the foreign merchants to hand over their stocks of opium, which amounted to 1,100,000 kg in over 20,000 boxes.

Lin Zexu had the confiscated opium piled up on the seashore at Humen, and destroyed. Starting June 3, 1839, it took 23 days to complete the destruction of the drug.

For his bold action, Lin Zexu became a national hero in modern Chinese history.

小资料 Data

虎门销烟的方法

虎门销烟的方法不是用火烧，而是用石灰水浸泡鸦片，产生化学反应，把鸦片分解、销毁掉。

The Destruction of the Opium at Humen

The opium was not burned, but immersed in pits of lime, which produced a chemical change that decomposed it.

1. 林则徐像
   A portrait of Lin Zexu

2. 林文忠公政书 (林则徐任湖广总督期间，曾两次上书清政府，主张严禁鸦片。)
   The official documents written by the viceroy of Hubei and Hunan, Lin Zexu, who urged the Qing government to ban opium.

3. 广东虎门销烟处是进出珠江战略要地，设有炮台
   Equipped with cannon ports, the seashore at Humen of Guangdong Province (where over one million kilograms of opium were destroyed) was a strategic position in war.

3

鸦片战争
The Opium Wars

　　鸦片生意利润很高，不但英国商人能从中赚很多钱，而且英国政府也能从中得到很大好处，因此，林则徐在广州的禁烟措施，使他们遭受了巨大的损失。公元1840年6月，英国派出48艘共装备有540门大炮的舰队开到广东海面，发动了第一次鸦片战争。

　　由于林则徐率广州军民早已严加防备，英军只好沿海岸线北上，攻陷浙江的定海，8月到达天津。清朝皇帝非常害怕，派主张求和的大臣琦 (qí) 善去谈判，保证只要英军退回广东，清政府就一定惩治林则徐。英军撤退后，朝廷就把林则徐撤职查办，把琦善派到广州去。

　　1841年1月，英军强行占领香港岛。清政府被迫宣战，并派大臣奕山到广州指挥。2月，英军猛攻虎门炮台，守将关天培在没有援军的情况下英勇奋战。炮台失守后，关天培和将士们用大刀和敌人拼杀，最后全部壮烈牺牲。英军进攻广州城，胆小如鼠的奕山举白旗投降。攻下广州的英军作恶多端，激起了人民的反抗。广州郊区三元里人民自发地组织起来，与侵略者展开斗争，保卫家乡，给侵略者以沉重的打击。

　　英军继续扩大侵华战争，进攻浙江省的定海、镇海、宁波等地。以葛云飞为代表的沿海爱国军民拼死抵抗，但终因武器落后，加上朝廷腐败、指挥不利而连连失败。1842年6月，英军进攻上海吴淞口，年近70的老将陈化成率军迎战，虽身受多处重伤，血染战袍，仍紧握令旗指挥战斗，直到牺牲。吴淞失守后，英军沿长江入侵，8月打到南京。清政府慌忙投降，与英方签订了出卖中华民族权益的《南京条约》，内容有：赔款2,100万银元；割让香港岛，开放广州、上海、厦门、福州、宁波五个城市为通商口岸等等，这是外国侵略者强迫清政府签订的第一个不平等条约。中国从此开始沦为半殖民地半封建国家。

Not only did British traders profit from the trade in opium, the British government did too. Lin Zexu's destruction of the opium stocks in Guangzhou brought huge losses to Britain, which, in June 1840, dispatched 48 warships equipped with 540 cannons to the coast of Guangdong, launching the First Opium War against China.

Under the command of Lin Zexu, the army and the people of Guangzhou had made abundant preparations for the war, and repelled the British fleet, which then turned northward along the coast, captured Dinghai in Zhejiang Province, and reached Tianjin in August. Panic-stricken, Emperor Daoguang sent Minister Qi Shan to sue for peace with the British. The emperor promised to dismiss Lin Zexu as long as the British troops went back to Guangdong. They did so, and Qi Shan was sent to Guangzhou.

In January 1841, the British occupied Hong Kong Island. To recover the territory, the Qing government sent troops under Minister Yi Shan to Guangzhou. In February, the British

鸦片战争形势图
Sketch Map of the Opium Wars

1. 鸦片战争海战图
   Painting: Sea Battle of the Opium War
2. 广东虎门鸦片战争博物馆，纪念作战牺牲的军民的雕像
   Museum of Opium War, Humen, Guangdong Province, exhibits statues of soldiers killed in wars.

2

圆明园是清朝皇帝的别宫，位于北京西北郊，是世界著名的皇家园林，被西方称为"万园之园"。1856年，英国和法国联合发动了第二次鸦片战争。1860年，英法联军攻陷北京，闯入圆明园，将园内无数的珍宝抢劫一空，毁坏了无法运走的珍贵文物，为了掩盖罪行，他们最后放火烧毁了圆明园。

The Burning of the Yuanmingyuan Garden

Situated in the northwest of Beijing, the Old Summer Palace (Yuanmingyuan) was a retreat for the Qing emperors during the height of summer. In 1860, during the Second Opium War, British and French allied forces captured Beijing. They plundered the Old Summer Palace, destroying what they could not take away. Finally, they burned it to the ground.

1. 圆明园遗址
    Ruins of the Yuanmingyuan Garden

troops bombarded the city's defenses. When the Chinese fort in Humen fell, the defenders, under General Guan Tianpei, engaged the enemy with swords, but were overwhelmed and slaughtered. Yi Shan surrendered Guangzhou, but resistance to the invaders among the local people continued, notably in Sanyuanli in the suburb of Guangzhou.

The British then turned their attention to other parts of the coast. They attacked several places in Zhejiang Province, including Dinghai, Zhenhai and Ningbo. Outdated weapons, inexperienced officers and corrupt court officials were the major factors that caused defeat after defeat for the Chinese army. In June 1842, the British troops captured the Wusong Fort in Shanghai. In August, they advanced on Nanjing. The Qing court was forced to sign the humiliating "Treaty of Nanking". Under the terms of the treaty, China was to pay 21 million silver dollars in reparations; cede Hong Kong Island to Britain; and open the cities of Guangzhou, Shanghai, Xiamen, Fuzhou and Ningbo as trading ports. The "Treaty of Nanking" was the first unequal treaty signed by the Qing court, and its signing marked the start of China's decline to the status of a semi-colonial and semi-feudal country.

1

太平天国运动
The Taiping Heavenly Kingdom

太平天国运动形势图
Sketch Map of the Taiping Heavenly
Kingdom Movement

🚩 太平天国起义地点
　Site of Hong Xiuquan's uprising

→ 太平军从金田到南京进军路线
　Taiping army's march on Nanjing
　from Jintian Village

➡ 北伐进军路线
　The route of the northern expedition

➡ 西征路线
　The route of the western expedition

◁ 拜上帝宗教活动地区
　The areas of God Worship Society activities

◁ 太平军主要活动地区
　The main areas of the Taiping army's operations

1. 洪秀全塑像
　A sculpture of Hong Xiuquan

鸦片战争以后，清朝的统治更加腐败，社会黑暗，广大人民生活非常贫苦。公元1843年，一个叫洪秀全的青年受基督教思想的启发，创立了一个宗教组织——拜上帝会，宣传人人平等的思想，号召人民跟清朝统治者斗争。拜上帝会发展得很快。1851年1月11日，这天正好是洪秀全38岁的生日，他领导农民在广西桂平县金田村起义，建号太平天国。

太平军作战勇猛，连连打败清军，队伍也从两万人很快扩大到几十万人。1853年3月，太平军攻占南京。洪秀全把南京改名为天京，定为首都。太平天国颁布了《天朝田亩制度》，中心内容是要实现"有田同耕、有饭同食、有衣同穿、有钱同使，无处不均匀，无人不饱暖"的理想社会。太平军出师北伐，打了很多胜仗，逼近北京，吓得清朝皇帝准备逃跑。

1856年8月，就在太平天国各方面事业都轰轰烈烈地展开的时候，领导集团内部却为了争夺权力而爆发了自相残杀的"天京事变"。这场变乱大大削弱了太平天国的力量，清军趁机全面反攻，特别是曾国藩(fān)领导的湘军成为太平天国最强大的敌人。虽然洪秀全为了扭转局面而选拔任用了陈玉成、李秀成等一批年轻的将领，并取得了一些成效，但还是没能挽救太平天国失败的命运。1863年底，湘军开始围困天京。1864年6月3日，洪秀全病逝。7月，湘军攻破天京，这场历时近14年的大规模农民起义被镇压了。

1. 南京太平天国天王府石舫
The stone boat in the royal palace of the Taiping Heavenly Kingdom in Nanjing

Following China's disastrous defeats in the Opium War, the Qing Dynasty became more corrupt and weaker than ever, and the misery and poverty of populace increased. In 1843, Hong Xiuquan, under the influence of Christianity, set up a religious organization called the God Worship Society, which advocated human equality and called for the overthrow of the Qing rulers. The new group quickly gathered adherents. On January 11, 1851, Hong Xiuquan put himself at the head of a peasant revolt which had broken out in Jintian Village, Guiping County, in the present-day Guangxi Zhuang Autonomous Region, and declared the establishment of the "Taiping Heavenly Kingdom (Taiping Tianguo)".

The Taiping army grew to hundreds of thousands. It was at first successful in battle wherever it went. In March 1853, the Taipings occupied Nanjing, and made the city their capital, changing its name to Tianjing (heavenly capital). Hong Xiuquan's aim was to achieve an ideal society here on earth, where all the people would "share land, food, clothing and money. There will not be inequality and nobody will suffer from hunger or cold". The Taiping army, victorious everywhere, marched northward, and soon threatened Beijing itself. Emperor Xianfeng prepared to abandon the capital.

However, power struggles weakened the Taiping leadership, and the Qing government took advantage of the Taiping army's wavering to raise local militias to counterattack. The most powerful and best-trained of these militias was the Xiang (Hunan Province) army, organized and led by Zeng Guofan. In late 1863, the Xiang army besieged Tianjing. On June 3, 1864, Hong Xiuquan died of illness, and in July Tianjing fell. After 14 years of civil war, this peasant uprising which turned into an experiment in utopian government was finally quashed.

中日甲午战争
The Sino-Japanese War of 1894

1. 中日甲午战争海战图
Painting: Sea Battle of the Sino-Japanese War

中日甲午战争形势示意图
Sketch Map of the Sino-Japanese
War of 1894

日本是中国的近邻。明治维新以后，日本的资本主义得到迅速的发展，国力大大增强，侵略扩张的野心也越来越大。公元1894年(农历甲午年)，日本出兵朝鲜，并袭击中国运兵船，中日甲午战争爆发。

战争初期，清朝军队在朝鲜的平壤(rǎng)与日军展开了战斗，清军战败，日军占领了平壤。接着战火烧到了中国境内。

9月17日上午，中国北洋水师10艘军舰在丁汝昌、刘步蟾(chán)的指挥下，与由12艘日舰组成的日本海军在黄海展开激战。虽然敌舰数量多、力量强，但中国海军大部分将士都英勇奋战。致远号弹药用尽、船身中炮后，舰长邓世昌命令开足马力撞击敌舰，结果军舰不幸被鱼雷击中沉没，全舰200多名官兵壮烈牺牲。经远舰舰长林永升也率领将士战斗到生命的最

洋务运动

19世纪60年代至90年代,以曾国藩、李鸿章、左宗棠、张之洞为代表的清政府高层官僚主张学习采用一些西方资本主义生产技术,以挽救中国的封建统治,历史上称为"洋务运动"。洋务派引进西方一些近代科学技术,开办江南制造局、福州船政局和各省机器局等近代军事和民用工业,派遣留学生学习技术,还购买军舰,成立北洋海军。由于封建制度和官僚机构的腐败,洋务运动没能使中国走向富强,但在客观上刺激了中国资本主义的发展,对外国经济势力的扩张,也起到了一些抵制作用。中日甲午战争的失败宣告了洋务运动的破产。

The Westernization Movement

From the 1860s to the 1890s, high officials and military officers of the Qing government, represented by Zeng Guofan, Li Hongzhang, Zuo Zongtang and Zhang Zhidong, advocated learning and adopting Western technology to save the dynasty. This is called the "Westernization Movement" by historians. The "Westernizers" set up modern military and civilian industries, including the Jiangnan Machinery Factory and Fuzhou Shipyard, and dispatched students abroad to learn advanced technology. They also bought warships and founded the Northern Fleet. However, the Westernization Movement foundered on the corruption of the feudal system and its bureaucratic inertia. Yet, this movement did contribute in a small way to the development of capitalism in China and the ideology of resistance to the expansion of foreign economic forces in China. The defeat of China in the Sino-Japanese War of 1894 sounded the death knell of the Westernization Movement.

后一刻。经过几个小时的激战,北洋水师损失严重,日方军舰也受到重创。

11月,日军攻占了大连、旅顺,并在旅顺进行了疯狂的大屠杀。在四天的时间里,用各种极为残忍的手段杀害了18,000多中国同胞。

1895年1月,甲午战争以清朝的失败求和而结束。中日签订了《马关条约》,中国赔偿日本军费白银2亿两,还把辽东半岛、台湾等地割让给日本(由于沙俄等国出面干涉,日本把辽东半岛归还中国。中国给日本3,000万两白银,作为"赎辽费")。甲午战争以后,中国半殖民地化的程度进一步加深了。

After the Meiji Restoration, which started in 1868 AD, capitalism developed rapidly in Japan, and the country's strength increased greatly. At the same time, the Japanese government turned its attention to building an empire on the mainland of Asia. In 1894, Japan dispatched an army to the Korean Peninsula, which clashed with Chinese ships carrying troops to defend the Korean king. Thus, the Sino-Japanese War of 1894 broke out.

Defeated in the city of Pyongyang, the Qing army was forced to retreat, and the war was carried into China itself.

On the morning of September 17, 1894,

under the command of Ding Ruchang and Liu Buchan, 10 warships from China's Northern Fleet engaged 12 Japanese warships in the Yellow Sea. When the warship "Zhiyuan"

ran out of ammunition, its captain, Deng Shichang, tried to ram a Japanese ship. The *Zhiyuan* was torpedoed and sank, and all its 200 officers and men died heroically. Lin Yongsheng, captain of the warship *Jingyuan*, also fought alongside his men to the last moment of his life.

In November, the Japanese army occupied Dalian and Lushun. In a period of only four days, the Japanese massacred more than 18,000 of the inhabitants of Lushun.

In January 1895, the Sino-Japanese War ended, with the Qing Dynasty suing for peace. China and Japan signed "Treaty of Shimonoseki", according to which China had to pay Japan 200 million taels (unit of weight) of silver as war reparations and to cede the Liaodong Peninsula and Taiwan to

Japan (Japan was later forced to return the Liaodong Peninsula to China, in return for 30 million taels of silver, due to pressure from Tsarist Russia and other countries). This war accelerated the semi-colonization of China.

1. 山东威海刘公岛炮台
   The casemate on Liugong Island, Weihai, Shandong Province
2. 甲午抗日名将丁汝昌雕像
   A statue of Ding Ruchang, the famous general of the Sino-Japanese War
3. 清代洋学堂的学生在操练
   The foreign school of the Qing Dynasty
4. 日军在旅顺残杀中国平民
   Massacre of civilians by the Japanese army in Lushun
5. 负责与日方谈判，签订《马关条约》的李鸿章(中)与大臣合照
   Li Hongzhang (middle) negotiated with Japan and signed the "Treaty of Shimonoseki" on behalf of China.

小资料 Data

台湾人民的抗日斗争

《马关条约》签订后，台湾人民纷纷组织起来，奋勇抗日，反对割台。在刘永福、徐骧(xiāng)等的领导下，台湾军民坚持抗战半年多，打死打伤日军3万多人。虽然日本侵略者依靠强大的兵力最终占领了台湾，但此后的几十年里，台湾人民反日斗争从未停止过。1945年，根据《波茨坦公告》，被日寇侵占了近半个世纪的台湾终于回到了中国的怀抱。

The Taiwan People's Struggle Against the Japanese
Following the signing of the "Treaty of Shimonoseki", the people of Taiwan organized to fight against the Japanese invaders and refused to be put under Japan's control. Led by Liu Yongfu and Xu Xiang, soldiers and civilians resisted the Japanese invaders for over half a year, and killed and injured more than 30,000 Japanese soldiers. Although the Japanese invaders finally captured Taiwan, the Taiwan people never stopped their resistance in the following decades. In 1945, in accordance with the Potsdam Proclamation, Taiwan, which had been occupied for nearly half a century by the Japanese, was returned to China.

戊戌变法
The Reform Movement of 1898

1. 光绪皇帝像 (公元1871年—1908年)
   A portrait of Emperor Guangxu (1871—1908 AD)
2. 谭嗣同 (公元1865年—1898年)
   Tan Sitong (1865—1898 AD)
3. 康有为 (公元1858年—1927年)
   Kang Youwei (1858—1927 AD)
4. 梁启超 (公元1873年—1929年)
   Liang Qichao (1873—1929 AD)
5. 慈禧太后 (公元1835年—1908年)
   Empress Dowager Cixi (1835—1908 AD)

公元1895年，《马关条约》签订的消息传到北京。当时正在北京参加科举考试的康有为，联合1,300多个考生一起给皇帝上书，反对向日本求和，要求变法。上书虽然没有到达皇帝手中，但维新变法思想的影响迅速扩大。历史上称这一事件为"公车上书"。

康有为认为中国的危亡局势都是腐败的制度、落后的思想造成的。"公车上书"后，他和他的学生梁启超一起办报纸、组织强学会，宣传改革旧制、变法维新的新思想，在全国掀起了爱国救亡运动的高潮。

1898年，中国农历叫戊戌 (wùxū) 年，光绪皇帝终于下决心重用维新派，在全国实行变法。变法的主要内容有：政治上改革旧机构，经济上保护、奖励工商业，教育上创办新学校、改革科举考试、学习西方的科学技术和文化思想等等。

维新派的主张和措施大大触怒了以慈禧 (cíxǐ) 太后为代表的守旧派。慈禧太后准备废掉光绪皇帝。维新派求救于手握重兵的袁世凯，但是却被袁世凯出卖了。慈禧发动政变，派人把光绪皇帝关了起来，同时抓捕维新党人。康有为、梁启超逃到了国外。另一位重要的维新党人谭嗣同本来也有机会逃走，但是他不愿走。他说："各国变法，没有不流血的，而中国还没有为变法而流血的人，所以国家不强盛，今天就从我开头吧。"不久，谭嗣同、康广仁等六人被杀害了，历史上称他们为"戊戌六君子"。

戊戌变法从开始到失败一共只有103天，所以又叫"百日维新"。

In 1895 AD, when the news reached Beijing that the "*Treaty of Shimonoseki*" had been signed, Kang Youwei, who was taking the imperial civil examinations at that time in Beijing, rallied over 1,300 examinees to submit a petition to the emperor to oppose the peace treaty with Japan and to demand political reform.

Kang Youwei thought that China's perilous situation had resulted from its corrupt bureaucracy and backward ideology. After he submitted the petition to the emperor, he and his student Liang Qichao started newspapers and organized the Qiangxue (Learn-to-be-Strong) Society to press for political reform.

In 1898, the year Wuxu by the Chinese lunar calendar, Emperor Guangxu decided to put reformers in important positions in the government, and to carry out reform measures all over the country. The main contents of the reform were: overhaul of the old institutions; protection, encouragement and rewards for industry and commerce; the introduction of modern educational

methods; abolition of the imperial civil examination system; and the wholesale introduction to Western science, technology and culture. The reformers hoped to enlist the

support of Yuan Shikai, a powerful general and minister, but Yuan saw danger looming, and refused to lend his support.

These proposed changes alarmed and infuriated the conservatives, represented by Empress Dowager Cixi. A palace coup masterminded by Cixi put Emperor Guangxu under house arrest, and most of the reformers were arrested. Kang Youwei and Liang Qichao fled abroad. Tan Sitong, another important reformer, who had had the chance to escape, refused to do so. He said, "There can be no reform without blood. In China there's no one who has shed blood for the reform, that's why our country is still poor and weak. Now I am willing to give my life for the reform." Before long, Tan Sitong, Kang Guangren and four other leading reformers were executed. They are known to history as the "Six Gentlemen of Wuxu".

The Reform Movement lasted for only 103 days, and so it is also called the "Hundred Days Reform".

小资料 Data

慈禧太后

又称西太后 (公元1835～1908年)。原为清朝咸丰皇帝的妃子。1861年，咸丰去世，六岁的同治皇帝即位。慈禧作为同治的母亲垂帘听政，掌握了国家大权。1875年同治病死，五岁的光绪皇帝即位，仍由慈禧听政。慈禧太后是同治、光绪两朝实际的统治者。

Empress Dowager Cixi

Empress Dowager Cixi (1835-1908 AD) was a concubine of Emperor Xianfeng. In 1861, Emperor Xianfeng died, and six-year-old Emperor Tongzhi succeeded to the throne. As the emperor's mother, Empress Dowager Cixi sat behind a screen when the young emperor was "holding court", and wielded the actual power of the throne. In 1875, Emperor Tongzhi died of illness, to be succeeded by five-year-old Emperor Guangxu. State power remained in the hands of Cixi.

义和团运动
The Yihetuan (Boxer) Movement

　　鸦片战争以后，外国传教士凭借不平等条约给他们的特权，强占中国的大量田地、房屋、庙宇，极力扩大教会势力。每当教民与平民发生矛盾时，教会总是无视中国法律，无条件地庇护（bìhù）教民。外国教会与中国平民之间的矛盾越来越尖锐。

　　公元1898年，在民间习武组织义和拳的基础上，山东兴起了反教会、反侵略的义和团运动。义和团遭到清军的严厉镇压。1900年，山东、河北两省义和团联合起来向北京进军。由于这场爱国运动得到了人民的热烈支持，义和团队伍迅速壮大。慈禧太后害怕继续镇压会危及自己的统治，又想利用义和团来对付外国势力，就暂时承认了义和团的合法地位，义和团先后进入北京、天津城内。

　　义和团运动的发展引起了外国势力的极大恐慌。他们先是逼迫清政府镇压，后来看到清政府无法控制局面，就决定出兵。1900年6月，英、美、德、法、俄、日、意、奥八国组成联军向北京进犯。清政府向列强宣战。义和团与八国联军展开了激烈的战斗。但由于清政府抗敌决心并不坚定，而义和团又组织松散，且战斗的方式和武器都十分落后，终于失败，北京陷落。慈禧太后带着皇帝逃到西安。八国联军在北京烧杀抢掠，犯下了滔天罪行。

　　为了向列强求和，清政府出卖了义和团，宣布义和团是"拳匪"，并与外国军队勾结在一起绞杀了义和团运动。1901年，列强强迫清政府签订了卖国的《辛丑条约》。从此以后，清政府完全成为帝国主义统治中国的工具。

Following the Opium Wars, relying on the privileges given to them by the unequal treaties, foreign missionaries spread all over China. They used their considerable influence to protect their converts, often in defiance of Chinese laws.

Resentment against foreign encroachment on China, as exemplified by the activities of the missionaries, grew day by day. Finally, in 1898, a semi-mystical movement known as Yihetuan (Society of Righteousness and Harmony) arose in Shandong Province, which soon took on an anti-Christian and anti-foreign coloring. They were called "Boxers" by

Westerners, as their leaders practiced forms of martial arts. The Yihetuan clashed with the Qing army, and soon a full-scale insurrection was under way. In 1900, the Yihetuan organizations in Shandong and Hebei allied, and marched on Beijing, their numbers growing rapidly all the time. Empress Dowager Cixi, fearing to alienate the Yihetuan, and at the same time wishing to use them as a weapon against the foreign forces which were bent on dismembering China, gave her recognition to the Yihetuan as a patriotic movement.

When the foreigners realized that the Qing government either could not or would not rein in the Yihetuan, they decided to dispatch troops to quash the movement themselves. In June 1900, eight countries — Britain, the United States, Germany, France, Tsarist Russia, Japan, Italy and Austria — formed an allied army, which occupied the foreign legation quarters in Beijing. The Qing government declared war on these powers. But the occupation troops defeated the combined Qing and Yihetuan forces, and the whole of Beijing fell into the hands of the foreign allies. Empress Dowager Cixi and the emperor fled to Xi'an. The foreign troops committed buring, killing, looting and other heinous crimes in Beijing.

The Qing government then betrayed the Yihetuan, calling them "bandits", and joined the foreign forces in suppressing them. In 1901, the foreign powers forced the Qing government to sign the "Protocol of 1901". From then on, the Qing government was no more than a tool with which the imperialists enforced their will on the Chinese people.

1. 武装起来的义和团员
   Yihetuan members
2. 向北京进发的八国联军
   The Eight-Power Allied Forces marched toward Beijing

小资料 Data

庚子赔款

根据《辛丑条约》的规定，清政府要向侵略者支付战争赔款4.5亿两白银，分39年还清，本息合计9.8亿两。由于八国联军入侵北京发生在1900年，农历称为庚(gēng)子年，所以这笔巨额赔款又称"庚子赔款"。

The Indemnity for the 1900 War

According to the "Protocol of 1901", the Qing government had to pay 450 million taels (unit of weight) of silver to the invaders as war reparations over a 39-year period. The principal and interest amounted to 980 million taels altogether.

孙中山与辛亥革命
Dr. Sun Yat-sen and the Revolution of 1911

公元1866年11月12日，孙中山生于广东省香山县（今中山市）一个农民家里。孙中山小时候喜欢听洪秀全的故事，非常崇拜这位敢于反抗清政府，创立新国家的英雄。12岁时，孙中山去了夏威夷（Hawaii）。在那里学习到西方的科学文化知识。那时，孙中山最爱读的是华盛顿（George Washington）和林肯（Abraham Lincoln）的传记，进一步坚定了为国家和民族的大业而奋斗的志向。

1894年，孙中山在檀（tán）香山（Honolulu）的爱国华侨中组织了一个反清革命团体——兴中会。1905年，孙中山又在日本联合一些革命团体的成员成立了全国规模的统一革命政党——中国同盟会，立志要推翻清政府，振兴中华，建立资产阶级民主共和国。孙中山还将他的革命理想概括为"民族、民权、民生"的"三民主义"。

孙中山和革命党人秘密组织了多次武装起义，但都失败了。大批革命党人献出了宝贵的生命。1911年4月27日，广州起义爆发。起义之前，广大爱国华侨积极捐助了大量钱物，有的爱国华侨还回到广州，与国内的革命党人一起组成"敢死队"，参加起义。起义失败后，有72位烈士的遗体被合葬在广州黄花岗，他们的精神激励着国内外爱国志士继续奋斗。

1911年10月10日，长期在军队中开展革命活动的湖北革命团体文学社和共进会联合发动了武昌起义，取得成功。武昌起义的胜利掀起了革命的高潮，各省纷纷响应。一个多月当中，共有10多个省宣布独立，清王朝的统治迅速崩溃。1911年是中国农历辛亥年，历史上把这场推翻清政府的革命叫辛亥革命。

1911年12月，孙中山回国。由于他对革命事业作出的巨大贡献和他在革命党人当中的崇高威望，孙中山被推选为临时大总统。1912年1月1日，孙中山在南京宣誓就职，中华民国临时政府成立。

中华民国成立不久，袁世凯在帝国主义的支持下，逼走孙中山，窃取了临时大总统的职位，政权落入腐败的北洋军阀的手中。为了对抗北洋军阀的统治，1912年8月，以中国同盟会为主的6个政团在北京合并，成立了中国国民党。孙中山被选为理事长。

Sun Yat-sen was born into a farmer's family in Xiangshan County (now Zhongshan City), Guangdong Province, on November 12, 1866. In his childhood he heard stories about the Taiping Heavenly Kingdom, and developed an admiration for the Taiping leader Hong Xiuquan. At the age of 12, he went to Hawaii, where he studied Western science and culture. He read biographies of George Washington and Abraham Lincoln, which planted in him a resolve to strive to do something for his country and people.

In 1894, Sun Yat-sen organized an anti-Qing revolutionary organization, the Society for the Revival of China (Xingzhonghui), among patriotic Chinese

1. 广州黄花岗72烈士陵园
   The tomb of the 72 martyrs in Huanghuagang, Guangzhou
2. 武昌起义军政府旧址
   The site of the Wuchang Uprising government
3. 推翻满清统治的孙中山先生
   Mr. Sun Yat-sen organized a revolution that overthrew the Qing Dynasty.
4. 1912年1月1日，孙中山在南京宣誓就职时的誓词
   The oath Sun Yat-sen took when establishing the interim government of the Republic of China in Nanjing, Jan 1, 1912

1

2

 小资料 Data

秋瑾 (jǐn)

浙江省绍兴人，是中国近代史上最著名的女英雄。她在日本留学时参加了革命党。秋瑾喜欢身着男装，骑马练剑，被人称为"鉴(jiàn)湖女侠"。公元1907年，秋瑾在浙江准备发动起义，不幸被捕，英勇牺牲。

Qiu Jin

Qiu Jin was born in Shaoxing, Zhejiang Province. She is the most famous heroine in modern Chinese history. She joined the China Revolutionary League when she was studying in Japan. Qiu Jin liked to wear men's clothes and practiced horsemanship and fencing. In 1907, she was arrested and executed for preparing an uprising in Zhejiang.

1. 江苏南京临时大总统孙中山办公室
   The office of the interim President Sun Yat-sen, Nanjing, Jiangsu Province
2. 秋瑾塑像
   A statue of Qiu Jin

in Honolulu. In 1905, he set up a nationwide united revolutionary party — the China Revolutionary League (Zhongguo Tongmenghui) by allying some revolutionary group members in Japan. He was determined to put an end to the Qing Dynasty, rejuvenate China and establish a bourgeois democratic republic. He generalized his revolutionary ideas into the "Three People's Principles", viz., the Principle of Nationalism, the Principle of Democracy and the Principle of the People's Livelihood.

Sun Yat-sen and other revolutionaries secretly organized many armed uprisings, but all of them failed, with the sacrifice of the lives of many revolutionaries. On April 27, 1911, an uprising broke out in Guangzhou, supported financially and in person by patriotic overseas Chinese and revolutionaries in China. After the uprising was crushed, the remains of 72 martyrs were buried together in Huanghuagang in Guangzhou. Their spirit impelled patriots at home and abroad to go on fighting.

On October 10, 1911, the Hubei revolutionary organizations known as the Literary Association (Wenxueshe) and Society for Mutual Progress (Gongjinhui), which had been developing revolutionary activities in the army, started the Wuchang Uprising, which triggered nationwide revolts against the dynasty. Within one month, a dozen provinces had declared their independence from the Qing government. The year 1911 was the year Xinhai by the Chinese lunar calendar, so this revolution which overthrew the Qing Dynasty is also called the "Xinhai Revolution".

In December 1911, Sun Yat-sen returned to China. Because of the enormous contributions he had made to the revolution and his prestige among the revolutionaries, he was elected interim president of the Republic of China. On January 1,1912, he took the oath of office in Nanjing, and the interim government of the Republic of China was founded.

Not long after the foundation of the Republic of China, Yuan Shikai managed to elbow Sun Yat-sen aside, and get himself elected president, with the support of the imperialist powers. Political power then fell into the hands of the Northern Warlords. As a counter to warlord rule, the Kuomintang was founded in Beijing in August 1912 by the China Revolutionary League together with five other political parties. Sun Yat-sen was elected chairman of the new party.

五四运动
The May 4 Movement

1918年，第一次世界大战结束，德国战败。1919年，英、法、美等国在巴黎召开"巴黎和会"，中国作为战胜国之一也参加了。会上，中国代表团提出从德国手中收回山东的主权，但是这个合理的要求被拒绝了，列强决定把德国在山东的特权转交给日本，强迫中国代表签字。

消息传来，全国人民万分悲愤。1919年5月4日，北京大学等10几所北京的大专院校的学生们在天安门集会，喊着"还我青岛"、"打倒卖国贼"等口号抗议示威。愤怒的学生还冲进卖国贼曹汝霖 (lín) 的家，痛打了正在曹家的驻日公使章宗祥，并放火烧了曹宅。北洋政府派军警镇压，抓走了30多名学生。

第二天，北京大学生开始罢课，他们走上街头进行爱国讲演和宣传。山东、天津、上海等地的学生也纷纷起来声援。反动的北洋政府逮捕了近千名学生，激起了全国人民更大的愤怒。6月，上海工人首先罢工支援学生的爱国行为。接着，学生罢课、工人罢工、商人罢市的运动在全国展开。同时，在巴黎参加和会的中国代表团收到几千份全国各界群众要求他们拒签和约的通电。6月28日，旅居法国的华侨和留学生还包围了中国代表团的住所，不让他们在卖国条约上签字。在巨大的压力面前，北洋政府只好释放了爱国学生，撤了卖国贼曹汝霖、章宗祥、陆宗舆 (yú) 的官职，中国代表团也拒绝在条约上签字，"五四运动"取得了胜利。

"五四运动"的意义不仅仅在外交方面。在运动发生前的几年中，具有民主与科学精神的新思想、新文化在以北京大学为中心的知识界迅速传播。"五四"以后，新的政治力量开始萌芽，中国社会进入了一个新的阶段。

北京大学

北京大学的前身是京师大学堂，创办于1898年，是中国近代最早由国家创办的大学。它是戊戌变法的"新政"措施之一。

Peking University

Peking University grew out of the Metropolitan University, which was founded in 1898 and was the first national university to be set up in modern China. It was an outcome of the Reform Movement of 1898.

1. 北京天安门人民英雄纪念碑"五四运动"浮雕
   A relief sculpture featuring the May 4 movement on the Monument to the People's Heroes in Tiananmen Square, Beijing

![Data icon] 小资料 Data

新文化运动

1915年，陈独秀创办《青年杂志》，在发刊词《敬告青年》中，鲜明地提出"人权，平等，自由"的思想，由此发起了新文化运动。《青年杂志》从第二期起改名为《新青年》。《新青年》集结了当时中国先进的知识分子，他们提倡民主与科学的精神，大力抨击中国的封建专制思想，展开了轰轰烈烈的思想启蒙运动。除了陈独秀以外，新文化运动的代表人物还有李大钊、胡适、蔡元培、鲁迅等。

The New Culture Movement

In 1915, Chen Duxiu started *Youth Magazine*. In its foreword, titled, "To Youth", he clearly advanced the thought of "human rights, equality and freedom", which inspired the New Culture Movement. *Youth Magazine* changed its name to *New Youth* from the second issue. *New Youth* attracted progressive intellectuals who advocated the spirit of democracy and science, fiercely attacked Chinese feudal autocratic thought and developed a vigorous enlightenment movement. Besides Chen Duxiu, the representatives of the New Culture Movement included Li Dazhao, Hu Shi, Cai Yuanpei and Lu Xun.

1. 鲁迅像
   A portrait of Lu Xun
2. 北京大学校门匾
   The signboard of Peking University
3. "五四运动"时学生使用的标语和纪念章
   Badges bearing slogans worn by students during the May 4 Movement

In 1918, the First World War ended, with the defeat of Germany. In 1919, Britain, France, the United States and other victor countries held Paris Peace Conference. As one of the victor countries China also attended the conference. At the conference, the imperialist powers handed the parts of Shandong Province which had previously been seized by Germany over to Japan. This caused explosions of outrage in China, and on May 4, 1919, students of Peking University and other institutions of higher learning gathered in Tiananmen Square to protest. In the unrest that followed, officials considered subservient to the imperialist powers were attacked, and dozens of students were arrested. The protests spread to other cities around China. The reactionary Northern Warlord government arrested nearly 1,000 students. In June, workers in Shanghai went on strike to support the students' patriotic demands, to be followed in other cities by students suspending classes, workers downing tools and merchants closing shops. Meanwhile, the Chinese delegation to the Paris Peace Conference received thousands of telegrams sent by people of all walks of life in China asking them not to sign the treaty. On June 28, overseas Chinese residents and students in France surrounded the residence of the Chinese delegation, to stop them signing the treaty. Confronted with huge pressure, the Northern Warlord government had to release the arrested students and remove the pro-treaty ministers Cao Rulin, Zhang Zongxiang and Lu Zongyu from office. Finally, the Chinese delegation refused to sign the treaty.

However, the significance of the May 4 Movement lay not only in this diplomatic victory. Several years before the movement, a new ideology and new culture full of a democratic and scientific spirit had been spreading rapidly in intellectual circles, with Peking University as the center. Following the May 4 Movement, a new political force began to sprout, and China's history entered a new phase.

中国共产党的成立
The Founding of the Communist Party of China

1917年，俄国发生了十月革命，建立了世界上第一个社会主义国家。当时，中国知识界正在开展新文化运动，一方面要打倒封建旧思想，一方面放眼全世界，希望从别国的发展变革中寻找适合中国的救国道路。因此，十月革命的胜利和社会主义思想引起了中国先进知识分子的关注。

1919年，工人阶级积极参加五四爱国运动，并对斗争取得最后的胜利起到了重要作用，这使全社会看到了劳动人民的力量。运动结束后，广大知识分子展开了关于如何改造中国的大讨论。许多先进的知识分子主张以马克思主义为指导，依靠无产阶级，通过革命的方式来打倒旧制度，建立新社会。全国各地以及海外留学生中间出现了很多研究、宣传马克思主义的报刊和组织。一批满怀爱国热情的马克思主义者涌现出来，他们当中最突出的有北京大学教授李大钊（zhāo）、陈独秀、湖南《湘江评论》主编毛泽东、天津南开大学学生领袖周恩来等等。

1921年7月23日，来自全国的十

1. 中国共产党第一次全国代表大会从上海移至浙江嘉兴南湖一船上举行。图为南湖烟雨楼
   Chinese Communist party's first general conference adjourned from Shanghai to a pleasure-boat on Nanhu Lake, Jiaxing, Zhejiang Province. This photo shows the Yanyulou mansion of the Nanhu Lake.
2. 上海中共"一大"会址
   The site of the First National Congress of the CPC in Shanghai

李大钊（1889—1927年）

李大钊，字守常，北京大学经济系教授和图书馆主任，《新青年》杂志编辑，中国最早的马克思主义者，中国共产党的创始人之一。1920年在北京组织共产党的早期组织。中国共产党成立后，他负责北方区党的工作。第一次国共合作期间，在帮助孙中山确定联俄、联共、扶助农工三大政策和改组国民党的工作中，起了重要作用。1927年4月6日被军阀张作霖逮捕，28日在北京英勇就义。

Li Dazhao

Li Dazhao was a professor in the Department of Economics and curator of the library at Peking University. As an editor of the magazine *New Youth*, he was one of the first Marxists in China, and one of the founders of the CPC. He was responsible for Party work in northern China. He played an important role in helping Dr. Sun Yat-sen establish the three cardinal policies of allying with Russia, uniting with the CPC and assisting peasants and workers, and the work of reorganizing the Kuomintang during the first round of cooperation between the two parties. On April 6, 1927, he was arrested by warlord Zhang Zuolin, and was executed in Beijing on April 28.

1. 参加中国共产党成立大会时的毛泽东
   Mao Zedong as he looked when he attended the founding conference of the CPC.

多位代表在上海秘密召开成立中国共产党的会议。会议进行到30日时，会场受到了警察的搜查和密探的注意。为了安全，代表们赶紧离开上海，到嘉兴南湖的一条游船上继续开会。这次会议后，在中国社会的政治舞台上，出现了一支崭新的力量——中国共产党，它给灾难深重的中国人民带来了光明和希望。

In 1917, the October Revolution took place in Russia, and the first socialist state in the world was established. At that time, the New Culture Movement was in the ascendant among Chinese intellectuals. The movement on the one hand aimed to destroy the old feudal ways of thinking, and on the other sought a modern, all-embracing world view. The victory of the October Revolution and socialist thought attracted the attention of progressive Chinese intellectuals.

In 1919, the working class actively took part in the patriotic May 4 Movement, which caused many intellectuals to advocate breaking away from the old system and building a new society relying on the proletariat to bring about a revolution under the guidance of Marxism. Chinese students both at home and abroad founded newspapers, periodicals and organizations to study and publicize Marxism. A group of patriotic Marxists emerged, among whom the most outstanding were Peking University professors Li Dazhao and Chen Duxiu, chief editor of Hunan's *Xiangjiang Review* Mao Zedong, and student leader of Tianjin's Nankai University Zhou Enlai.

On July 23, 1921, a dozen representatives of Marxist groups from around the country held a secret conference in Shanghai to found the Communist Party. Fearing arrest by the secret police, the conference adjourned to a pleasure-boat on Nanhu Lake in nearby Jiaxing. Following this conference, the Communist Party of China (CPC) — a brand-new force — became active on China's political stage, bringing hope to the suffering Chinese people.

黄埔军校
The Whampoa Military Academy

1. 广州黄埔军校旧址
   The site of the Whampoa Military Academy, Guangzhou

20世纪20年代初，为了推翻北洋军阀和帝国主义在中国的统治，中国共产党与孙中山领导的国民党合作。1924年1月，中国国民党第一次全国代表大会在广州召开，李大钊、毛泽东等共产党员也参加了会议，第一次国共合作正式形成。

国共合作实现后，为了培养军事人才，建立革命武装力量，孙中山在苏联和中国共产党的帮助下，在广州创办了陆军军官学校——黄埔军校。

黄埔军校的校长由蒋介石担任，周恩来等许多共产党人在军校中担任了重要的职务。学员入学后主要学习军事和政治两类课程。注重政治教育，培养学生的爱国思想和革命精神，是黄埔军校与所有旧式军校根本不同的地方。在军事教育方面，军校主要采用当时苏联最新的军事理论和技术进行分学科的训练。

从1924年到1927年，黄埔军校培养了6期共12,000多名毕业生，其中涌现了一批优秀的军事和政治人才，许多人成为国共两党的高级将领。黄埔军校为中国革命作出了巨大贡献。

In the early 1920s, in order to overthrow the rule of the Northern Warlords and the imperialists, the CPC and the Kuomintang (KMT) led by Sun Yat-sen agreed to cooperate. In January 1924, the first national congress of the KMT was held in Guangzhou. Some CPC members, such as Li Dazhao and Mao

小资料 Data

省港大罢工

在国共合作的形势下，中国南方掀起了革命的高潮。1925年6月，广州、香港工人举行反对英帝国主义的大罢工。这次罢工规模大、时间长。香港有25万工人参加了罢工，罢工坚持了16个月。

The Guangzhou-Hong Kong Strike

Revolutionary fervor increased in southern China under the influence of the cooperation between the CPC and KMT. In June 1925, workers in Guangzhou and Hong Kong went on strike to protest British imperialism. In Hong Kong alone, 250,000 workers participated in the strike, which lasted 16 months.

1. 任黄埔军校政治部主任的周恩来
   Zhou Enlai, director of the Political Department of the Whampoa Military Academy
2. 孙中山(中)主持黄埔军校开学典礼(前排右四为蒋介石)
   Sun Yat-sen (center) presided at the opening ceremony of the Whampoa Military Academy (Chiang Kai-shek stood fourth from right, front row)

Zedong, also attended the conference, which marked the debut of the first period of cooperation between the two parties.

With the help of the Soviet Union and the CPC, Sun Yat-sen set up an academy for army officers — the Whampoa Military Academy — in Guangzhou, which trained members of both the CPC and KMT as the spearhead of the new revolutionary forces.

Chiang Kai-shek was appointed president of the Whampoa Military Academy, and many CPC members, including Zhou Enlai, held important posts in the academy. Both military and political courses were taught. Whampoa differed from the old-style military academies in that it stressed political education and cultivated the students' patriotism and revolutionary spirit. As for military education, it adopted the latest military theories and techniques from the Soviet Union.

From 1924 to 1927, the Whampoa Military Academy trained in six terms over 12,000 students, from among whom there emerged prominent military and political personnel in large numbers. Many of them later became senior officers of the two parties. The academy made brilliant contributions to China's revolution.

北伐战争
The Northern Expedition

1. 有"铁军"之称的第四军叶挺独立团
The Fourth Corps, an Independent Regime, won the title "iron army".

1924年国共合作实现后，国共两党以广州为革命基地，准备进行北伐。北伐的目的就是要推翻军阀的黑暗统治，打破帝国主义国家对中国的政治军事控制，使人民摆脱苦难。

1925年，国民党在广州成立广东国民政府。1926年国民政府正式决定北伐。为了全力支持北伐，中国共产党深入工人农民当中，积极进行宣传和组织工作，为北伐战争打下了广泛而坚实的群众基础。

1926年7月，国共合作的广东革命军开始北伐。北伐军先攻占了湖南的省会长沙，接着直逼武汉。敌人在武汉外围选择地势极其险要的地方派重兵防守。北伐军浴血奋战，特别是叶挺领导的，以共产党员为主力的第四军独立团冲锋在前，英勇无比，为第四军赢得了"铁军"的称号。北伐军突破防线，渡过长江，占领武汉。1927年3月中旬，周恩来率领上海工人武装起义，使北伐军顺利进驻上海。3月下旬北伐军攻占南京。

国共合作的北伐战争得到了全国人民的热烈拥护和支持。在不到一年的时间里，北伐军就占领了长江以南的大部分地区，沉重地打击了反动军阀，使国民革命的火焰燃遍了半个中国。

In their cooperation the two parties (CPC and KMT) made Guangzhou their revolutionary base, and prepared for the Northern Expedition, which would sweep away the rule of the warlords and break the military and political control of imperialist countries over China.

In 1925, The KMT formed the Guangdong National Government in Guangzhou. In 1926, the National Government decided to launch the Northern Expedition. In order to drum up support for the Northern Expedition, the CPC went deep among the workers and peasants doing publicity and organization work, which established a broad and firm mass base for the Northern Expedition.

![icon] 小资料 **Data**

孙中山逝世

1925年3月12日，孙中山先生在北京病逝。北伐胜利后，国民政府按照孙中山先生生前的愿望，将其遗体从北京运到南京。1929年安葬于中山陵。

The Passing away of Dr. Sun Yat-sen

On March 12, 1925, Dr. Sun Yat-sen died of illness in Beijing. After the victory of the Northern Expedition, the National Government moved his remains from Beijing to Nanjing according to his will. In 1929, his remains were buried in the Sun Yat-sen Mausoleum.

In July 1926, the Northern Expeditionary Army, including the Independent Regiment of the Fourth Corps, which was composed mainly of Communists and commanded by Ye Ting, set off on its northward march. The Northern Expeditionary Army first captured Changsha, the capital of Hunan Province, and then pressed on toward Wuhan, which was heavily fortified. The Independent Regiment, in particular, fought courageously, and won for the Fourth Corps the title of "iron army". The Northern Expeditionary Army broke through the Northern Warlords' line of defense, crossed the Yangtze and occupied Wuhan. In the middle of March 1927, Zhou Enlai led the workers of Shanghai in staging an armed uprising, ensuring the smooth entry of the Northern Expeditionary Army into Shanghai. At the end of March, the Northern Expeditionary Army occupied Nanjing.

The Northern Expedition was warmly welcomed and supported by people all over China. In less than a year, it had occupied most of the area south of the Yangtze, which struck a heavy blow at the reactionary warlords and kindled the flame of revolution over half of China.

1. 南京中山陵
   Sun Yat-sen Mausoleum, Nanjing

南昌起义
The Nanchang Uprising

1. 南昌起义浮雕
   A relief sculpture depicting the Nanchang Uprising

北伐战争的胜利打击了军阀和帝国主义在中国的统治，但是，随着形势的发展，国民党右派敌视共产党、破坏国共合作的面目也日益暴露出来。1927年4月12日，蒋介石在上海发动反革命政变，杀害了300多名共产党员和革命群众，另外还有500多人被捕，数千人失踪。接着，广东、江苏、浙江、湖南等省都发生了屠杀共产党人的惨案。蒋介石叛变革命以后，在南京建立了国民政府。7月15日，以汪精卫为首的武汉国民政府也背叛了革命，大规模逮捕杀害共产党人。至此，第一次国共合作彻底破裂，中国出现了白色恐怖的局面。

面对危急的形势，共产党人为了挽救革命进行了英勇顽强的斗争。1927年8月1日，周恩来、贺龙、叶挺、朱德、刘伯承等领导了南昌起义。经过4个多小时的激战，起义军打败了国民政府军队，占领了南昌城。

南昌起义引起了国民政府的恐慌，蒋介石调动军队进攻南昌，起义军撤离南昌，向广东进军，准备重建广东革命根据地。这一计划由于受到敌人的围攻而失败。

南昌起义打响了武装反抗国民党反动派的第一枪，中国共产党

从此创建了自己的军队，开始走上独立领导革命、武装夺取政权的新道路。

The victory of the Northern Expedition greatly weakened the power of the warlords and imperialists in China. But as time went on, the Right wing of the KMT began to sabotage the cooperation with the CPC. On April 12, 1927, Chiang Kai-shek staged a reactionary coup d'etat in Shanghai, killing over 300 CPC members and other revolutionaries, and arresting over 500. In addition, thousands went missing. The purge spread to Guangdong, Jiangsu, Zhejiang, and Hunan provinces, where CPC members were slaughtered. After he betrayed the revolution, Chiang set up his National Government in Nanjing. On July 15, the National Government in Wuhan, led by Wang Jingwei, also betrayed the revolution, arresting and killing CPC members en masse. By this time, the cooperation between the two parties had completely dissolved, and a period of White terror commenced in China.

At this critical moment, the Communists rose in a brave struggle to save the revolution. On August 1, 1927, Zhou Enlai, He Long, Ye Ting, Zhu De, Liu Bocheng and others seized the city of Nanchang.

The Nanchang Uprising alarmed the National Government. Chiang dispatched an army which retook Nanchang. The insurgents then marched toward Guangdong, planning to rebuild the Guangdong revolutionary base.

The Nanchang Uprising marked the first shot of the CPC's armed struggle against the KMT reactionaries. From then on, the CPC built its own army to lead the revolution independently and seize state power by armed force.

1. 周恩来等人领导的南昌起义
   The Nanchang Uprising led by Zhou Enlai

二万五千里长征
The Long March

南昌起义后，毛泽东也领导了武装起义，并在江西的井冈山建立了第一块革命根据地。此后，共产党领导的革命根据地广泛建立，并得到农民的热烈支持和拥护，根据地不断扩大。

1930年到1932年，国民政府调集重兵，发动了四次大规模的"围剿"(jiǎo)，企图破坏根据地，消灭共产党。共产党领导的红军在根据地人民的支持下，一次又一次地粉碎了敌人的"围剿"。

1933年，蒋介石调集了100万军队开始第五次"围剿"。由于当时共产党中央领导人在斗争中犯了严重的错误，使红军第五次反"围剿"失败。1934年10月，红军被迫从福建、江西的中央根据地撤退，向西突围，开始著名的万里长征。

长征初期，红军人员损失大半。在这种危急的形势下，共产党中央于1935年1月在贵州省的遵义召开会议，及时纠正了错误，确立了毛泽东在党和红军中的领导地位。遵义会议在最危急的关头，挽救了红军，挽救了共产党，挽救了中国革命。

长征路线图
Sketch Map of the Long March

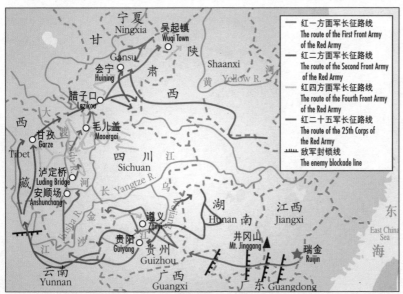

遵义会议以后，红军采取了正确的战略，变被动为主动，打了很多胜仗：四渡赤水、强渡大渡河、飞夺泸定桥……打破了国民政府军队的围追堵截。长征的道路十分艰难，红军爬雪山、过草地，没有粮食时就挖野菜，啃树皮，克服了今天人们难以想像的困难。1935年10月中央红军到达陕北吴起镇，与刘志丹领导

177

1. 遵义会议会址 (贵州省遵义市)
   The site of Zunyi Conference, Zunyi City, Guizhou Province
2. 四川大渡河上的泸定桥
   Luding Bridge over Dadu River, Sichuan Province
3. 四川若尔盖——红军通过的若尔盖水草地，到处是发黑的死水潭，很多地方人一踩就会陷下去，再也挣脱不出来
   The Red Army had to cross the treacherous marshy grassland in Ruoerga, Sichuan Province. There were many lives lost in the swamps.

的陕北红军胜利会师。1936年10月，红军三大主力在会宁等地会师，二万五千里长征胜利结束。

Soon after the Nanchang Uprising, Mao Zedong also led an armed uprising, and established the first revolutionary base area. He chose the Jinggang Mountains in Jiangxi Province for the base, which was followed by several others set up in other parts of China.

From 1930 to 1932, the National Government launched four large-scale campaigns of "encirclement and suppression", attempting to destroy the revolutionary base areas and eliminate the CPC. But with the support of the people in the base areas, the Red Army, directed by the CPC, repulsed the enemy time and again.

In 1933, Chiang Kai-shek assembled a force of one million men, and launched an "encirclement and suppression" campaign for the fifth time. Because of grave mistakes made by leaders of the Central Committee of the CPC, in October 1934 the Red Army was forced to retreat from its central base areas in Fujian and Jiangxi provinces. It broke through the encirclement to the west, and began the famous Long March.

In the early period of the Long March, the Red Army lost more than half of its members. Facing this critical situation, the Central Committee of the CPC convened the Zunyi Conference in Zunyi, Guizhou Province, in January

1935. This conference established Mao Zedong's leadership of the Party and the Red Army. At a particularly perilous moment, the Zunyi Conference saved the Red Army, the CPC and the Chinese revolution.

After the Zunyi Conference, the Red Army adopted correct strategies, took the initiative in its hands and won many battles. Famous episodes at this time included crossing the Chishui River four times, forcing a way across the Dadu River and capturing the Luding Bridge. The Long March was an arduous trek. The Red Army had to cross snow-covered mountains and uninhabited grassland. When there was no food, the Red Army soldiers ate tree barks and wild herbs. In October 1935, the central column of the Red Army reached Wuqi Town in northern Shaanxi Province and joined up with the Red Army column of northern Shaanxi led by Liu Zhidan. In October 1936, the three major columns of the Red Army converged at Huining and other places, which marked the end of the Long March.

九一八事变
The September 18 Incident

在20世纪30年代，中国到处传唱着一首歌："九一八，九一八，从那个悲惨的时候，脱离了我的家乡……"那么，"九一八"到底是一个什么日子呢？

从19世纪后期开始，日本多次发动侵华战争，并且武装占领了台湾。但是，日本对这一切并不满足。20世纪日本准备大规模向国外军事扩张，中国是其主要目标。为了先侵吞中国的东北三省，日本制造了"九一八事变"。

1931年9月18日晚上，沈阳附近的日军在一个叫柳条湖的地方炸毁了一段铁路，反而说是中国军队破坏铁路，想袭击日本军队，随即向东北军大营和沈阳城发起了突然进攻。东北军伤亡很大。一夜之间，日军就占领了沈阳。

"九一八事变"发生时，国民政府正忙于"剿共"，即消灭共产党。蒋介石一再命令东北军指挥官张学良不许抵抗日本的侵略，说如果抵抗会把事情闹大，还说现在不是对日作战的时候，共产党才是最大的敌人。由于中国军队不抵抗，日军仅用了四个多月的时间就轻而易举地占领了东北三省，3,000万同胞沦为亡国奴。

为了稳固统治，日本侵略者在东北三省成立所谓"满洲国"，让早已退位的清朝末代皇帝溥仪来当傀儡 (kuílěi) 皇帝，实际上，权力完全控制在日本人手中。日本的侵略和统治激起了当地人民的激烈反抗，抗日义勇军在十分艰苦危险的环境中与日本人展开了英勇的斗争。

1. 溥仪当了"伪满洲国"的傀儡皇帝
   Puyi was the puppet emperor of the state (Manchukuo) established by Japanese invaders.
2. "九一八"纪念碑 (辽宁沈阳)
   The Memorial Tablet of the September 18 Incident, Shenyang, Liaoning Province
3. 伪满洲国皇帝溥仪 (左五) 与日军司令官 (左四) 等人合影
   Puyi (fifth from left, front row), emperor of the puppet state of Manchukuo, and the Japanese army commander in northeast China (on Puyi's right)
4. 日军侵入沈阳城内架枪准备射击
   Japanese troops invaded Shenyang

In the 1930s, a song became popular all over China. Its lyrics went: "September 18, September 18. That tragic day I

was forced to leave my hometown...." What happened on September 18?

Japan had harbored designs on Chinese territory since the late 19th century. It had unleashed wars of aggression against China, and seized Taiwan. Following the First World War, Japan made preparations for a large-scale invasion of China's mainland. Its first target was the three northeastern provinces.

On the evening of September 18, 1931, Japanese troops stationed in Liaoning Province blew up part of a railway line at Liutiaohu, near Shenyang, capital of the province, and blamed the Chinese army for it. The Japanese then attacked the barracks of the Northeast Army and Shenyang.

At this time, the National Government was busy trying to eliminate the CPC. Chiang Kai-shek ordered Zhang Xueliang, commander of the Northeast Army, not to resist the Japanese, claiming that the CPC was the government's greatest enemy. Because of this weak-kneed policy, the Japanese army easily occupied the three provinces of northeast China, with a population of 30 million, in the space of only four months.

In order to consolidate their rule over northeast China, the Japanese invaders established a puppet state called Manchukuo, with Puyi, the abdicated last emperor of the Qing Dynasty, as its titular ruler. This aroused great indignation among the local people, who formed volunteer units to fight against the invaders.

小资料 Data

末代皇帝

溥仪（pǔyí）（公元1906年—1967年），满族，姓爱新觉罗。1908年光绪皇帝死后，不满三岁的溥仪登上皇位，年号宣统。1912年，中华民国成立，不久后，溥仪退位，清朝灭亡。溥仪是中国二千多年封建社会里的最后一个皇帝。

The Last Emperor of China

Aisin-Gioro Puyi (1906-1967 AD) was of the Manchu ethnic group. In 1908, after the death of Emperor Guangxu, Puyi, who was only two years old at that time, came to the throne with the reign title Xuantong. In 1912, the Republic of China was founded. Soon after, Puyi abdicated, and the Qing Dynasty came to an end. Puyi was the last emperor of China's 2,000-year-old feudal society.

西安事变
The Xi'an Incident

1

日本占领中国东北三省后，又不断制造事端，准备侵略华北，形势十分危急。全国人民要求政府停止内战，抵抗日本侵略。但蒋介石却顽固地坚持先消灭共产党，再抵抗日本侵略者的政策。

1936年，蒋介石到西安逼迫张学良和杨虎城两位将军继续"剿共"。已经丢失了自己的故乡东北三省的张学良一再表示要去抗日，甚至哭着请求蒋介石不要再打内战了，救国要紧。可是他不但没能感动蒋介石，反而受到严厉训斥。张学良、杨虎城看到劝说无效，只好另想办法，逼蒋抗日。

12月9日，西安的大学生举行游行集会，他们步行前往蒋介石的住地，要求停止"剿共"，一致抗日。蒋介石大怒，命令张学良派兵把学生挡回去，如果学生不听，就开枪。张学良非常同情学生，他赶到学生们那儿，极力劝他们先回去，并且说用自己的生命作保证，实现大家的爱国愿望。当天晚上，张学良向蒋介石反映学生们的要求，并再一次恳求抗日救国，但仍然遭到拒绝。

12月12日夜里，张学良、杨虎城发动兵变，抓住了蒋介石。西安事变发生后，应张学良、杨虎城的邀请，共产党派周恩来到西安，商讨解决问题的办法。经过各方面的努力，终于迫使蒋介石答应停止内战，一致抗日，西安事变和平解决了。

After occupying the three provinces in northeast China, the Japanese army indulged in a series of provocations designed to give itself an excuse to penetrate deeper into China. People throughout China demanded that the

National Government stop the civil war and switch to resisting the Japanese army. But Chiang Kai-shek stubbornly persisted in his policy of eliminating the CPC first before making a stand against the Japanese.

In 1936, Chiang went to Xi'an to press generals Zhang Xueliang and Yang Hucheng to pursue the operations against the Communists more vigorously. Zhang Xueliang, who was from the Northeast, pleaded with Chiang to stop the civil war, otherwise, he said, the country would be lost. When all attempts at persuasion turned out to be in vain, Zhang and Yang decided to force Chiang to resist the Japanese.

On December 9, students in Xi'an held a demonstration, demanding that Chiang halt the civil war and turn his guns on the Japanese. Zhang Xueliang and Yang Hucheng sympathized with the students, and early on the evening of December 12, the two generals arrested Chiang. They then invited the CPC to send Zhou Enlai to Xi'an to discuss how to solve the

problem. Under pressure from all sides, Chiang Kai-shek finally agreed to stop the civil war and cooperate with the CPC to resist the Japanese invaders. Thus, the Xi'an Incident was solved peacefully.

小资料 Data

"千古功臣"

西安事变和平解决后，为了表示自己的忠诚，张学良亲自陪蒋介石回南京，从此被软禁，失去了人身自由。杨虎城后来被蒋秘密杀害。这两位将军在民族危急关头为抗日事业作出了巨大的贡献，周恩来后来称赞他们是"千古功臣"。

"Heroes of All Time"

After the Xi'an Incident had come to a peaceful conclusion, Chiang Kai-shek had Zhang Xueliang put under house arrest, and Zhang lost his freedom for decades since then. Yang Hucheng was murdered later, upon Chiang's order. These two generals, who had made a great contribution to the cause of resisting Japan at a moment when the nation was in great danger, were praised by Zhou Enlai as "Heroes of All Time".

1. 西安事变前夕的张学良（左）、杨虎城
   Zhang Xueliang (left) and Yang Hucheng on the eve of the Xi'an Incident
2. "西安事变"前，蒋介石在华清池的办公室
   Shortly prior to Xi'an Incident, Chiang Kai-shek was at his office near the Huaqingchi Pond, Lintong, Xi'an.
3. "西安事变"发生在临潼华清池。当年蒋介石听到枪声，马上逃跑到背后的骊山上，但在半山被士兵捉获
   The Xi'an Incident took place at the Huaqingchi Pond, Lintong. As soon as Chiang Kai-shek heard the gun shot, he immediately fled to the Lishan Mountain behind the pond, but was caught halfway by soldiers.
4. 西安事变和平解决时蒋介石（左一）、杨虎城（左二）、张学良（右一）等人合影
   Chiang Kai-shek (first left), Yang Hucheng (second left) and Zhang Xueliang (first right) after the peaceful conclusion of the Xi'an Incident

七七事变
The July 7 Incident

芦沟桥

芦沟桥位于北京的西南郊，建于1192年，长265米，宽8米，由11孔石拱组成。桥旁建有石栏，上面有485个精雕细刻的石狮。"芦沟晓月"曾是北京著名的风景点。

Lugouqiao Bridge

Lugouqiao Bridge is located in the southwest of Beijing. It was built in 1192. It is 265 m long and eight meters wide, and is composed of 11 stone arches. On both sides of the bridge there are stone balustrades, on which there are 485 exquisitely carved stone lions. The "Morning Moon over Lugouqiao Bridge" used to be one of old Beijing's famous sights.

为了实现侵占全中国的企图，日本发动了"七七事变"。1937年7月7日晚上，驻扎在北平（今北京）郊区芦沟桥一带的日本军队举行军事演习。演习结束后，日军藉口有一个士兵失踪了，又说好像听到宛平城内（芦沟桥附近）有枪声，要强行进入宛平县城搜查，遭到中国守军的拒绝。日军随即炮轰芦沟桥，向宛平城发起进攻。中国军队奋起还击，驻守芦沟桥的100多名士兵战斗到只剩下4人，其余全部牺牲，终于打退了敌人的进攻。由于这次事件发生在芦沟桥，所以又叫"芦沟桥事变"。

"七七事变"后，面对危急的形势，中国共产党发出通电，指出"平津危急！华北危急！中华民族危急！"呼吁"只有全民族实行抗战，才是我们的出路！"全国各界群众、爱国党派和团体、海外华侨也纷纷举行集会，强烈要求政府抗战。不少大城市相继组织了"抗敌后援会"，募捐了大量钱物，送往抗日前线，支援和慰劳驻守华北、积极抗日的中国军队。

在严峻的形势和全国人民高昂的抗日热情面前，蒋介石发表谈话，表示准备抗战的决心。国共两党经过谈判，决定将共产党领导的主力红军改编为国民革命军第八路军，开赴华北抗日前线。另一部分红军被改编为新四军。9月，国共合作宣言发表，全国抗日民族统一战线正式形成。

On the night of July 7, 1937, Japanese troops stationed in the Lugouqiao area in the suburbs of Beiping (today's Beijing) held a military exercise. Claiming to have heard gunshots in the nearby town of Wanping and that one of their men was missing, the Japanese launched an attack on Wanping and bombarded Lugouqiao. The 100-strong Chinese unit stationed in the Lugouqiao area fought back bravely and repulsed the enemy attack, but only four soldiers survived the battle. The July 7 Incident is also called the Lugouqiao Incident.

The July 7 Incident made Japan's intention to conquer the whole of China clear to the the world. The CPC issued an open telegram calling upon the whole nation to fight against the Japanese aggressors. People from all walks of life, all the patriotic parties and groups, and overseas Chinese assembled, and demanded that the government mount all-out resistance. Aid associations were organized in many big cities to collect money for the war effort.

The CPC and the KMT agreed to reorganize the main force of the Communist-led Red Army into the Eighth Route Army of the National Revolutionary Army, to be dispatched to the north China front to fight against the Japanese. Another part of the Red Army was reorganized into the New Fourth Army. In September, the declaration of the cooperation of the two parties was publicized, and the national united front to resist Japan formally came into being.

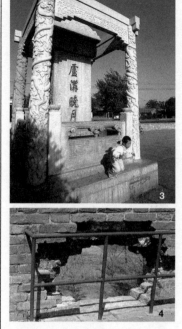

3

4

小资料 Data

"八一三事变"

1937年8月13日，日军在炮火的掩护下，突然对上海发起猛烈攻击。中国军队英勇抵抗，淞沪战役爆发。

The August 13 Incident

On August 13, 1937, the Japanese army mounted a surprise attack on Shanghai. The Chinese army fought back bravely, and the campaign to defend Shanghai started.

1. 芦沟桥
   Luogouqiao Bridge
2. 准备东渡黄河抗日的红军骑兵队伍
   Mounted troops of the Red Army prepared to cross the Yellow River eastward to fight the Japanese army.
3. 芦沟桥"芦沟晓月"石碑
   The stone tablet celebrating the "Morning Moon over Luogouqiao Bridge"
4. 北京宛平城"七七事变"日军第一炮弹残壁洞
   This hole in Wanping City, Beijing, was lasted by the first bomb from the Japanese army during the July 7 Incident.

2

平型关大捷
The Victory at Pingxing Pass

小资料 Data

八路军

"芦沟桥事变"爆发不久,国共两党合作抗战。1937年8月22日,国民政府宣布,将红军主力部队改编为国民革命军第八路军,简称"八路军",下辖三个师:第115师、第120师和第129师,朱德任总指挥,彭德怀任副总指挥。

The Eighth Route Army

Not long after the Lugouqiao Incident, the CPC and KMT joined hands to resist the Japanese invasion. On August 22, 1937, the National Government reorganized the main forces of the Red Army into the Eighth Route Army of the National Revolutionary Army. The Eighth Route Army had three divisions: the 115th Division, the 120th Division and the 129th Division. Zhu De was the commander-in-chief of the Eighth Route Army, and Peng Dehuai was his deputy.

1937年红军改编为八路军后,立即开赴华北战场,积极配合正面战场作战。

1937年9月,华北日军侵入山西,以精锐部队进攻雁门关等长城关隘,企图夺取太原。

国民政府组织太原会战,林彪、聂荣臻(zhēn)率领八路军115师在山西参加会战。平型关地形险要,是晋北交通要道。115师利用平型关的有利地形,于9月25日伏击日军,歼灭日军板垣师团1,000多人,缴获大批军用物资,取得平型关大捷。这是抗战以来中国军队的第一次大捷。平型关大捷,粉碎了日军不可战胜的神话,摧毁了日军直取太原的军事计划,支援了国民党军队正在准备的忻(xīn)口会战,鼓舞了全国人民抗战胜利的信心。

After the Red Army had been reorganized into the Eighth Route Army in 1937, it was immediately deployed in the north China battlefield.

In September 1937, the Japanese army in north China invaded Shanxi Province, through Yanmen and other strategic passes along the Great Wall, in an attempt to seize Taiyuan, the capital of Shanxi.

Lin Biao and Nie Rongzhen led the 115th Division of the Eighth Route Army to defend the strategic Pingxing Pass. On September 25, the 115th Division ambushed the Japanese army and wiped out over 1,000 soldiers of the Itagaki Division, and seized a lot of military materials. This was the first victory won by the Chinese army since the beginning of the anti-Japanese war, dispelling the myth that the Japanese army was invincible, and boosting the spirit of resistance of the Chinese people. The victory also halted the Japanese advance on Taiyuan.

平型关战役形势示意图
Sketch Map of the Battle of Pingxing Pass

寒水村
Hanshui Village

老爷庙
Laoyemiao

石灰沟
Shihuigou

东跑池
Dongpaochi

关沟
Guangou

白崖台
Baiyatai

东长城村
Dongchangcheng Village

山 西

Shanxi Province

八路军开进方向
The marching direction of the Eighth Route Army

八路军进攻方向
The attacking direction of the Eighth Route Army

八路军防御阵地
The defense line of the Eighth Route Army

八路军歼敌地区
The area where the Eighth Route Army wiped out the enemy

南京大屠杀
The Nanjing Massacre

1. 日军在国民政府门前举行入城仪式
   Japanese troops held a march-in before the National Government office building to mark their occupation of Nanjing.
2. 日军屠杀中国平民情形
   Atrocities carried out against Chinese civilians by the Japanese army

1937年11月12日，日军侵占上海后，下一个攻击目标便是当时中国的首都——南京。12月13日上午，以松井石根为司令官的日军侵入城内，占领国民政府，南京沦陷。日军采用极其野蛮的手段，对居民及解除武装的中国军人进行了长达6个星期的血腥屠杀。

日军在南京下关江边、草鞋峡、煤炭港、上新河、燕子矶、汉中门外等地制造了多起集体屠杀事件，还实行了分散屠杀。屠杀之后，日军又采用抛尸入江、火化焚烧、集中掩埋等手段，毁尸灭迹。据调查统计，被日军屠杀的人数总计达30万以上。日军屠杀南京人民的手段很残忍，主要有砍头、刺杀、枪击、活埋、火烧等，还有惨无人道的"杀人比赛"。在日本侵略者的屠刀下，南京这座原来和平繁华的大都市，变成了阴森可怕的人间地狱。日军在南京的暴行，为现代世界文明史留下最为黑暗的一页。

1945年8月15日，日本无条件投降。中国军事法庭（于1946年12月设立）及东京军事法庭都对南京大屠杀进行了严肃认真的调查、审理，并作出审判。集体屠杀列为28案，零散屠杀列为858案。东京军事法庭对东条英机等28名日本甲级战犯进行了审判。至此，国际社会对侵华日军南京大屠杀事件定下了铁案。

半个多世纪过去了，一些日本军国主义者想粉饰自己不光彩的过去，甚至为那些双手沾满鲜血的刽子手唱赞歌。但历史不会被忘记，任何人都无法将他们的名字从历史的耻辱柱上抹去。

After capturing Shanghai on November 12, 1937, the Japanese army attacked Nanjing, China's capital at that time, on the morning of December 13. For six weeks, the occupying troops engaged in an orgy of slaughter by

1. 南京大屠杀遇难同胞纪念馆
   Nanjing Massacre Memorial Hall
2. 展示日军南京大屠杀的展览
   Exhibition of the horrific slaughter — the Nanjing
   Massacre

the most brutal means. It is estimated that over 300,000 civilians and disarmed Chinese soldiers were murdered. The Nanjing Massacre has gone down in the annals of history as a horrific incident and a stain on modern civilization.

Following Japan's surrender on August 15, 1945, war crimes trials investigated the Nanjing Massacre. The court came to the conclusion that there had been 28 cases of collective slaughter and 858 cases of scattered slaughter.

台儿庄战役
The Taierzhuang Campaign

台儿庄战役示意图
Sketch Map of the Taierzhuang
Campaign

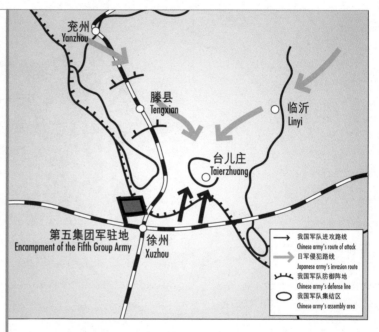

台儿庄战役是国民党军队保卫徐州的一次外围战役。

台儿庄位于徐州东北约50公里处，临近津浦铁路，同时又是运河要道，具有十分重要的战略地位。

1937年12月，日军占领南京以后，为了打通津浦路，连结南北战场，决定先夺取徐州。1938年春，日军从山东分两路进攻徐州。国民政府第五战区司令长官李宗仁，指挥中国军队作战，将两路日军分别阻挡在山东临沂和台儿庄。

在台儿庄战役中，池峰城师长率领中国守军坚守半个月之久，将日军主力吸引到台儿庄附近，李宗仁调集大量兵力包围日军，形成内外夹击之势，在台儿庄消灭日军1万余人，击毁日军坦克30余辆，并缴获大量武器，取得台儿庄大捷，这是抗战以来正面战场取得的最大胜利。台儿庄战役沉重地打击了日军，鼓舞了全国军民的抗战信心。

1. 台儿庄守军与日军在激战
The fierce battle between the Chinese and Japanese armies at Taierzhuang

The Taierzhuang Campaign was launched by the KMT army to protect Xuzhou.

Located about 50 km northeast of Xuzhou, Taierzhuang is a vital transportation hub, commanding the main north-south railway line and the Grand Canal.

After the Japanese army occupied Nanjing in December 1937, it moved to capture Xuzhou, in order to link their northern and southern forces. In the spring of 1938, the Japanese army launched a two-pronged attack on Xuzhou from Shandong Province. Li Zongren, commander of the Fifth War Zone of the National Government, deployed his men to block both paths of the Japanese advance at Linyi and Taierzhuang, respectively, in Shandong.

Division Commander Chi Fengcheng held fast to Taierzhuang for half a month, drawing the main forces of the Japanese army to the Taierzhuang area, while Li Zongren mustered his main force to pincer attack the Japanese. Finally, the Chinese army annihilated over 10,000 Japanese soldiers, destroyed 30-odd Japanese tanks and seized a large number of weapons. The Taierzhuang victory was another great morale booster for the Chinese army and people in their struggle against the aggressors.

🔲 小资料 Data

李宗仁

1891年出生于广西桂林，后成为桂系军阀首领。1948年，他在当时的国民政府选举中当选为副总统，蒋介石下野后任代总统。新中国成立后去美国治病。1965年，在中国政府的关怀帮助下，李宗仁回到北京。1969年去世。

Li Zongren

Born in Guilin, in what is now the Guangxi Zhuang Autonomous Region, in 1891, Li Zongren was a hero of the Taierzhuang Compaign. He was elected vice-president of the National Government in 1948. After Chiang Kai-shek resigned as president, Li acted as president of the National Government. He went to the US for medical treatment after the New China was founded in 1949. In 1965, Li Zongren returned to Beijing. He passed away in 1969.

1. 李宗仁司令在台儿庄留影
Commander Li Zongren in Taierzhuang

华侨与抗日战争
Overseas Chinese and the War of Resistance against Japan

1. 陈嘉庚铜像
   A bronze statue of Tan Kah-kee
2. 爱国华侨领袖陈嘉庚在厦门集美的墓园
   The mausoleum of the patriotic overseas Chinese leader, Tan Kah-kee, Jimei, Xiamen

海外华侨有着爱国的光荣传统。孙中山领导的辛亥革命就曾得到广大华侨的积极响应和支持。

海外华侨是中华民族抗日战争中的重要力量。从1931年"九一八事变"到1945年抗日战争胜利,他们同祖国人民一起,为世界反法西斯战争作出了巨大的贡献,是中华民族的骄傲,炎黄子孙的光荣,受到世人的称颂。

他们的贡献主要表现在以下几个方面:

建立广泛的爱国抗日统一组织。抗战爆发后,德、意、日结成法西斯同盟,支持日本对中国的侵略,而美、法、英等国采取了"中立政策"。华侨利用自己侨居海外的便利条件,在欧洲、美洲、大洋洲以及东南亚建立了各种爱国抗日组织,为抗日战争争取广泛的国际同情和援助。

积极捐款捐物,支持祖国抗战。他们提供的大量物资,补充了军队的给养和人民的生活费用。

支持团结抗战,反对分裂投降。"九一八事变"后,海外华侨强烈要求全国抗战,实行各党联合作战,成为推动第二次国共合作的进步力量。

全面抗战开始后,华侨纷纷组织抗日团体,宣传抗日,回国参战。美国华侨成立航空学校,为祖国培训航空人才。1938年10月以后,中国东南的海陆交通被日军切断,新开辟的滇缅公路工程完成后,急需大批汽车司机和修理工,1939年,南侨总会受国民政府委托,招募约3,200名华侨机工回国效力。《南洋商报》、《星洲日报》等10余家侨报的记者联合组织"南洋华侨战地记者通讯团"，于1938年回国进行战地采访。

Overseas Chinese have a glorious patriotic tradition. The Revolution of 1911 led by Sun Yat-sen received an enthusiastic welcome and support from numerous overseas Chinese.

Overseas Chinese played an important role in the anti-Japanese war too. From the September 18 Incident in 1931 to V-J Day in 1945, overseas Chinese, together with people back home, made great contributions to the worldwide anti-Fascist war. They were part of the pride and glory of the Chinese nation, and were praised by people all over the world.

The contributions of overseas Chinese were manifested mainly in the following aspects:

They set up united patriotic anti-Japanese organizations in Europe, the Americas, Oceania and Southeast Asia, to win international sympathy and help for beleaguered China.

The overseas Chinese enthusiastically donated money and goods for the anti-Japanese cause, and were solidly behind calls for the whole Chinese people to unite against the common enemy, especially after the September 18 Incident. Many of them volunteered to defend their homeland. Overseas Chinese were a progressive force in promoting the second period of cooperation between the CPC and KMT.

Chinese people in the US established an aviation school to train flyers for their motherland. When the Japanese army cut off marine and land transportation in southeast China in October 1938, the Yunnan-Burma Highway was quickly constructed. In 1939, entrusted by the National Government, the General Association of Overseas Chinese in Southeast Asia for Relieving Fellow Countrymen in Distress, set up in October 1938, recruited about 3,200 overseas Chinese mechanics to help maintain trucks that supplied the Chinese army via the new road. Reporters from the *Nanyang Commercial News*, *Sinchew Daily* and many other overseas Chinese newspapers formed the "Communications Team of War Correspondents of Overseas Chinese from Southeast Asia" to report on the war from China in 1938.

重庆谈判
The Chongqing Negotiations

1. "双十协定"签订后毛泽东和蒋介石在重庆合影
   Mao Zedong posed with Chiang Kai-shek in Chongqing after they signed the "Double 10th Agreement".
2. 1945年8月28日，毛泽东、周恩来等人在美方代表赫尔利的陪同下前往重庆谈判
   On August 28, 1945, Mao Zedong, Zhou Enlai and other members of the CPC negotiating team left for Chongqing accompainied by the US representative Patrick Hurley.

　　抗日战争胜利后，蒋介石一方面准备发动内战，一方面又受到国内外要求和平、反对内战的舆论压力，于是采取了"假和平，真内战"的策略。1945年8月，蒋介石三次邀请毛泽东去重庆"商讨"国内和平问题。他的意图是：如果毛泽东不去，就宣传共产党没有和平诚意，把发动内战的责任加在共产党身上；如果去了，就可以借谈判，逼共产党交出人民军队和解放区政权。

　　1945年8月28日，为谋求和平，毛泽东、周恩来、王若飞等中共领导人从延安前往重庆，开始了重庆谈判。国民党派王世杰、张治中、邵力子为谈判代表。

　　这次谈判共进行了43天。中共代表团提出了和平建国的基本方针，即坚决避免内战，在和平、民主、团结的基础上实现全国统一，建立独立、自由、富强的新中国。蒋介石不得不表面同意结束专制统治，召开各党派政治协商会议，保障民主自由，保障各党派平等合法地位等主张，并于10月10日公布了《国共代表会谈纪要》（即"双十协定"）。

这次谈判，国共双方在解放区的政权问题和军队问题上争论激烈。中共代表团要求承认人民军队和解放区民主政权的合法地位，蒋介石则要求中共交出军队和解放区。为了争取和平，中共代表团作出让步，在普遍裁减全国军队的条件下，将人民解放军减少为24个师，并自动退出广东、湖南等8个解放区。

这次谈判迫使蒋介石承认了和平建国等政治方针。同时也揭穿了国民党假和平、真备战的阴谋，使得中共在政治上取得主动，国民党在政治上陷入孤立。

1. 毛泽东、周恩来在重庆谈判期间下榻于桂园，《双十协定》即在此签订
   During the negotiation in Chongqing, Mao Zedong and Zhou Enlai stayed at Guiyuan, where the "Double 10th Agreement" was signed.

With the end of the anti-Japanese war, Chiang Kai-shek prepared to restart the civil war. But pressure from home and abroad forced him to adopt a policy of "phony peace and real civil war". In August 1945, Chiang invited leaders of the CPC to Chongqing, ostensibly to discuss the issue of domestic peace. Mao Zedong, Zhou Enlai, Wang Ruofei and other leaders of the CPC went from Yanan to Chongqing on August 28, 1945, and began the Chongqing negotiations. The representatives of the the KMT were Wang Shijie, Zhang Zhizhong and Shao Lizi.

The negotiations lasted 43 days. Chiang Kai-shek agreed to the convening of a consultative conference of all political parties, the guaranteeing of democracy and freedom, and the equal, legal status of all political parties. Finally, Chiang published the "Summary of Talks Between the CPC and the KMT Representatives". This was called the "Double 10th Agreement", as it was published on October 10, i.e. the 10th day of the 10th month.

However, there still remained disputes over the liberated areas and the armed forces of the two sides. The delegation of the CPC demanded legal status for the people's army and the democratic government of the liberated areas, while Chiang demanded that the CPC surrender the army and the liberated areas. In order to achieve peace, the CPC delegation made concessions, reducing the People's Liberation Army to 24 divisions on condition of an overall reduction of armed forces in China, and retreating from eight liberated areas, including those in Guangdong and Hunan.

These negotiations forced Chiang to agree to a peaceful settlement and exposed his policy of "phoney peace and real civil war". The CPC gained the political initiative.

解放战争
The War of Liberation

1946年6月，蒋介石下令全面进攻解放区，解放区军民奋起抗击，解放战争正式开始。

全面内战爆发时，国民党政府在军事力量上占有明显优势，拥有430多万人的庞大军队，控制着全国所有的大城市和绝大部分交通干线，还得到美国在军事上和财政上的支持。

1

1947年2月，解放区军民取得了自卫战争的初步胜利。1947年3月起，国民党政府从原来对解放区的全面进攻，改为对陕甘宁和山东两个解放区的重点进攻，但也失败了。到1947年6月，国共双方力量对比已发生了显著的变化。国民党军队总兵力下降到373万人，士气低落。国民党政府在政治上、经济上也陷入严重危机。人民解放军总兵力不断上升，充满胜利的信心。解放军开始转入战略进攻阶段。

1947年7月起，解放军三支大军先后南下中原，展开进攻。到1948年8月，双方力量对比发生了进一步的变化。人民解放军的人数上升到280万，解放区面积也扩大了。中共中央作好了大决战的准备，先后组织了辽沈、淮海、平津三大战役，基本上消灭了国民党的主力部队，解放了全国大部分地区，加速了全国解放战争胜利的到来。

三大战役以后，国民党政府继续在长江南岸部署兵力，妄图凭借长江天险，阻止人民解放军渡江南进。1949年4月21日，毛泽

 小资料 Data

北平和平解放

1949年1月，华北"剿总"总司令傅作义将军与人民解放军经过谈判，签署了和平解放北平的声明。1949年1月31日，解放军举行了正式的入城仪式，北平和平解放。这大大推动了全国解放的到来。

The Peaceful Liberation of Beiping

In January 1949, general Fu Zuoyi, commander-in-chief of the KMT's North China "Bandit Suppression" Headquarters, signed a statement on the peaceful liberation of Beiping (Beiping, now Beijing) after negotiating with the PLA. On January 31, 1949, the PLA held a ceremony to enter the city, and Beiping was liberated peacefully, which greatly propelled the liberation process of the whole of China.

1. 1949年3月25日，毛泽东在北平西苑机场检阅部队
   Mao Zedong inspected troops at the Beiping Xiyuan Airport on Mar 25, 1949.

总统府

总统府位于南京市长江路292号。明初这里是汉王府，1912年，孙中山临时大总统也曾在此办公。蒋介石在抗战前后14年内以此为国民政府，所以称总统府。

The Presidential Palace

The Presidential Palace is located at No.292 Changjiang Road, Nanjing. It was the residence of Prince Han at the beginning of the Ming Dynasty. Sun Yat-sen used it as his headquarters when he was interim president in 1912. Chiang Kai-shek made it the site of the National Government for 14 years before and after the anti-Japanese war.

1. 江苏南京国民党总统府旧址
   The PLA occupied the Presidential Palace in Nanjing, Jiangsu Province.

东和朱德下达命令，人民解放军在东起江阴，西至湖口，长达500多公里的战线上，分三路发起渡江战役。23日，人民解放军占领南京，蒋介石集团逃往台湾。

In June 1946, Chiang Kai-shek launched an all-out attack on the liberated areas. Both soldiers and civilians of the liberated areas rose as one against the enemy. The War of Liberation had started.

At the beginning of the civil war, the KMT had obvious military superiority. They possessed a massive army of over 4,300,000 men, controlled all the big cities and most of the main lines of transportation in China, and received military and financial support from the US.

In February 1947, the liberated areas won initial victories. In March 1947, the KMT began to focus their forces against the Shaanxi-Gansu-Ningxia and Shandong liberated areas, but these two areas held out against all the odds. By June 1947, the strength of the armed forces of the CPC had grown remarkably, while that of the KMT had shrunk to 3,730,000 men. At the same time, the National Government fell into grave political and economic crises. By now the People's Liberation Army (PLA) had began to move to the phase of strategic offensive.

From July 1947, three wings of the PLA advanced southward to the Central Plains area. By August 1948, the strength of the armed forces of the two sides had changed further, with the PLA increasing to 2,800,000 men and the liberated areas having expanded rapidly. The Central Committee of the CPC made full preparations for decisive campaigns to end the war. They launched the three major campaigns of Liaoxi-Shenyang, Huai-Hai and Beiping-Tianjin, which basically destroyed the main forces of the KMT army, and liberated most of China.

After the three decisive campaigns, the KMT deployed its troops on the south bank of the Yangtze, which is a natural barrier. On April 21, 1949, Mao Zedong and Zhu De ordered the PLA to force the river in three places along a front of over 500 km, starting from Jiangyin in the east and ending at Hukou in the west. On April 23, the PLA occupied Nanjing, and the Chiang Kai-shek clique fled to Taiwan.

概述
Introduction

　　1949年10月1日，毛泽东主席登上雄伟的天安门城楼，向全世界人民庄严宣告：中华人民共和国成立了！中国人民从此站起来了！10月1日就是中国的国庆节，这一天也是中国现代史的开端。新中国成立后，在中国共产党和新中国第一代领导人毛泽东的领导下，中国恢复了国民经济，建立了社会主义制度，改善了人民生活，加强了民族团结，发展了对外关系，恢复了中国在联合国和联合国常任理事国的合法席位，政治、经济面貌得到了巨大改观。

　　1978年，在中国共产党和新中国第二代领导人邓小平的领导下，在第三次科技革命的影响和推动下，中国进入改革开放和社会主义现代化建设的新时期，经济发展速度大大加快，科技、教育、文化、体育、卫生事业不断进步，国际地位迅速提高，成功地运用"一国两制"政策解决了香港问题、澳门问题，并将以此来解决台湾问题。

　　目前，中国人民正在以胡锦涛总书记为核心的中共中央领导下，朝着现代化的目标继续前进。

On October 1, 1949, Chairman Mao Zedong solemnly declared to the world from the magnificent Tiananmen Rostrum. "The People's Republic of China is founded! The Chinese people have risen!" That day marked the beginning of China's contemporary history. After the founding of New China, under the direction of the CPC and her first-generation leader Chairman Mao, New China recovered her war-torn national economy, established the socialist system, improved the people's living standard, strengthened the unity of all ethnic groups, developed relations with foreign countries and resumed her legal status in the UN and that of a permanent member of the UN Security Council. China took on an entirely new look both politically and economically.

In 1978, under the direction of the CPC and her second-generation leader Deng Xiaoping, New China entered a new period of reform, opening-up and socialist modernization, with her economy developing rapidly, her undertakings in the scientific, educational, cultural, sports and health fields making constant progress and her international status increasing by leaps and bounds. Using the policy of "one country, two systems", China successfully solved the questions of Hong Kong and Macao that were left over by history (and she will use the same approach to the solution of the Taiwan question).

Now China is continuing to advance steadily toward the goal of modernization under the direction of the CPC Central Committee headed by General Secretury Hu Jintao.

毛泽东与新中国的建立
Mao Zedong and the Founding of New China

1949年9月，中国人民政治协商会议第一届全体会议在北平开幕，会议决定成立中华人民共和国，选举毛泽东为中华人民共和国中央人民政府主席，朱德、刘少奇等人为副主席，决定把北平改名为北京，作为中华人民共和国的首都，以《义勇军进行曲》为国歌，以五星红旗为国旗。

10月1日下午2时，国家领导人宣布就职，任命周恩来为中央人民政府政务院总理。

10月1日下午3时，举行开国大典。北京30万群众齐集天安门广场，毛泽东站在天安门城楼上，向全世界庄严宣告："中华人民共和国中央人民政府成立了！"在礼炮声中，他亲自升起了第一面五星红旗。接着举行了盛大的阅兵式和礼花晚会。

中华人民共和国的成立，标志着100多年来半封建半殖民地的旧中国历史的结束，揭开了中国历史的新篇章，使一个占世界人口近四分之一的大国成为独立统一的国家，人民从此成为国家的主人。

In September 1949, the First Plenary Session of the Chinese People's Political Consultative Conference (CPPCC) was held in Beiping. The Session decided to found the People's Republic of China (PRC), and elected Mao Zedong Chairman of the Central People's Government of the PRC, and Zhu De, Liu Shaoqi and others Vice-Chairmen. The Session also decided to change the name of Beiping to Beijing and make it the capital of the PRC, and decided to adopt *March of the Volunteers* as the national anthem and the five-starred red flag as the national flag.

At 2 p.m. on October 1, the state leaders were sworn into office, and Zhou Enlai was appointed Premier of the Government Administration Council of the Central People's Government.

At 3 p.m., the founding ceremony of the PRC was held. In Beijing, 300,000 people gathered in Tiananmen Square. Standing on the Tiananmen Rostrum, Mao Zedong solemnly declared to the world, "The Central People's Government of the People's Republic of China is founded!" He raised in person the first five-starred red flag to the accompaniment of an artillery salute. This was followed by a grand military review, and a fireworks display in the evening.

The founding of the PRC marked the end of over a century of the semi-colonial, semi-feudal old China, and opened a new chapter in Chinese history. Since then, China, with nearly a quarter of the world's population within her territory, has been a united and independent country, and her people have become their own masters.

1. 毛泽东
   Mao Zedong
2. 1949年10月1日，毛泽东主席在天安门城楼上庄严宣告："中华人民共和国中央人民政府成立了！"
   On October 1, 1949, Chairman Mao Zedong solemnly declared from Tiananmen Rostrum, "The Central Government of the People's Republic of China is founded!"

2

抗美援朝保家卫国
The War to Resist US Aggression and Aid Korea

1950年6月25日，朝鲜内战爆发。美国立即出兵干涉朝鲜内政；同时，美国海军侵入台湾海峡。7月7日美国操纵联合国安理会通过了决议，组成以美军为主的"联合国军"，扩大侵朝战争。美国总统杜鲁门任命麦克阿瑟(sè)为"联合国军"总司令。

中国主张和平解决朝鲜问题，对于美国武装干涉朝鲜内政和侵入中国领空表示强烈抗议。

9月15日，美军在朝鲜西海岸登陆，进攻朝鲜人民军，并于10月初越过北纬38度线(简称"三八线")，企图迅速占领整个朝鲜。同时，美军空军不断轰炸中朝边境的中国乡镇，海军不断炮击中国船只，中国安全受到严重威胁。

10月初，中国政府根据朝鲜民主主义人民共和国政府的请求，作出"抗美援朝、保家卫国"的决策。中国人民志愿军于1950年10月19日，在司令员彭德怀率领下，跨过鸭绿江，开赴朝鲜战场，与朝鲜人民军并肩作战抗击美国侵略者。从1950年10月到1951年6月，连续进行了五次战略性战役，将"联合国军"打回"三八线"，扭转了朝鲜战局。1951年7月，战争双方开始举行朝鲜停战谈判。1953年7月27日，战争双方在朝鲜停战协定上签字，抗美援朝战争结束。

抗美援朝战争粉碎了帝国主义扩大侵略的野心，维护了亚洲与世界和平，提高了中国的国际威望，为新中国的建设赢得了相对稳定的和平环境。

On June 25, 1950, civil war broke out on the Korean Peninsula. The US immediately sent troops to shore up the Syngman Rhee regime in the south. At the same time, it sent warships into the Taiwan Straits. On July 7, the US manipulated the UN Security Council to pass a resolution to organize a "UN Command", consisting mainly of US troops in order to enlarge the aggression against Korea. US president H.S. Truman appointed General Douglas MacArthur Commander-in-Chief of the "UN Command".

China insisted on a peaceful solution to the Korean question and strongly protested against the US armed interference in Korea's internal affairs as well as intrusion into China's territorial air space.

In early October 1950, US troops crossed the 38th Parallel, which had been the demarcation line between the Democratic People's Republic of Korea (DPRK) and the Republic of Korea (ROK), attempting to seize the whole of Korea. At the same time, the US air force bombed Chinese villages and towns near the Chinese-Korean border, and the US navy bombarded Chinese ships. With national security thus endangered, and upon the request of the government of the DPRK, the Chinese government made the decision to "resist the US and aid Korea, and protect our motherland". On October 19, 1950, under Commander-in-Chief Peng Dehuai, the Chinese People's Volunteers crossed the Yalu River and marched to the Korean battlefield to fight side by side with the Korean People's Army against the US invaders. From October 1950 to June 1951, they launched five strategic campaigns in succession, which forced the "UN forces" back to the 38th Parallel. In July 1951, the two belligerent parties began armistice talks. On July 27, 1953, they signed the armistice agreement, and the Korean War ended.

The War to Resist US Aggression and Aid Korea crushed the imperialists' aggressive ambitions, helped to safeguard Asian and global peace, enhanced China's international prestige and won a peaceful environment of relative stability for the construction of New China.

小资料 Data

毛岸英牺牲

像千千万万英雄儿女一样，毛泽东主席的长子毛岸英主动要求参加志愿军到朝鲜参战。后来在一次美军飞机轰炸中牺牲，长眠在朝鲜的土地上。

The Heroic Death of Mao Anying

Like thousands of heroic Chinese young people, Mao Anying, the eldest son of Chairman Mao, joined the Chinese People's Volunteers to fight in Korea. He died a heroic death during a US bombing attack. He sleeps eternally on Korean soil.

1. 中国人民志愿军跨过鸭绿江，开赴朝鲜战场
   Chinese People's Volunteers crossed the Yalu River and marched to the Korean battlefield.

2. 彭德怀（左）、金日成（右）等中朝指挥人员在一起
   Peng Dehuai (left), Kim Il Sung (right) and other Chinese and Korean commanding personnel

3. 1953年7月27日，朝鲜停战协定签字仪式在板门店举行
   On July 27, 1953, the signing ceremony of the Korean armistice agreement was held in Panmunjom, on the 38th Parallel.

周恩来与新中国外交
Zhou Enlai and New China's Diplomacy

周恩来是一位杰出的政治家、外交家，是中国共产党的重要领导人。他在北伐战争、南昌起义、遵义会议、万里长征、西安事变、重庆谈判，以及中华人民共和国的创建等一系列重大历史事件中都发挥了重要的作用。他是新中国的首任总理兼外交部长，具有高超的外交艺术和人格魅力。他在外交场合的每一次出现，都会给爱好和平的人们带来希望，是成功和胜利的象征。

1954年4月至7月，美国、苏联、中国、法国，还有朝鲜战争和印度支那战争的交战各方，在瑞士日内瓦举行会议，讨论停战问题。这是新中国第一次以大国身份参加的重要国际会议。周恩来率领中国代表团出色地完成了任务，为恢复和平作出了巨大贡献。

周恩来还为中美关系的改善作出了杰出的贡献。新中国成立后，中美两国关系中断了20多年。20世纪60年代末，中美两国政府都决定改善中美关系。1970年10月1日，天安门广场举行国庆节庆祝活动，周恩来邀请美国记者埃德加·斯诺夫妇登上天安门城楼观礼，向美国发出了友好的信息。

1972年2月21日，美国总统尼克松在和中国没有外交关系的情况下，到长期相互敌视的中国进行友好访问。周恩来在机场迎接。当他们的手握在一起时，周恩来微笑着说："你把手伸过了世界上最辽阔的海洋来和我握手。"中美关系开始走上了正常化的道路。周恩来在其中发挥了任何人都无法代替的关键性作用，在制定和执行这一时期中国对美国的方针方面表现了极大的创造性、灵活性，以及卓越的外交艺术。

1. 1972年2月21日，美国总统尼克松来华访问，周恩来在机场迎接
   On February 21, 1972, Premier Zhou Enlai greeted US President Richard Nixon at Beijing International Airport.
2. 周恩来总理（1898—1976年）
   Premier Zhou Enlai (1898-1976 AD)

Zhou Enlai was an important leader of the CPC. He was an outstanding statesman and diplomat who played an important role in a series of major historical events, such as the Northern Expedition, Nanchang Uprising, Zunyi Conference, Long March, Xi'an Incident, Chongqing negotiations and the founding of the PRC. As the first premier and concurrently minister of foreign affairs of New China, he possessed superb diplomatic skills and personality charm. Every time he appeared on diplomatic occasions, he would bring hope to those who loved peace. He was a symbol of success and victory.

From April to July 1954, the US, the Soviet Union, China, France and the belligerent parties in the Korean War and the Indo-China War held a conference in Geneva, Switzerland, to discuss the armistice issue. This was the first important international conference in which New China participated as a great nation. The Chinese delegation, led by Zhou Enlai, accomplished their task at the conference with flying colors, and made a great contribution to the restoration of peace.

Zhou Enlai also made exceptional contributions to the improvement of Sino-US relations. Relations between China and the US were suspended for over 20 years after the founding of New China. But in the late 1960s, the Chinese and US governments decided to improve their relations. On October 1, 1970, during National Day celebrations held in Tiananmen Square, at Zhou Enlai's invitation, the US reporter Edgar Snow and his wife appeared on the Tiananmen Rostrum, sending a signal of friendship to the US.

On February 21, 1972, US President Richard Nixon visited China, despite the fact that the two countries had no formal diplomatic relations. Zhou Enlai went to the airport to welcome him, and said, as they shook hands, "You stretched out your hand across the broadest ocean in the world to shake hands with me." From that moment on, relations between the two countries began to be orbited on to the road of normalization. Zhou Enlai played a critical role in this process, displaying great creativity, flexibility, and extraordinary diplomatic skills in working out and implementing China's policy concerning the US.

小资料 Data

乒乓外交

1971年4月10日至17日，美国乒乓球代表队来中国进行友好访问和比赛，这是自新中国成立以来，第一个应邀访问中华人民共和国的美国代表团。美国乒乓球队访华在美国引起强烈的反响，掀起一股"中国热"，在国际上也引起了广泛的关注。1972年4月12日至29日，中国乒乓球代表团赴美进行回访。中美两国乒乓球队之间的互访，打开了两国人民友好往来的大门，"小球转动了大球"，推进了两国关系正常化的进程，被国际舆论誉为"乒乓外交"。

The "Ping-Pong Diplomacy"

From April 10 to 17, 1971, a US table tennis (Ping-Pong) delegation toured China, and played matches with their Chinese counterparts. This was the first US delegation to be invited to visit China since the founding of the PRC. From April 12 to 29, 1972, a Chinese table tennis delegation toured the US. This "Ping-Pong diplomacy" gave momentum to the process of normalizing relations between the PRC and the US.

邓小平与改革开放
Deng Xiaoping and the Reform and Opening-up

中国的改革开放，开始于1978年召开的中国共产党十一届三中全会，经历了从农村改革到城市改革，从经济体制的改革到各方面体制的改革，从对内搞活到对外开放的进程。

邓小平是这场改革的主要领导人，是中国改革开放的总设计师。

邓小平提出了"建设有中国特色的社会主义"的理论：以经济建设为中心，进行现代化建设，在农村实行家庭联产承包责任制，在城市推行打破"大锅饭"的各种经济责任制，建立公有制基础上的社会主义市场经济体制。同时，改革政治体制，如党政分开、下放权力、精简机构、发扬民主等等。

把改革和开放结合起来，设置经济特区。1979年7月，国务院确定广东、福建两省试办经济特区。1980年，正式设立了深圳、珠海、汕头、厦门四个经济特区。又相继开放了沿海10几个城市，在长江三角洲、珠江三角洲、闽东南地区、环渤海地区开辟经济开放区，批准海南建省并成为经济特区。1984年1月，邓小平等人视察了深圳和珠海两个经济特区。1992年，又视察了武昌、深圳、珠海、上海等地，发表重要讲话，强调改革开放胆子要大一些，要抓住时机，关键是发展经济。

邓小平提出"科技是第一生产力"，提出要尊重知识，尊重人才，发展教育事业，加强社会主义精神文明建设。

在解决香港和澳门回归的问题上，邓小平提出了用"一国两制"的方针实现祖国统一的构想，取得了成功。

经过20多年的改革开放，中国在政治、经济、文化等领域都取得了巨大成就，综合国力显著增强，人民生活水平日益提高。

1. 邓小平是中国改革开放的总设计师
   Deng Xiaoping was the mastermind behind China's reform and opening-up policies.
2. 邓小平参观深圳先科激光公司
   Deng Xiaoping visited the Shenzhen Xianke Laser Company.
3. 邓小平在上海观看小学生操作电子计算机
   Deng Xiaoping watched a schoolboy operating a computer in Shanghai.

The Third Plenary Session of the 11th Central Committee of the CPC, held in late 1978, saw the introduction of China's reform and opening-up policies. The process of the new policies was from rural reform to urban reform, from reform of the economic structure to structures in all aspects, and from internal vitalization to external opening-up.

Deng Xiaoping was the major leader and general designer of China's reform and opening-up policies.

Deng Xiaoping initiated the theory of "building socialism with Chinese characteristics", e.g., carrying out construction to realize modernization with economic construction as the central task, implementing the household contract responsibility system with remuneration linked to output in rural areas, and, in urban areas practicing various economic systems of responsibility to prevent people from "eating from the same big pot" (getting the same reward or pay as everyone else regardless of one's work performance) and establishing a socialist market economic system based on public ownership of the means of production. At the same time, the political systems were also reformed, such as by separating the functions of the Party and the government, transferring power to lower levels, simplifying the administrative structure and developing a democratic style of work.

Deng Xiaoping advocated combining reform and opening-up, and set up special economic zones (SEZs) to attract foreign investment and boost

the economy. In July 1979, the State Council decided to set up the first group of SEZs in Guangdong and Fujian provinces on a trial basis. In 1980, the four SEZs of Shenzhen, Zhuhai, Shantou and Xiamen were formally set up. Then over a dozen coastal cities were opened in succession, and open economic regions were established in the Yangtze Delta, the Pearl River Delta, southeast Fujian area and the area around the Bohai Sea. Hainan Island was made a full-fledged province and an SEZ. In January 1984, Deng Xiaoping and other leaders went on an inspection tour of the Shenzhen and Zhuhai SEZs. In 1992, Deng inspected Wuchang, Shenzhen, Zhuhai and Shanghai, and issued instructions, emphasizing boldness in the reform and opening-up tasks, telling people to grasp opportunities, taking economic development as the key to progress.

Deng emphasized that "Science and technology are the first productive forces", and urged more respect for knowledge and talented people. He also noted the need to develop education and strengthen the construction of socialist spiritual civilization.

As for the Hong Kong and Macao questions, Deng initiated the principle of "one country, two systems" to realize the reunification of the country. This principle underlay the successful reunion of Hong Kong and Macao with the motherland.

After more than 20 years of reform and opening-up, China has made enormous achievements in the political, economic, cultural and other fields. As a result, China's comprehensive national power and people's living standards have increased greatly.

1. 邓小平在深圳视察
   Deng Xiaoping visited Shenzhen.
2. 深圳经济特区
   Shenzhen Special Economic Zone
3. 2001年11月11日，在卡塔尔首都多哈举行了中国加入世贸组织议定书签字仪式。当时的中国外经贸部部长石广生（右）在签字后与世贸组织总干事穆尔（左）举杯庆祝中国入世成功
   On November 11, 2001, the signing ceremony for China's accession to the Word Trade Organization (WTO) was held in Doha, the capital of Qatar. Shi Guangsheng, the then current China's Minister of Foreign Trade and Economic Cooperation, and Mr. Moore, General Secretary of the WTO, celebrated the accession.

香港回归
Hong Kong's Return to China

1840年6月，中英鸦片战争正式爆发。英国在1841年1月26日占领香港岛。1842年8月29日，清政府被迫与英国签订了屈辱的《南京条约》，将香港岛割让英国。

1984年12月19日，邓小平在会见英国首相撒切尔夫人时提出"一国两制"这一解决香港问题的方法，也就是实行"一个国家，两种制度"，"港人治港"、"高度自治"，保持香港原有的资本主义制度和生活方式50年不变。经多次协商，中英达成协议，签订了《中华人民共和国与大不列颠及北爱尔兰联合王国关于香港问题的联合声明》，宣告"中国政府将于1997年7月1日对香港恢复行使主权，英国将在同时把香港交还中国"。

1997年6月30日午夜，中英两国政府香港政权交接仪式在香港隆重举行。7月1日零点，中华人民共和国国旗和香港特别行政区区旗在香港升起，中华人民共和国主席江泽民在香港会议展览中心庄严宣告：根据中英关于香港问题的联合声明，两国政府举行了香港政权交接仪式，宣告中国对香港恢复行使主权，中华人民共和国香港特别行政区正式成立。之后，香港特区首任行政长官董建华宣誓就职。英国在香港一个半世纪的殖民统治结束了，香港终于回到祖国的怀抱。

1. 香港回归后的夜景
   A night scene after Hong Kong's return to China
2. 江泽民主席与查尔斯王子在香港政权交接仪式上
   President Jiang Zemin and Prince Charles of Britain at the ceremony to mark Hong Kong's return to China

On January 26, 1841, Britain seized Hong Kong Island, after its victory in the aggressive First Opium War. On August 29, 1842, the government of the Qing Dynasty was forced to sign the *Treaty of Nanking* with Britain, formally ceding Hong Kong Island.

On December 19, 1984, Deng Xiaoping proposed the principle of "one country, two systems" to solve the Hong Kong question when he met with British Prime Minister Margaret Thatcher. Under this principle, Hong Kong would be administered by Hong Kong people as a highly autonomous region, and Hong Kong's capitalist system and life style would not be changed for 50 years. After many rounds of consultation, China and Britain reached an agreement, and signed the *"Sino-British Joint Declaration on the Question of Hong Kong"*, which declared that "the Chinese government will resume exercise of its sovereignty over Hong Kong from July 1, 1997, and at the same time Britain will return Hong Kong to China."

On the midnight of June 30, 1997, the hand-over ceremony was held solemnly at the Hong Kong Convention and Exhibition Centre. At zero hour on July 1, the national flag of the PRC and the regional flag of the Hong Kong Special Administrative Region (HKSAR) were raised. Jiang Zemin, president of the PRC, solemnly declared the founding of the HKSAR. Then Tung Chee Hwa, the first Chief Executive of the HKSAR, took the oath of office. The one and a half centuries of Britain's colonial rule of Hong Kong came to an end, and Hong Kong finally returned to the motherland.

小资料 Data

东方之珠——香港

香港位于珠江三角洲南部、珠江口东侧，是国际尤其是亚太地区的贸易、金融、交通、旅游中心。经济以贸易为主，制造业、金融业、房地产业、旅游业等很发达。维多利亚港是世界上最繁忙的港口之一；大屿山的香港国际机场为世界最先进的机场之一。

Hong Kong—Pearl of the Orient

Situated south of the Pearl River Delta, Hong Kong is a trading, financial, communication and tourism center both for the Asian-Pacific region and the world as a whole. Its economy is based mainly on trade. Its manufacturing, financial, real estate and tourism sectors are flourishing. Victoria Harbor is one of the world's busiest ports, and the Hong Kong International Airport on Lantau Island is one of the world's most advanced airports.

澳门回归
Macao's Return to China

从公元1553年开始，澳门逐渐被葡萄牙殖民者攫取了管治权，成为西方殖民者在中国领土上建立的第一个侵略基地。

20世纪70年代末，中葡两国就澳门问题达成了原则协议。1986年至1987年，中葡两国经过和平友好谈判，最终于1987年4月13日签字发表了《中华人民共和国政府和葡萄牙共和国政府关于澳门问题的联合声明》，确认澳门地区是中国领土，中国政府将于1999年12月20日对澳门恢复行使主权。

1999年12月19日23时42分，澳门政权交接仪式正式开始，葡萄牙总统桑帕约等政府要员参加仪式。12月20日零时，中华人民共和国主席江泽民宣告，中国政府对澳门恢复行使主权。而后，澳门特区首任行政长官何厚铧 (huá) 宣誓就职。

Macao was the first Chinese territory to fall into the hands of Western colonialists, as, starting in 1553, the Portuguese gradually asserted their power over it.

At the end of the 1970s, China and Portugal reached agreement in principle on the question of Macao. From 1986 to 1987, after peaceful and friendly negotiations, China and Portugal signed the *"Sino Portuguese Joint Declaration on the Question of Macao"* on April 13, 1987. The Declaration affirmed that Macao is a part of China, and the Chinese government would resume exercise of its sovereignty over the territory on December 20, 1999.

At 23:42 on December 19, 1999, the hand-over ceremony formally opened, in the presence of PRC President Jiang Zemin, Portuguese President Jorge Sampaio, and other leading governmental officials. At zero hour on December 20, Jiang Zemin declared the resumption of exercise of China's sovereignty over Macao by the Chinese government. Then, Ho Hau-Wah, the first Chief Executive of the Macao Special Administrative Region took the oath of office.

小资料 Data

澳门

地处珠江三角洲西岸,面积约23.5平方公里,人口约44万,是一个中西文化交汇的地方。

澳门实行的是自由经济制度,近年来,旅游博彩业以及其他服务业正逐步取代制造业而成为主要的经济支柱。

Macao

Situated on the west bank of the Pearl River Delta, Macao covers an area of 23.5 km², with a population of about 440,000. It is a place where Eastern and Western cultures converge.

Macao has a free economic system. In recent years, tourism and gambling and various service trades have gradually replaced manufacturing industry, to become the economic mainstay.

1. 澳门政权交接仪式现场
   A scene of the hand-over ceremony
2. 江泽民主席与桑帕约总统在澳门政权交接仪式上
   President Jiang Zemin and Portuguese President Sampaio at the handover ceremony to mark the return of Macao to China
3. 1999年12月20日零点整,澳门市政厅广场万众欢庆回归
   A midnight scene at Largo do Senado Square after Macao's return to China, Dec 20, 1999
4. 美丽的澳门
   Beautiful Macao

中国体育走向世界
China as a World Sporting Power

1. 中国第一位国际奥委会委员王正廷
   Wang Zhengting, the first Chinese member on the International Olympic Committee
2. 第一位参加奥运会的中国运动员刘长春，他是1932年第10届奥运会唯一的中国运动员
   Liu Changchun, the first Chinese athlete to compete in the Olympics, in 1932
3. 2008年北京奥运网站
   The 2008 Beijing Olympic website
4. 1984年8月7日，中国女排获得第23届奥运会女排冠军，实现了在世界大赛中"三连冠"
   On August 7, 1984, the Chinese women's volleyball team won the championship in the 23rd Olympic Games and achieved a "triple crown" in international matches.
5. 伏明霞在亚特兰大第26届奥运会上获女子跳台、跳板的双料冠军
   Fu Mingxia won the championships in both the platform diving and springboard diving events at the 26th Olympic Games.
6. 21岁的刘翔以平世界的纪录，勇夺雅典奥运男子110米栏的金牌
   The 21-year-old Liu Xiang stormed to the champion of 110-m hurdles at the Athens Olympics with a stunning world record-equalling time.

1924年，在张伯苓 (líng)、王正廷等人的活动下，中华全国体育协进会成立了。1931年国际奥委会正式承认中华全国体育协进会为中国奥林匹克委员会。1932年第10届奥运会在美国洛杉矶举行，中国第一次派选手刘长春参加。

1960年第17届奥运会，台湾选手参加比赛，杨传广获十项全能银牌，这是中国运动员在奥运史上取得的第一枚奖牌。1968年第19届奥运会，台湾选手纪政获得女子80米栏铜牌，这是中国女运动员在奥运会上首次获得奖牌。

1979年国际奥委会恢复了中华人民共和国的合法席位。

1984年7月，在第23届洛杉矶奥运会上，中国射击运动员许海峰夺得本届奥运会的第一枚金牌，中国运动员获得的金牌总数居第4位，中国女子排球队取得冠军，实现了世界杯冠军、世界锦标赛冠军、奥运会冠军"三连冠"。

中国又相继参加了第24届汉城奥运会、第25届巴塞罗那奥运会、第26届亚特兰大奥运会。

2000年9月，在第27届悉尼奥运会上，中国运动员共获得59枚奖牌，总数列第三名。

2004年8月，在第28届雅典奥运上，中国运动员再创佳绩，获得了63枚奖牌，其中32枚金牌。至此中国共参加了14届奥运会的比赛。

2001年7月13日，中国申办2008年奥运会获得成功；很快又于9月成功举办了第21届世界大学生运动会，这有力地促进了中国体育事业的发展。同时也显示出中国综合国力的增强，以及在国际上的地位进一步提高。

In 1924, the All-China Sports Association was founded, with the efforts of Zhang Boling, Wang

Zhengting and others. In 1931, the International Olympic Committee formally recognized the Association as the Chinese Olympic Committee. China was represented for the first time, by runner Liu Changchun, at the Olympic Games when the 10th Olympics were held in Los Angeles in 1932.

China won its first Olympic medal when Yang Chuanguang from Taiwan won the silver medal for the decathlon at the 17th Olympics in 1960. In the 19th Olympics in 1968, Taiwan athlete Ji Zheng won the bronze medal in the women's 80-meter hurdle race, which was the first Olympic medal won by a Chinese female athlete.

In 1979, the International Olympic Committee restored the PRC's legal seat on the committee.

In July 1984, Chinese marksman Xu Haifeng won China's first gold medal, at the 23rd Olympics held in Los Angeles. At the 23rd Olympics, China ranked fourth in the gold medal standings. The Chinese women's volleyball team also won a gold medal, attaining three successive Championships for the sport (the other two being World Cup and World Championships).

China attended the Seoul (24th), Barcelona (25th) and Atlanta (26th) Olympics.

At the 27th Olympics, held in Sydney in September 2000, Chinese athletes won 59 medals, ranking China third in the medal standings.

At the 28th Athens Olympics in August 2004, Chinese athletes won a record of 63 medals, among which 32 were gold. By then, China had been represented at 14 sessions of the Olympic Games.

On July 13, 2001, China's bid for the 2008 Olympics was successful; in September that year, China hosted the 21st Universiade, which vigorously promoted the development of China's sports, demonstrated the increase of China's overall national strength and enhanced China's international status.

小资料 Data

"东方玫瑰"

中国女子足球自20世纪80年代组建国家队以来，在国际比赛中取得了很好的成绩，如1986年—1999年女足亚洲杯7连冠；亚运会女足3连冠；1996年亚特兰大奥运会女足亚军；1999年第3届女足世界杯亚军等等，被人们誉为"东方玫瑰"。

Oriental Roses

The Chinese women's national football team has achieved very good results in international matches since its founding in the 1980s. Its achievements include seven Asian Cup championships in succession—from 1986 to 1999; three Asian Games championships in succession; runner-up in the 1996 Atlanta Olympics; and runner-up in the Third Women's Football World Cup in 1999. The women players are popularly known as "Oriental Roses".

中国历史年代简表
A Brief Chronology of
Chinese History

中国古代史	约170万年前—1840年
旧石器时代	约170万年前—约1万年前
新石器时代	约1万年前—4,000年前

夏	约公元前21世纪—前16世纪
商	约公元前16世纪—前11世纪
西周	约公元前11世纪—前771年
春秋	公元前770—前476年
战国	公元前475—前221年
秦	公元前221—前206年
汉（西汉·东汉）	公元前206—公元220年
三国（魏、蜀、吴）	公元220—280年
晋（西晋、东晋）	公元265—420年
南北朝	公元420—589年
隋	公元581—618年
唐	公元618—907年
五代	公元907—960年
辽	公元907—1125年
宋（北宋、南宋）	公元960—1279年
西夏	公元1038—1227年
金	公元1115—1234年
元	公元1271—1368年
明	公元1368—1644年
清（鸦片战争以前）	公元1644—1840年

中国近代史	公元1840—1949年
清（鸦片战争以后）	公元1840—1911年
中华民国	公元1912—1949年

现代中国	公元1949—
中华人民共和国	公元1949—

Ancient Period	c. 1,700,000 years ago-1840 AD
Paleolithic Period	c.1, 700,000 years ago-c.10,000 years ago
Neolithic Period	c.10,000 years ago-4,000 years ago

Xia Dynasty	c. 21st century BC-16th century BC
Shang Dynasty	c. 16th century BC-11th century BC
Western Zhou Dynasty	c. 11th century BC-771 BC
Spring and Autumn Period	770 BC-476 BC
Warring States Period	475 BC-221 BC
Qin Dynasty	221 BC-206 BC
Han Dynasty	206 BC-220 AD
(Western Han and Eastern Han)	
Three Kingdoms (Wei, Shu, Wu)	220-280 AD
Jin Dynasty	265-420 AD
(Western Jin and Eastern Jin)	
Southern and Northern Dynasties	420-589 AD
Sui Dynasty	581-618 AD
Tang Dynasty	618-907 AD
Five Dynasties	907-960 AD
Liao Dynasty	907-1125 AD
Song Dynasty	960-1279 AD
(Northern Song and Southern Song)	
Western Xia Dynasty	1038-1227 AD
Jin Dynasty	1115-1234 AD
Yuan Dynasty	1271-1368 AD
Ming Dynasty	1368-1644 AD
Qing Dynasty	1644-1840 AD
(before the Opium War of 1840)	

Modern Period	1840-1949 AD
Qing Dynasty	1840-1911 AD
(after the Opium War of 1840)	
Republic of China	1912-1949 AD

Contemporary Period	1949 AD-
People's Republic of China	1949 AD-

再版后记
Postscript for New Edition

《中国历史常识》、《中国地理常识》和《中国文化常识》于2002年1月与海外广大华裔青少年读者见面，及时缓解了海外华文教学辅助读物短缺的局面，并以其通俗易懂、生动活泼的编写风格受到了社会各界的热烈欢迎和好评。

由于初版时间比较仓促，三本书中尚存在一些不尽完善之处，诸位作者与编辑本着精益求精、认真负责的态度，对书中的某些内容和数据进行了全新的修订，以求进一步完善；全书并以中、英文对照再版。在修订再版工作中，潘兆明、杨伯震两位教授在百忙之中审读书稿并提出了许多宝贵意见，对我们的再版工作给予了大力支持和热情帮助，对此，我们谨表诚挚的谢意。

书中考虑不周或疏漏之处，期盼广大读者不吝赐正，以供今后再修订时参考。

编者
2006年5月

Common Knowledge about Chinese History, Common Knowledge about Chinese Geography, Common Knowledge about Chinese Culture were published in January 2002 and are now available to overseas young readers of Chinese origin. This has helped meet the demand for reference material for Chinese teaching abroad. The plain language and lively way of writing are both acclaimed by the general reading public.

There are places in the first edition of the three books for improvement. The authors and editors have carefully revised the books and updated some data and content. This editon is printed in bilingual format. Professor Pan Zhaoming and Yang Bozhen have, despite their own busy schedule, read the books and gave very valuable comments. We are most grateful to them for their time and support.

In case of any error or omission, please let us know. They will be used as reference for the next edition.

Compilers
May 2006

主编　王恺

编写人员　李　华　张美霞　徐正龙　夏小芸　钱玉莲

　　　　　　赵　玉　王　浩　唐晓丹　薛蓓蓓

责任编辑　马耀俊

英文编辑　林美琪　王娉婷

封面设计　阮永贤

美术编辑　阮永贤　刘玉瑜

Chief Compiler : Wang Kai

Writers : Li Hua, Zhang Meixia, Xu Zhenglong, Xia Xiaoyun, Qian Yulian,

Zhao Yu, Wang Hao, Tang Xiaodan, Xue Beibei

Executive Editor : Ma Yiu Chun

English Editors : Maggie Lam, Kristy Wong

Cover Design : Yuen Wing Yin

Designers : Yuen Wing Yin, Lau Yuk Yu

中国历史常识

Common Knowledge about Chinese History

图书在版编目 (CIP) 数据

中国历史常识/王恺主编.—香港：香港中国旅游出版社，2006.5

ISBN 962-8746-47-2

I. 中… II. 王… III. 历史—中国—儿童读物　IV. K209

中国版本图书馆CIP数据核字 (2001) 第081771号

出版：香港中国旅游出版社 (中国·香港)

电话：(852)2561 8001

2006年5月第4版/2006年5月第1次印刷

印制：香港美雅印刷制本有限公司